An Introduction to Ergodicity Economics

Ole Peters and Alexander Adamou

LML PRESS

An Introduction to Ergodicity Economics

Edition 1.1
ISBN: 978-1-0686491-3-4 (hardback)

Published by
LML Press
8 Margravine Gardens
London, W6 8RH, UK

Visit https://ergodicityeconomics.com/an-introduction-to-ergodicity-economics/ for book-related news, including discussion and errata.

For permissions or inquiries, contact: info@lmlpress.org.uk

Acknowledgements

This book would not have been possible without the community which has grown around the nascent field of ergodicity economics. This community is too large to name everyone, so we say "thank you" to all who feel part of it. We do want to name one institution, though – the London Mathematical Laboratory. It has unwaveringly supported all of the unusual work which has now led to this book. Its fellows, trustees, sponsors, and staff have created a space and an atmosphere which have allowed us to learn and to unlearn, to sit with a problem, to develop fresh perspectives, and to give them time to mature. We are deeply grateful to all of you.

London, 26 April 2024.

Contents

Chapter 1

Introduction

Welcome to the first-ever textbook on ergodicity economics (EE), written for upper-level undergraduates, graduate students, researchers, and practitioners. EE places the ergodicity question centre-stage in individual and collective decision-making: is what happens over time well represented by expected value? This question challenges and expands traditional economic models, where expected values appear frequently, often by default and without explicit motivation. It has been asked repeatedly by thinkers dotted around the globe and across the centuries. Over the last decade, we have collected instances of such work, made original contributions, and begun to build a coherent formalism.

Traditional economic theory defines rational behaviour as maximising the expected value of utility, an average of all possible outcomes in risky situations. However, this approach overlooks the fact that real-life decisions unfold over time. The ergodicity question highlights that expected values align with time averages only under restrictive conditions. When these conditions do not hold, we are led to different notions of rationality and to new understandings of risk and decision-making.

EE is producing new results at an accelerating pace, and a comprehensive survey of everything our community has achieved is no longer feasible. Nor would such a survey make a good textbook. Instead, we start by introducing the necessary mathematical tools, and then we develop a single EE idea in depth: we design behavioural protocols which maximise the growth of wealth in the long run. This yields powerful models of individual decision-making, cooperation, insurance, economic inequality, and financial markets.

The material presented here is roughly that of a one-semester lecture course. If you clear your desk and do absolutely nothing else, we think you can work through this book in a fortnight. By the end, you will be equipped to contribute to the development and application of EE, and to help us pave the way for more robust and equitable economic systems.

1.1 The game

Imagine we offer you the following game: we toss a coin, and if it comes up heads we increase your monetary wealth by 50%; if it comes up tails we reduce your wealth by 40%. We're not only doing this once, we will do it many times, say once per week for the rest of your life. Would you accept the rules of our game? Would you submit your wealth to the dynamic our game will impose on it?

Your answer to this question is up to you and will be influenced by many factors, such as the importance you attach to wealth that can be measured in monetary terms, whether you like the thrill of gambling, your religion and moral convictions and so on.

In this book we will mostly ignore these factors. We will build a simple model of your wealth, which will lead to a simple model of the way you make decisions that affect your wealth. We are interested in analysing the game mathematically, which requires a translation of the game into mathematics. We introduce the variable $x(t)$, which we refer to as "wealth", and which is a function of the variable t, which we refer to as "time". It should be kept in mind that "wealth" and "time" are just names that we've given to mathematical objects. We have chosen these names because we want to compare the behaviour of the mathematical objects to the behaviour of wealth over time, but we emphasise that we're building a model – whether we write $x(t)$, or wealth(time), or ☺(↯) makes no difference to the mathematics.

The usefulness of our model will be different in different circumstances, ranging from completely meaningless to very helpful. There is no substitute for careful consideration of any given situation.

Let us define our model of the dynamics of your wealth under the rules we just specified.[1] At regular intervals of duration δt, we randomly generate a factor r with each possible value $r_i \in \{0.6, 1.5\}$ occurring with probability $1/2$,

$$r = \begin{cases} 0.6 & \text{with probability } 1/2 \\ 1.5 & \text{with probability } 1/2 \end{cases} \tag{1.1}$$

and multiply current wealth by that factor, so that

$$x(t + \delta t) = x(t) r. \tag{1.2}$$

To make this concrete, let's imagine further that your starting wealth is $x(0) = \$100$ and the duration between coin tosses is $\delta t = 1$ week.

[1] For those in the know: this coin game is a discrete version of geometric Brownian motion, the workhorse model of financial mathematics and much more. The game itself is sometimes called the multiplicative binomial process [55], and we thank Sidney Redner for pointing this out to us.

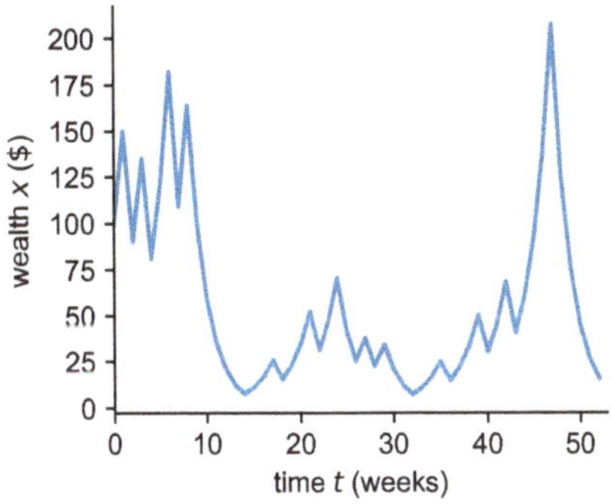

Figure 1.1: Wealth $x(t)$ resulting from a computer simulation of our game, as specified by (Eq. 1.1) and (Eq. 1.2), starting from $x(0) = \$100$ and playing for one year.

We have good reasons to suspect that this model will do something interesting. It's not just a silly game because it has one important property: it's multiplicative. Every time the coin is tossed, wealth is *multiplied* by one of the two possible factors. This introduces a reference point, or state-dependence, of the absolute size of the change. Processes with this property are very common in nature – the amount of anything that reproduces changes in proportion to what's already there. In the absence of other constraints, such as limited resources, this applies to the dynamics of the biomass of a cell culture. In fact, life itself has been defined as that which produces more of itself [41]: life and evolution begin with the minimal chemical structure that can copy itself. The rest, in a sense, is details. We will see, especially in Chap. 9, how multiplicativity generates interesting structure, both in economics and in other areas.

Without discussing in depth how realistic a representation of your wealth this model is (for instance your non-gambling related income and spending are not represented in the model), and without discussing whether randomness truly exists and what the meaning of a probability is, we simply switch on a computer and simulate what might happen. You may have many good ideas of how to analyse our game with pen and paper, but we will just generate possible trajectories of your wealth and pretend we know nothing about mathematics or economic theory. Figure 1.1 is a trajectory of your wealth, according to our computer model, as it might evolve over the course of 52 one-week time steps, i.e. a year.

A cursory glance at the trajectory does not reveal much structure. Of course there are regularities, for instance at each time step $x(t)$ changes, but no trend is discernible – does this trajectory have a tendency to go up, does it have a tendency to go down? Neither? What are we to learn from this simulation? Perhaps you conclude that playing the game for a year is quite risky, but is the risk worth taking?

1.1.1 Averaging over many trials

The trajectory in Fig. 1.1 doesn't tell us much about overall tendencies. There is too much noise. A common strategy for getting rid of noise is to try again. And then try again and again, and look at what happens on average.[2]

So let's try this in our case and see if we can make sense of the game. Consider the average over a finite number, N, of wealth trajectories,

$$\langle x(t)\rangle_N = \frac{1}{N}\sum_{i=1}^{N} x_i(t), \tag{1.3}$$

where $x_i(t)$ is an individual trajectory indexed by i. The average wealth is a function of time, t, and in Fig. 1.2 we plot it for different values of N, from one to one million trajectories.

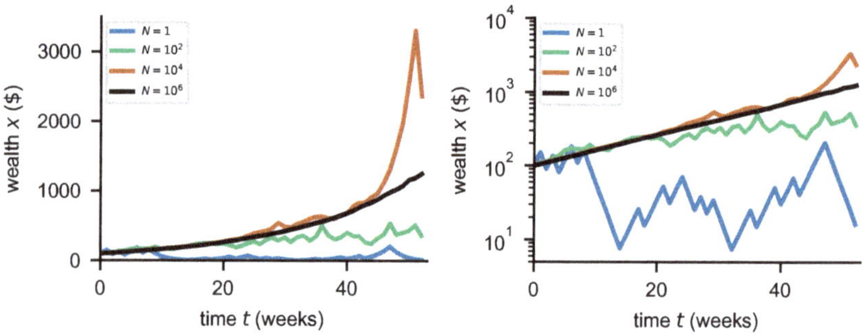

Figure 1.2: Averages $\langle x(t)\rangle_N$ over N wealth trajectories in the coin game for $N = 1, 10^2, 10^4, 10^6$. The noise in the average wealth diminishes systematically as N increases. **Left:** on linear scales the multiplicative (non-linear) nature of the process is apparent. **Right:** on logarithmic scales the multiplicative process is additive in time, and the average wealth for $N = 10^6$ is a straight line except for small fluctuations.

As anticipated, the more trajectories included in the average, the smaller the fluctuations of the average. For $N = 10^6$, hardly any fluctuations are visible. Since this almost noise-free average points up, you might conclude that your own wealth will similarly go up and, therefore, that the game is worth playing. We will see later that this type of thinking, and specifically of averaging, is at the heart of many important models of decisions in economics.

[2] An example of this technique is Shannon's error-correcting code: instead of sending a message 0 or 1 once, send it three times. The recipient averages over the received digits and takes the closest possibility. If one out of three digits was miscommunicated because of noise, the code nonetheless recovers the original message. The averaging gets rid of the noise.

1.1.2 Averaging over time

Does the conclusion that the game is worth playing follow from our analysis? To answer this, let's consider the mechanistic meaning of the average we computed. It is as if N copies of you played the game in parallel for a fixed period of time (a year), then pooled their end wealths together, and then shared the total equally between them.[3] This is very different from you playing one game for all your wealth for a long time, as would correspond to our original instructions of repeating the coin toss once a week for the rest of your life.

We therefore try a different analysis. Figure 1.3 shows another, different simulation of your wealth. This time we don't show an average over many trajectories but a simulation of a single trajectory over a long time. Noise is removed also in this case, but in a different way. To capture visually what happens over a long time we have to zoom out – more time has to be represented by the same amount of space on the page. In the process of this zooming-out, small short-time fluctuations will be diminished. Eventually the noise will be removed from the system just by the passage of time.

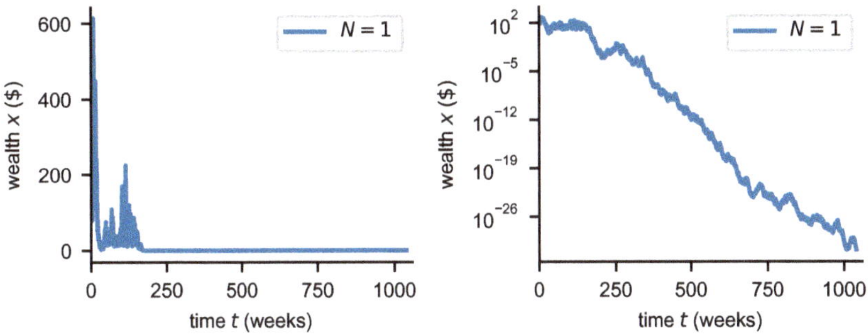

Figure 1.3: Single trajectory over 1,040 time steps, corresponding to 20 years in our setup. **Left:** on linear scales all we see is wealth quickly dropping to zero. **Right:** logarithmic scales are more appropriate for the multiplicative process and reveal systematic exponential decay.

The trajectory in Fig. 1.3 is, of course, random, but the apparent trend emerging from the randomness implies that our initial analysis in Fig. 1.2 does not reflect what happens over time in a single system. In one long game, your wealth seems to decay systematically, which suggests the game is best avoided. Several important messages can be derived from the observation that an individual trajectory grows more slowly (or decays faster) over time than an average of a large number of

[3] Or, equivalently, it is as if you split your wealth into N equal parts and invested each part in N independent coin games. The rules of the game as we defined it did not allow that.

trajectories.

1. If my wealth follows (Eq. 1.2), I will make poor decisions if I use the finite-ensemble average of wealth as an indication of what is likely to happen to my own wealth.

2. The performance of the average (or aggregate) wealth of a large group of individuals differs systematically from the performance of an individual's wealth. In our case large-group wealth grows (think gross domestic product (GDP)), whereas individual wealth decays.

3. For point 2 to be possible, *i.e.* for the average to outperform the typical individual, wealth must become increasingly concentrated in a few extremely rich individuals. The wealth of the richest individuals must be so large that the average becomes dominated by it, so that the average can grow although almost everyone's wealth decays. Inequality increases in our system.

The two methods we've used to eliminate the noise from our system are well known. We will see in Chap. 2 that the first method is closely related to the mathematical object called the "ensemble average," and the second is closely related to the object called the "time average."

Part I

Tools

Preview of Part I

In this part, we introduce the mathematical concepts and machinery used in the rest of the book.

We start in Chap. 2 with the random variable – the atom of all mathematical models of uncertainty. We examine its expectation value and its ensemble average, which we show to be equivalent under the frequentist interpretation of probability. Then we introduce time and move from the random variable to the stochastic process, for which two types of average become possible: the ensemble average and the time average.

These two averages lead us to the central concept in this book – ergodicity – which we treat in Chap. 3. We define the ergodic property as the equality of the ensemble and time averages of a stochastic process, and we give examples of ergodic and non-ergodic stochastic processes that illustrate ways in which ergodicity can hold or be broken.

Finally, in Chap. 4, we introduce the specific models we will use later in applications. We start with two key probability distributions – the normal and the lognormal – before introducing Brownian motion as the limiting case of the random walk. After a short interlude on Itô calculus, which greatly simplifies our handling of stochastic differential equations, we introduce our workhorse model of wealth evolution, geometric Brownian motion. In this stochastic process, wealth grows by random multiplication, much like in the coin game of Sec. 1.1.

Chapter 2

Averages

2.1 Random variables

When we toss a coin, we perform an *experiment* with unknown outcome. In the game, the two possible outcomes – heads or tails – correspond to wealth multipliers with the numerical values 1.5 and 0.6. A *random variable* is a very simple model of an experiment like this. Although much more can be said about random variables, the key idea is this: a random variable is a collection of pairs of numbers, like $\{(1.5, 0.5), (0.6, 0.5)\}$, see also [68, p. 2]. The first number in the pair is a possible *realisation* of the random variable, and the second number in the pair is the corresponding probability.

In general, a random variable, Z, is defined by:

- the set of its possible *realisations*, Ω;
- a *probability distribution*, $\mathrm{P}[\cdot]$, over this set.

Taking this as a starting point, we will spend the rest of this section developing all the random-variable-related concepts we will need later in the text.

2.1.1 Realisations

A realisation is one possible numerical outcome in our model of an experiment, for example "tails" or 0.6 in the coin game. The set of all possible realisations, Ω, is also called the *sample space*. It may be discrete, like the integers $\Omega = \mathbb{Z}$ or the set $\Omega = \{2/3, \sqrt{2}, 4\}$; continuous, like the real numbers $\Omega = \mathbb{R}$ or the interval $\Omega = (3, 12)$; or some combination of the two. The realisations must be mutually exclusive (meaning if one outcome occurs, the others do not) and collectively exhaustive (meaning the sample space describes all possible outcomes).

Clearly, a random variable is more than just a realisation of a random variable. When this distinction is important, random variables are usually denoted in upper case, Z, and realisations in lower case, z. When the sample space is discrete, it may help further to index realisations with an integer, $z^{(j)}$. Where it won't create confusion, we will use lower case letters for both random variables and realisations. This is less precise but easier on the eye.

2.1.2 Events

Consider a subset of the sample space. It might be a single realisation, a set of realisations, the empty set, or the entire sample space. For example, in the discrete sample space $\{2/3, \sqrt{2}, 4\}$, the realisation $\sqrt{2}$ is a subset (as is the set $\{2/3, 4\}$). In the continuous sample space $(3, 12)$, the interval $(8, 9)$ is a subset.

An *event* is a statement about the outcome of an experiment. Specifically, it is a statement that the realisation of a random variable, Z, belongs to some subset, E, of the sample space. We will refer to such events by writing $Z \in E$.[1] Where the situation allows, as in the examples above, we can write events in more everyday notation, for example $Z = \sqrt{2}$ (meaning the realisation of Z is $\sqrt{2}$) and $8 \leq Z \leq 9$ (meaning the realisation of Z is between 8 and 9).

There are two special events, corresponding to the empty set, $\varnothing$, and the sample space, Ω. As we have already said, one of the realisations in the sample space is guaranteed to occur (at least in our model, if not in reality). Therefore, the event $Z \in \varnothing$ is a statement about the experiment that cannot be true, so we call it the *impossible event*. Similarly, the event $Z \in \Omega$ is a statement that must be true, so we call it the *certain event*.

2.1.3 Probability distributions

We have said enough about realisations to turn to the second component of the random variable: the probability distribution. This is a function which assigns real numbers, called *probabilities*, to events. For example, if we write

$$\mathrm{P}[Z = z] = p, \tag{2.1}$$

we mean that the event $Z = z$ is associated with the probability p.

The probability distribution has the following properties:

[1] This notation from set theory is read as "Z is a member of the set E". Strictly speaking, Z is a random variable and E is a set of real numbers, so the former cannot be a member of the latter. What we really mean is that a realisation of Z, which is a real number, is a member of E. This mild abuse of notation is common and convenient, so we will use it.

- all events have non-negative probability, *i.e.* $\mathrm{P}[Z \in E] \geq 0$ for all $E \in \Omega$;
- the certain event has probability one, *i.e.* $\mathrm{P}[Z \in \Omega] = 1$.

The latter is a *normalisation condition* which fixes the scale of the probabilities. In effect, it is an agreement by all of us who use probabilities that the certain event has probability one, rather than, say, forty-two. This aids mutual understanding.

2.1.4 Discrete random variables

When the set of realisations is discrete, say $\{z^{(1)}, \ldots, z^{(M)}\}$, we assign a probability $p^{(j)}$ to each realisation $z^{(j)}$ such that

$$\mathrm{P}[Z = z] = \begin{cases} p^{(j)} & \text{if } z = z^{(j)} \\ 0 & \text{otherwise} \end{cases} \tag{2.2}$$

and

$$\mathrm{P}[Z \in \Omega] = \sum_{j=1}^{M} p^{(j)} = 1. \tag{2.3}$$

2.1.5 Continuous random variables

Most of the models in this book use random variables whose realisations form a continuous set. In this case, Z can take uncountably many values, to which we cannot assign non-zero probabilities while maintaining the normalisation condition. Instead, we assign probabilities to intervals.

We define a probability density function (PDF), $\mathcal{P}_Z(z)$, such that the probability of Z being realised in the interval (a, b) is

$$\mathrm{P}[a \leq Z \leq b] = \int_a^b \mathcal{P}_Z(z)\, dz. \tag{2.4}$$

The PDF is a non-negative function, $\mathcal{P}_Z(z) \geq 0$, normalised so that the probability of the certain event, *i.e.* the integral over the sample space, is one:

$$\mathrm{P}[Z \in \Omega] = \int_\Omega \mathcal{P}_Z(z)\, dz = 1. \tag{2.5}$$

Since we can assign zero probability density to any interval not in Ω without changing materially the random variable, we will often take the sample space to be the entire real line and write the normalisation condition as:

$$\int_{-\infty}^{\infty} \mathcal{P}_Z(z)\, dz = 1. \tag{2.6}$$

Note the difference between subscript and argument: $\mathcal{P}_Z(z)$ is the probability density of the random variable Z at value z. You might find it helpful to think of $\mathcal{P}_Z(z)\,\delta z$ as the approximate probability of Z being realised in the small interval, $(z, z+\delta z)$, close to z.

2.1.6 Frequentist interpretation

You may have noticed that we have said nothing about the meaning of probabilities. So far we have established only that they are numbers assigned to events. Giving these numbers meaning is the next step.

We will use the *frequentist interpretation* of probability. Imagine many separate experiments. For example, suppose we toss a coin N times and record the number of times, n_E, that the event $Z \in E$ occurs. Under the frequentist interpretation, the probability associated with this event is its relative frequency, n_E/N, in the limit $N \to \infty$, *i.e.*

$$\mathrm{P}\left[Z \in E\right] = \lim_{N\to\infty} \frac{n_E}{N}. \tag{2.7}$$

In the coin toss example, the probability assigned to the event of heads would be $1/2$ if the coin were unbiased; if biased, it would be some other number between 0 and 1.

The frequentist interpretation of probability is silent about whether the frequencies referred to are of outcomes in:

- one experimental system at many times, *e.g.* one coin flipped repeatedly;
- many experimental systems at one time, *e.g.* many coins flipped once.

Distinguishing between *temporal* (over time) and *spatial* (across systems) realisations will become important when we model quantities that vary over both dimensions, such as the wealth of individuals in an economy. As we shall see, this distinction lies at the heart of the ergodicity question. We introduce the mathematical machinery needed to disentangle time from systems in Sec. 2.4.

Unless otherwise stated, we will assume random variables carry neither temporal nor spatial information. They are just mathematical objects – paired sets of realisations and probabilities – from which we can build models of temporal and spatial phenomena. When the probability distribution of a random variable does not depend on time, as under this default assumption, we will say that the random variable is *stationary* or *time-independent*.

In Sec. 2.4 we will see that it is sometimes useful to use *non-stationary* or *time-dependent* random variables, with probability distributions parametrised by time. For example, wealth $x(t)$ in the coin game can be viewed as just such a random variable. When this is the case, we will make it explicit.

2.2 Expectation values

The *expectation value* is a property of a random variable.[2] Denoted by $\mathrm{E}[Z]$, it is the *probability-weighted average* of the realisations of Z.

DEFINITION: **Expectation value**

If Z is a discrete random variable, its expectation value is the sum of all possible realisations, $z^{(j)}$, weighted by their probabilities, $p^{(j)}$:

$$\mathrm{E}[Z] = \sum_j p^{(j)} z^{(j)}. \tag{2.8}$$

If Z is a continuous random variable, its expectation value is the integral over all realisations weighted by the probability density:

$$\mathrm{E}[Z] = \int_{-\infty}^{\infty} z \mathcal{P}_Z(z)\, dz. \tag{2.9}$$

The sum or integral may not exist, in which case the random variable does not have an expectation value. One example of this is the payout of the St. Petersburg lottery in Sec. 7.1. Another example is the Pareto random variable with PDF of the form:

$$\mathcal{P}_Z(z) = \begin{cases} \zeta z^{-(1+\zeta)} & z \geq 1 \\ 0 & z < 1 \end{cases} \tag{2.10}$$

for $\zeta \leq 1$.

Note what the operation of taking the expectation value has done. It has converted a random variable – a set of realisations and a corresponding set of probabilities – to single number. We often refer to such numbers as *scalars*, especially when we want to distinguish them from higher-dimensional mathematical objects, like vectors or random variables. The neat thing about scalars is their *transitivity property*: if $a > b$ and $b > c$, then $a > c$. This allows us to rank scalars. As a consequence, any object that can be collapsed to a scalar can be *ranked*. For this reason, theories of decision-making often involve extracting rankable scalars from models of economic variables.

[2]It is known by many names, including expected value, mathematical expectation, first moment, and mean.

2.3 Ensemble averages

The *ensemble average* is conceptually different from the expectation value, although we will see that, under the frequentist interpretation of probability, it is identical in value. Instead of taking the probability-weighted average of the members of the sample space of Z, we generate many independent realisations of Z and take the unweighted average of the *sample* thus obtained. If the sample is finite, we call this the *finite-ensemble average* and denote it by $\langle Z \rangle_N$.

DEFINITION: **Finite-ensemble average**

The finite-ensemble average $\langle Z \rangle_N$ of a random variable Z is the average over N independent realisations,

$$\langle Z \rangle_N \equiv \frac{1}{N} \sum_{i=1}^{N} z_i, \tag{2.11}$$

where z_i denotes the ith realisation of Z. (Note that z_i is not the same as $z^{(i)}$, which would denote the ith member of the sample space of Z, if Z were a discrete random variable.)

You may know $\langle Z \rangle_N$ as the *sample average* or *sample mean*. It is an additive average, *i.e.* the unique value by which each of the N realisations can be replaced without altering their sum. We have already encountered one type of finite-ensemble average – the average wealth in the coin game, (Eq. 1.3).

The finite-ensemble average is itself a random variable. Each sample of size N can contain different realisations of Z with a different average. As $N \to \infty$, this random average may converge to a unique constant. If it does, we call it the ensemble average and denote it by $\langle Z \rangle$.

DEFINITION: **Ensemble average**

The ensemble average $\langle Z \rangle$ of a random variable Z is the $N \to \infty$ limit of its finite-ensemble average,

$$\langle Z \rangle \equiv \lim_{N\to\infty} \langle Z \rangle_N = \lim_{N\to\infty} \frac{1}{N} \sum_{i=1}^{N} z_i, \tag{2.12}$$

where the limit exists.

The limit is not guaranteed to exist, in which case Z has no ensemble average (although we note that a finite-ensemble average can always be computed).[3] We sometimes refer to the imagined infinitely large sample as the *ensemble* of Z.

Unlike the expectation value, the ensemble average of a random variable is not defined directly in terms of probabilities. It is simply the quantity to which averages over realisations converge as the number of realisations grows. Recall, however, that we interpret probabilities as relative frequencies of realisations in an infinitely large sample, *i.e.* the ensemble. Under this interpretation, we can express the ensemble average in terms of probabilities and show it is equal to the expectation value *almost surely*.[4] We do this here for the case of a discrete random variable, noting that a similar proof can be offered for the continuous case.

Proof. Let $n^{(j)}$ be the number of times $z^{(j)}$ is observed in N realisations of Z. The finite-ensemble average is

$$\langle Z \rangle_N = \frac{1}{N} \sum_{i=1}^{N} z_i = \sum_j \frac{n^{(j)} z^{(j)}}{N}, \tag{2.13}$$

where i indexes the generated realisation of Z, and j indexes the members of the sample space, *i.e.* the possible realisations. Under the frequentist interpretation, (Eq. 2.7), the relative frequency of each possible realisation, $n^{(j)}/N$, converges almost surely to the probability $p^{(j)}$ as $N \to \infty$. Therefore,

$$\lim_{N \to \infty} \langle Z \rangle_N = \sum_j p^{(j)} z^{(j)} = \mathrm{E}[Z] \tag{2.14}$$

almost surely. □

This result is commonly known as the *law of large numbers.* It is exceedingly useful because it means we do not need to generate infinitely many realisations of a random variable to compute its ensemble average. Instead, if we know the probability distribution, we can compute its expectation value as a weighted average or integral. From now on, we will use ensemble average and expectation value interchangeably, happy that we understand the conceptual difference between the two.

[3]When $\langle Z \rangle$ is divergent, then $\langle Z \rangle_N$ will grow systematically with N. If $\langle Z \rangle_N$ represents an average taken over N successive measurements, *i.e.* a time series, then it will be non-stationary. In such situations, using a Z with a divergent ensemble average (*e.g.* with a fat-tailed PDF) may model the growing average as faithfully as using a $Z(N)$ with explicit N-dependence.

[4]You will encounter the equivalent phrases "almost surely", "for almost all", and "with probability one" several times in this book. These fragments of mathematical rigour allow us to claim as equal two different mathematical objects, like $\mathrm{E}[Z]$ and $\langle Z \rangle$, when strictly speaking their equality is only a certain event in some limit ($N \to \infty$ here). We include these phrases mostly to avoid offending serious mathematicians, some of whom are our friends.

History: The invention of the expectation value

Expectation values were developed to settle a moral question that arises in the following somewhat contrived context. Imagine playing a game of dice with a group of gamblers. The rules of the game are simple: we roll the dice three times; whoever rolls the most points gets the pot to which we've all contributed equal amounts. We've already rolled the dice twice when suddenly the police burst in because they've heard of our illegal gambling ring. We all avoid arrest, most of us escape through the backdoor, and to everyone's great relief you had the presence of mind to grab the pot before jumping out of a conveniently located ground-floor window. Later that day, under the cover of dusk, we meet behind the old oak tree just outside of town to split the pot in a fair way. But hold on – what does "fair" mean here? Some of us had acquired more points than others in the first two rolls of the dice. Shouldn't they get more? The game was not concluded, so wouldn't it be fair to return everyone's wager and thank our lucky stars that we weren't arrested? Should we split the pot in proportion to each player's points?

All of these solutions were proposed [15]. The question is fundamentally moral, and there is no mathematical answer. But Blaise Pascal, now famous for addressing theological questions using expectation values, put the problem to Pierre de Fermat, and over the course of a few months' correspondence (the two never met in person) Fermat and Pascal agreed that fairness is achieved as follows: think of all (equally likely) possible realisations of the third round of throws of the dice, call the number of all possibilities N. Now count those possibilities that result in player j winning, call this $n^{(j)}$. If q is the amount of money in the pot, then we split the pot fairly by giving each player $q \times n^{(j)}/N$. This is the expectation value of player j's winnings, according to (Eq. 2.8), because $n^{(j)}/N = p^{(j)}$ is the probability that player j would have won the amount q in the pot. Later researchers called this amount the "mathematical expectation" or simply the "expectation value". But this is really an unfortunate choice – no player during the game "expected" to receive their expectation value. Instead, each player expected to receive q or nothing.

2.4 Stochastic processes

Recall that a random variable carries no information about whether its realisations are temporal (drawn from one system at many times) or spatial (drawn from many systems at one time). Since we are interested in quantities like wealth, which vary over time and across people, we had better clear this up once and for all. Enter the *stochastic process.* This is a mathematical object, a sort of big brother to the random variable, whose realisations are labelled by the times and systems to which they correspond.

We motivate our treatment of the stochastic process with a familiar example. Wealth in the coin game of Sec. 1.1 evolves according to

$$x(t+\delta t) = x(t)R, \tag{2.15}$$

where R is a random variable, with realisations $\{0.6, 1.5\}$ and probabilities $\{0.5, 0.5\}$, and δt is the duration of a round.

Rules such as (Eq. 2.15), which map from the value of an observable at one time to its possible value at a later time, are known as *dynamics.* As we shall see, building and studying models of wealth dynamics are important activities in EE. Starting from wealth $x(0)$, successive applications of the dynamics in (Eq. 2.15) generate a function of time,

$$x(t) = x(0)\prod_{\tau=1}^{T} r_\tau, \tag{2.16}$$

where $T = \lfloor t/\delta t \rfloor$ is the number of rounds completed and r_τ is the realisation of R in the τth round.[5]

Equation (2.16) describes one possible evolution of wealth in the game. If we start again, generating fresh realisations of R at each round, we get a second function of time, likely different from the first. We imagine these two functions as describing the wealth of two different players or, more generally, in two different systems. Playing the game in N systems generates a finite ensemble, $\{x_1(t), \ldots, x_N(t)\}$, of functions of time, called *trajectories.* Now we have what we wanted, a way of distinguishing spatial from temporal realisations: $x_i(t)$ is the realisation of the stochastic process $X(t)$ in system i at time t.

This reminds us somewhat of the random variable. There we had a set of real numbers, the realisations, and an associated probability distribution. Here we have a set of real-valued functions of time, the trajectories, which are also generated randomly. If we know enough about how, then we can define a probability distribution over the set of trajectories. This is easy in the coin game: after T rounds, there are 2^T equally likely trajectories and we can assign the probability $1/2^T$ to each of them.

Thus we can view the stochastic process as a generalisation of the random variable from scalars to functions of time. For illustration, consider a generic stochastic process $X(t)$ with an ensemble of trajectories $\{x_i(t)\}$. Figure 2.1 shows the first five trajectories in the ensemble,

[5] $\lfloor t/\delta t \rfloor$ is the "floor" of $t/\delta t$, *i.e.* rounded down to the nearest integer.

$i = 1 \ldots 5$, plotted horizontally on a grid. Selecting a trajectory from this ensemble is equivalent to selecting at random a horizontal slice of the grid.

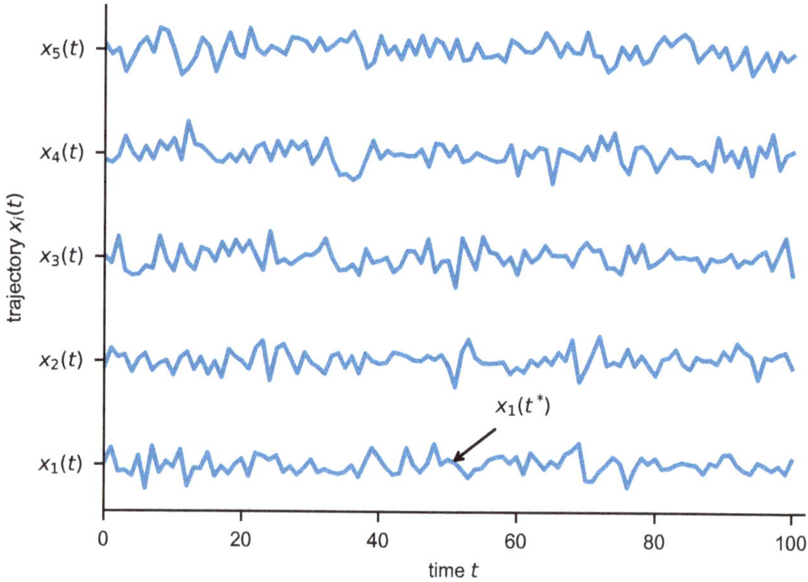

Figure 2.1: Five trajectories of a generic stochastic process $X(t)$. Each trajectory $x_i(t)$ is a function of time, plotted horizontally across the figure. Fixing time at $t = t^*$ results in a random variable $X(t^*)$, one realisation of which is indicated at $x_1(t^*)$.

To treat this generally, we could introduce a random variable Z, of which each realisation $z^{(j)}$ identifies a possible trajectory $x^{(j)}(t)$ of the stochastic process $X(t)$.[6] In this setup, the probability $p^{(j)}$ associated with $z^{(j)}$ is also the probability associated with $x^{(j)}(t)$. You might find this sort of treatment of the stochastic process in other textbooks, like [68, p. 52]. Conceptually, it corresponds to resolving all our uncertainty about the future values of x in a single initial act: the realisation of a random variable to select one of the possible trajectories. Note the distinction between members of the set of possible trajectories, denoted $x^{(j)}(t)$, and members of an ensemble of trajectories, denoted $x_i(t)$. You will recall we made a similar distinction for realisations of random variables.

Figure 2.1 suggests a second way of viewing the stochastic process.

[6] For simplicity, we have assumed that the possible trajectories are countable and, therefore, identifiable using realisations of a discrete random variable. For a stochastic process with uncountably many trajectories, we would use a continuous random variable instead.

Fixing the time, say at $t = t^*$, yields a random variable whose realisations form an ensemble of function values $\{x_i(t^*)\}$. If we change the time, say to $t = 2t^*$, we get a different random variable with different realisations. Therefore, we can also think of a stochastic process as a family of time-dependent random variables, each corresponding to a vertical slice of the grid in Fig. 2.1.

This second picture of the stochastic process is quite convenient. For any given time, we can extract a random variable, parametrised by time, that describes the spatial realisations of the observable we are studying. Of course, this random variable does not contain the full temporal detail of each trajectory: it will not tell us the story of how each system arrived at its value. But often we are not interested in that detail, like when we want to know how wealth is distributed in the coin game, or in an economy, at some point in time. In such situations, a time-dependent random variable is easy to work with and tells us everything we want to know.

In summary, then, a stochastic process, $X(t)$, is defined as:

- a set of possible trajectories, $\{x(t)\}$; and
- a probability distribution over this set.

The set of possible trajectories may be countable and associated with a discrete set of probabilities, or uncountable and associated with a PDF. We always interpret the parameter t as time. Fixing time collapses the stochastic process to a time-dependent random variable.

2.4.1 Ensemble average

We can define the ensemble average of a stochastic process similarly to how we defined the ensemble average of a random variable in Sec. 2.3. Indeed, if we view the stochastic process as a time-dependent random variable, we can use that definition directly. In essence, we take the average over a finite ensemble of N trajectories and then let $N \to \infty$.

DEFINITION: **Ensemble average of a stochastic process**

The ensemble average of a stochastic process $X(t)$ at time t is defined as

$$\langle X(t) \rangle = \lim_{N\to\infty} \frac{1}{N} \sum_{i=1}^{N} x_i(t), \tag{2.17}$$

where this limit exists. $x_i(t)$ is the ith trajectory in the ensemble of trajectories, which we interpret as the value of x in system i at time t. Thus $\langle X(t) \rangle$ is a spatial average at a specified time.

We can view $\langle X(t) \rangle$ in (Eq. 2.17) as an average over the ensemble of trajectories of the stochastic process or, equivalently, as the ensemble average of the time-dependent random variable formed by specifying time t in the stochastic process. In general, $\langle X(t) \rangle$ is a time-dependent quantity.

2.4.2 Expectation value

We can also take the expectation value of the stochastic process $X(t)$, if we know the probability distribution over the set of trajectories.

> DEFINITION: **Expectation value of a stochastic process**
>
> If the stochastic process $X(t)$ has countably many trajectories, then we can write its expectation value as
>
> $$\mathrm{E}[X(t)] = \sum_j p^{(j)} x^{(j)}(t), \tag{2.18}$$
>
> where $x^{(j)}(t)$ is the jth possible trajectory and $p^{(j)}$ is its probability.
>
> If the stochastic process $X(t)$ has uncountably many trajectories, then we can write its expectation value as
>
> $$\mathrm{E}[X(t)] = \int_{-\infty}^{\infty} x \, \mathcal{P}_X(x;t) \, dx, \tag{2.19}$$
>
> where $\mathcal{P}_X(x;t)$ is the time-dependent PDF of the random variable formed by specifying time t in the stochastic process.

Under the frequentist interpretation of probability, $\langle X(t) \rangle = \mathrm{E}[X(t)]$.

2.4.3 Generating trajectories

Switching to practical considerations, there are two approaches to generating a trajectory of a stochastic process, say on a computer. The first is to reproduce numerically the conceptual act of selecting one member from a set of trajectories. For example, if the possible trajectories were finitely many and equally probable, then we could label them with integers and draw one from a discrete uniform distribution. All the uncertainty is resolved at the start, in a single realisation of a random variable.

The other approach is to generate a trajectory on-the-fly by repeated application of the dynamics. This is how we generate wealth trajectories in the coin game, where the rule in (Eq. 2.15) tells us to multiply current wealth by the realisation of a random variable. Realising a random variable at every time step sounds laborious. However, in many models of natural phenomena, it is easier to write down realistic dynamics than a realistic PDF for all possible trajectories. There is an explanation for this: it is often about the changes of quantities, rather than the quantities themselves, that we can reason physically. Indeed, much of science is well described as the search for the unchanging rules of how things change.

Typically, then, we will generate trajectories of a stochastic process sequentially using dynamics. If it creates no ambiguity, we will not distinguish between the stochastic process and a single realisation of it, using lower case to denote both, such as $x(t)$ for wealth. When it is important to identify different trajectories, this will usually be in the context of a sample of systems, so we will use the system subscript already introduced, $x_i(t)$.

2.5 Time average

Equation (2.17) shows how to take the ensemble average of a stochastic process $X(t)$ by averaging over infinitely many systems at a fixed time. Now that we have distinguished spatial from temporal realisations, another type of average is possible: the *time average*. Instead of choosing a time and averaging across systems, we choose a system, *i.e.* a trajectory, and average over time.

We will start by taking the average for system i over a finite time period from time t_0 to $t_0 + \Delta t$. We call this a *finite-time average*.

DEFINITION: **Finite-time average**

The finite-time average of the trajectory $x_i(t)$ is the average value of the function from time t_0 to $t_0 + \Delta t$,

$$\bar{x}_i(t_0, \Delta t) \equiv \frac{1}{\Delta t} \int_{t_0}^{t_0+\Delta t} x_i(s) ds. \tag{2.20}$$

If $x_i(t)$ changes only at T discrete time intervals of δt, such that $\Delta t = T\delta t$, then the finite-time average can be written as

$$\bar{x}_i(t_0, \Delta t) = \frac{1}{T} \sum_{\tau=0}^{T-1} x_i(t_0 + \tau\delta t). \tag{2.21}$$

In the same way that the ensemble average is the many-systems limit of the finite-ensemble average, so the time average is the long-time limit of the finite-time average.

DEFINITION: **Time average**

The time average is the $\Delta t \to \infty$ limit of the finite-time average,

$$\bar{x}_i \equiv \lim_{\Delta t \to \infty} \bar{x}_i(t_0, \Delta t), \tag{2.22}$$

where this limit exists.

We have assumed that this limiting value does not depend on t_0, the time at which the averaging starts. This is a reasonable assumption. Suppose we start averaging later, say at time $t_1 > t_0$. We lose a contribution of $\int_{t_0}^{t_1} x_i(s)ds$ to the integral in (Eq. 2.20). If this contribution is finite, which imposes only a gentle constraint on the behaviour of $x_i(t)$ between t_0 and t_1, then losing it will not alter the time average after we divide by Δt and let $\Delta t \to \infty$.

In general, the time average depends on the choice of trajectory: $\bar{x}_1$ can be different from $\bar{x}_2$ and so on. Some stochastic processes do not have this dependence or, more formally, the time average of each trajectory converges to the same value almost surely. When this is the case, we can drop the system index i from the notation and denote the unique time average of the stochastic process as $\bar{x}$.

Expressed visually, the ensemble average operates along a vertical slice of Fig. 2.1, corresponding to many trajectories at a fixed time, while the time average operates along a horizontal slice, corresponding to one trajectory over long time. We show this explicitly in Fig. 2.2.

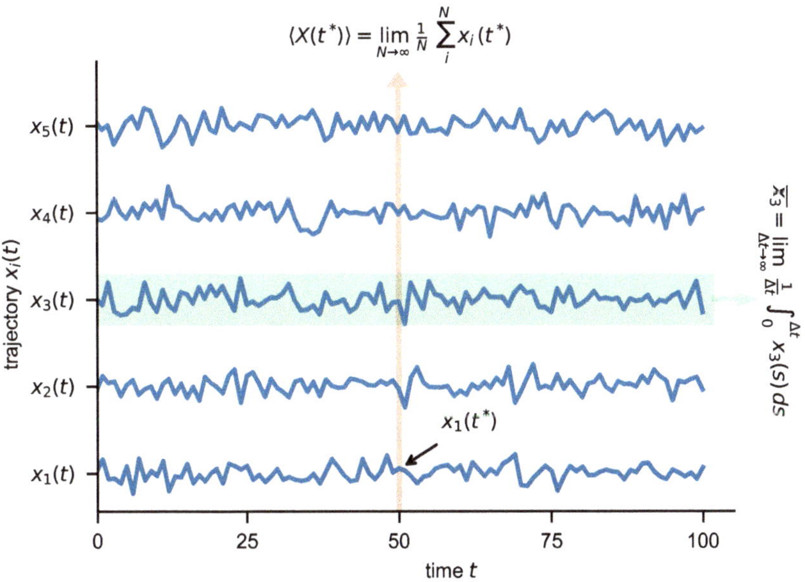

Figure 2.2: Realisations of a generic stochastic process $X(t)$, *cf.* Fig. 2.1. The ensemble average $\langle X(t^*)\rangle$ is obtained by choosing a time, say $t = t^*$, and averaging over systems (vertical red bar). The time average is obtained by choosing a system, say $i = 3$, and averaging over time (horizontal green bar).

Chapter 3

Ergodicity

3.1 The game, revisited

We have introduced some essential tools for studying models like the coin game, where outcomes are uncertain and vary over time. It makes sense, therefore, to apply these tools to the game to see how they deepen our understanding of it.

We pretended to be mathematically clueless when we ran the simulations in Sec. 1.1, hoping to understand the game simply by looking at many possible outcomes. We can now compute exactly the ensemble average of the stochastic process for wealth, $x(t)$, instead of approximating it numerically by a finite-ensemble average. We start by taking the ensemble average of the wealth updating equation, (Eq. 2.15),

$$\langle x(t+\delta t)\rangle = \langle x(t)r\rangle\,. \tag{3.1}$$

We assume the outcomes of coin tosses are independent of the player's wealth and of time, so that $\langle x(t)r\rangle = \langle x(t)\rangle \langle r\rangle$. Thus, (Eq. 3.1) can be written as

$$\langle x(t+\delta t)\rangle = \langle x(t)\rangle \langle r\rangle\,. \tag{3.2}$$

We can solve this recursively for the wealth after T rounds from a known starting wealth, $x(t_0)$:

$$\langle x(t_0+T\delta t)\rangle = x(t_0)\langle r\rangle^T\,. \tag{3.3}$$

δt is the duration of a single round of the game, so the total playing time is $\Delta t = T\delta t$.

Recall that r is a random variable with outcomes $\{0.6, 1.5\}$ and probabilities $\{0.5, 0.5\}$. The expectation value is $\langle r\rangle = 1.05$ and (Eq. 3.3) becomes

$$\langle x(t_0+T\delta t)\rangle = x(t_0)1.05^T\,. \tag{3.4}$$

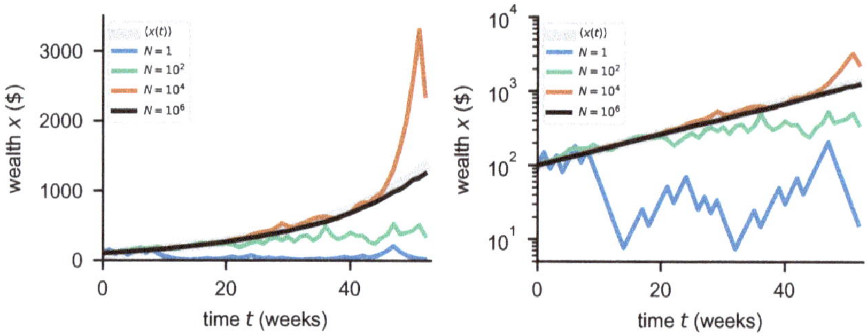

Figure 3.1: Ensemble average (thick grey line) and finite-ensemble averages for $N = 1, 10^2, 10^4, 10^6$ trajectories of the coin game. **Left:** wealth on a linear scale. **Right:** wealth on a logarithmic scale.

Thus the ensemble average wealth grows exponentially by a factor of 1.05 per round of the game.

It is useful to quantify this growth in a standard way, as a growth rate. We will say much more about this in Sec. 5.3, since it is a central concept in EE. For the moment, we will simply express the exponential growth of the ensemble average wealth using the exponential function,

$$\langle x(t_0 + \Delta t)\rangle = x(t_0)\exp(g_{\langle\rangle}\Delta t), \tag{3.5}$$

where we have labelled the growth rate as $g_{\langle\rangle}$ to indicate it is that of the ensemble average wealth. Equating (Eq. 3.5) with (Eq. 3.3), we get

$$g_{\langle\rangle} = \frac{T \ln\langle r\rangle}{\Delta t} = \frac{\ln\langle r\rangle}{\delta t}. \tag{3.6}$$

We must choose the units in which we measure time. For simplicity, let's just measure it in rounds of the game, *i.e.* $\delta t = 1$ round. This choice gives us a growth rate of $g_{\langle\rangle} = \ln(1.05)/1 \approx 4.9\%$ per round.

Finding $g_{\langle\rangle} > 0$ led us to think initially that the coin game was worth playing, when we analysed it numerically in Sec. 1.1. In Fig. 3.1 we compare the analytical result for the ensemble, derived above, to the numerical results of Fig. 1.2 for finite ensembles. We could now conclude that the case is closed. Mathematics and simulations agree there is some risk involved, but "on average" our wealth grows if we play the game.

However, we now know that there are two ways in which we can say "on average". Let's consider a single wealth trajectory over long time, as we did in Sec. 1.1, but using the tools we have since developed. Starting from $x(t_0)$ and playing for T rounds leads to wealth,

$$x(t_0 + T\delta t) = x(t_0)\prod_{\tau=1}^{T} r_\tau, \tag{3.7}$$

where r_τ is the realisation of the random wealth multiplier r at round τ. We have taken no kind of average yet and $x(t_0 + T\delta t)$ remains a random variable (it is, after all, the outcome of a stochastic process at a specified time).

We follow our previous strategy of expressing this as exponential growth

$$x(t_0 + \Delta t) = x(t_0) \exp(g_T \Delta t), \tag{3.8}$$

where g_T is the exponential growth rate measured after T rounds of the gamble. Equating (Eq. 3.7) and (Eq. 3.8) and rearranging for the growth rate, we get

$$g_T = \frac{1}{\Delta t} \ln \left(\prod_{\tau=1}^{T} r_\tau \right) = \frac{1}{\delta t} \left(\frac{1}{T} \sum_{\tau=1}^{T} \ln r_\tau \right), \tag{3.9}$$

where we used the property of the logarithm that $\ln(AB) = \ln A + \ln B$ to convert the product into a sum. Individual wealth grows exponentially at a random growth rate, g_T, whose distribution depends on the number of rounds played, T.

What happens to g_T in the long run? There are two ways of evaluating the $\Delta t \to \infty$ (or, equivalently, $T \to \infty$) limit of (Eq. 3.9). Both are illuminating. First, we can consider the product of wealth multipliers. The effective multiplier after T rounds (i.e. that which, if applied at each round, would yield the same product) is

$$r_T = \left(\prod_{\tau=1}^{T} r_\tau \right)^{\frac{1}{T}}. \tag{3.10}$$

This is the *geometric mean* of the $\{r_\tau\}$. Suppose heads appear n_{heads} times and tails n_{tails} times. Then

$$r_T = (1.5)^{\frac{n_{\text{heads}}}{T}} (0.6)^{\frac{n_{\text{tails}}}{T}}, \tag{3.11}$$

which is simply the product of possible realisations of the wealth multiplier raised to their relative frequencies. We know already what happens to relative frequencies as the number of rounds grows large: they converge almost surely to their corresponding probabilities, in this case both 1/2. So, in the many-rounds (or long-time) limit, the effective per-round multiplier of wealth converges to

$$r_{\text{time}} = \lim_{T \to \infty} r_T = (1.5)^{\frac{1}{2}} (0.6)^{\frac{1}{2}} = (0.9)^{\frac{1}{2}} \approx 0.95. \tag{3.12}$$

This tells a strikingly different story from that told by ensemble average wealth. Instead of growing exponentially by a factor 1.05 per round, a single wealth trajectory over long time decays exponentially by an effective factor of 0.95 per round. The corresponding exponential growth rate is

$$g_{\text{time}} = \frac{\ln r_{\text{time}}}{\delta t} \approx -5.1\% \text{ per round.} \tag{3.13}$$

The alternative route to this result is to take the $T \to \infty$ limit of the sum in (Eq. 3.9). Something rather interesting – and central to EE– happens when we do this:

$$g_{\text{time}} = \lim_{T\to\infty} \frac{1}{\delta t} \left(\frac{1}{T} \sum_{\tau=1}^{T} \ln r_{\tau} \right) = \frac{\langle \ln r \rangle}{\delta t}. \tag{3.14}$$

The first equality says that the growth rate of individual wealth over long time is the time average of the logarithm of the wealth multipliers, $\{\ln r_\tau\}$, divided by the round duration, δt. That's kind of believable. After all, we are trying to quantify how something is growing over time. The second equality, however, contains a remarkable conceptual insight: we can express this time average as the ensemble average of the random variable, $\ln r$. In other words, provided we know which observable to average over, we can investigate what happens in our model over long time by averaging over many systems!

To maintain sanity, let's confirm this is the same as the result obtained by finding the effective wealth multiplier:

$$\frac{\langle \ln r \rangle}{\delta t} = \frac{\frac{1}{2}\ln(1.5) + \frac{1}{2}\ln(0.6)}{\delta t} = \frac{\ln\left[(1.5)^{\frac{1}{2}}(0.6)^{\frac{1}{2}}\right]}{\delta t} = \frac{\ln r_{\text{time}}}{\delta t}. \tag{3.15}$$

It checks out.

There are two deep reasons why this works. The first is that the operation we perform on the product of the $\{r_\tau\}$ in (Eq. 3.9) – taking the logarithm and dividing by the duration – produces an arithmetic mean of the $\{\ln r_\tau\}$. In effect, by using the logarithm to transform multiplication to addition, we express the evolution of wealth in the form of a sum, specifically a finite-time average. The second reason is that the $\{\ln r_\tau\}$ are independent identically distributed (iid) random variables, with the same distribution as $\ln r$ and with no dependence on time. It follows that realisations over time and across systems are statistically indistinguishable, so that the time average in (Eq. 3.14) can be replaced by the ensemble average. Another way of seeing this is that the summation index, τ, in (Eq. 3.14) can just as well index different players as different rounds, because of the iid-ness of the $\{r_\tau\}$.

Observables whose time and ensemble averages are equivalent are very special, and we will say much more about them in the next section.

Our computations of g_{time} are consistent with the simulations in Sec. 1.1. Figure 3.2 (right panel) compares the single trajectory generated in Fig. 1.3 to exponential decay at rate g_{time}. The trajectory in

Fig. 1.3 was no fluke: *every* trajectory will decay in the long run, with a growth rate approaching −5.1% per round.

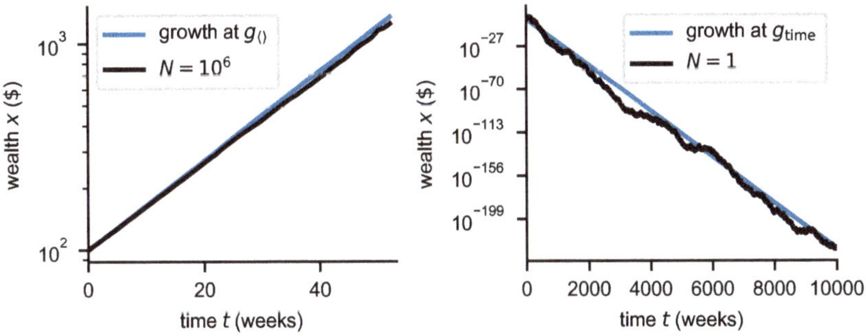

Figure 3.2: Ensemble and time averaging in the coin game. **Left:** a simulated finite-ensemble average of $N = 10^6$ trajectories (black line) grows at approximately $g_{\langle\rangle}$ (blue line) over 52 time steps. **Right:** a simulated single trajectory (black line) decays at approximately g_{time} (blue line) over 10,000 time steps.

There are two average wealth multipliers – $\langle r \rangle$ and r_{time} – and corresponding growth rates – $g_{\langle\rangle}$ and g_{time} – which we have determined numerically and analytically. Neither average is "wrong" *per se*. Instead, each average corresponds to a different property of the model and, therefore, answers a different question about the model. A statement like "wealth goes up, on average" is meaningless on its own. It should be countered with the question: "on what type of average?"

3.2 Ergodicity

We have now introduced all the concepts needed to ask the *ergodicity* question. The question is very simple: is the time average of a stochastic process equal to its ensemble average (or expectation value)? If so, then we say the stochastic process is *ergodic*. If not, then we say the stochastic process is *non-ergodic*.

Formally, we define the ergodic property of a stochastic process as follows.

DEFINITION: **Ergodic property**

A stochastic process $X(t)$ is ergodic[1] if its ensemble average is constant in time and its time average converges to this constant almost surely (a.s.), *i.e.* if for all j and t

$$\bar{x}_j = \langle X(t) \rangle, a.s., \tag{3.16}$$

or, writing it out in full, if

$$\lim_{\Delta t \to \infty} \frac{1}{\Delta t} \int_{t_0}^{t_0+\Delta t} x_j(s)\, ds = \lim_{N\to\infty} \frac{1}{N} \sum_i^N x_i(t), a.s. \tag{3.17}$$

We can write this condition equivalently as the equality of time average and expectation value, *i.e.* if for all j and t

$$\bar{x}_j = \mathrm{E}[X(t)], a.s., \tag{3.18}$$

or, in full,

$$\lim_{\Delta t \to \infty} \frac{1}{\Delta t} \int_{t_0}^{t_0+\Delta t} x_j(s)\, ds = \int_{-\infty}^{\infty} x\, \mathcal{P}_X(x;t)\, dx, a.s., \tag{3.19}$$

where $\mathcal{P}_X(x;t)$ is the time-dependent PDF of the random variable formed by $X(t)$ at time t.

We refer to (Eq. 3.19) (and generalisations of it) as *Birkhoff's equality*, after one of the founders of *ergodic theory* in the 1930s. Ergodic theory is a highly technical branch of mathematics which provides rigorous conditions for such equalities to hold. Mercifully, we do not need to study it in order to use the ergodicity concept in economics. Instead, we will make a brief excursion into some salient points.

Our definition of the ergodic property, (Eq. 3.17), assumes explicitly that the ensemble average is constant, *i.e.* does not change over time, and that convergence of the time average to this constant is almost sure. However, a stochastic process can exhibit *transient* behaviour, where $\mathcal{P}_X(x;t)$ is non-stationary but converges to a stationary function $\mathcal{P}_X(x)$ in the $t \to \infty$ limit. The idea is that the probability distribution, perhaps in a response to an initial disturbance, exhibits temporary behaviour

[1] Some researchers would call $X(t)$ "mean ergodic" and require further observables derived from it to be mean ergodic in order to call $X(t)$ "wide-sense ergodic." This extra nomenclature is not necessary for our work, but we leave a footnote here to avoid confusion. Ours is a working definition of ergodicity common in stochastic processes research. In dynamical systems research, ergodicity is a deeper property from which Birkhoff's ergodic theorem derives the equality of time averages and expected values.

before settling down to a unique stable form. We discuss this further in Sec. 9.2.3.

In such situations, we can take the expectation value in the long-time limit,

$$\lim_{t\to\infty} \mathrm{E}\left[X(t)\right] = \int_{-\infty}^{\infty} x\,\mathcal{P}_X(x)\,dx, \tag{3.20}$$

and compare it to the time average (assuming that is system-independent) to decide whether the ergodic property holds. In practical terms, we are allowing for transient behaviour in our definition of ergodicity by taking the expectation value after it has subsided.

What about the assumed system-independence of the time average? Well, it is sometimes possible to define weird trajectories of a stochastic process, whose time averages differ from the typical case. An example would be always flipping heads in the coin game of Sec. 1.1. Provided the probability of such trajectories becomes vanishingly small over time, then we can treat the time average as system-independent (in the "almost sure" sense). Of course, this is not relevant if there is no typical case, *i.e.* if the stochastic process produces trajectories with generally system-dependent long-time behaviours. This is one way of breaking ergodicity, as we shall see in Sec. 3.2.2.

A trick for avoiding nuanced questions of transients and atypical trajectories is to apply the $\Delta t \to \infty$ and $N \to \infty$ limits to both sides of (Eq. 3.17), and then to ask whether the order of taking the limits matters. Taking the ensemble average of the time average on the left-hand side eliminates the impossible trajectories, since they appear with zero relative frequency, while taking the time average of the ensemble average on the right-hand side eliminates any transient behaviour. If we get the same constant regardless of the order of averaging, *i.e.* if the long-time and many-systems limits are commutative, then we can say that the stochastic process is ergodic.

We note that ergodicity is a property of a stochastic process, *i.e.* of a mathematical model, which indicates whether its time and ensemble averages are equal. Ergodicity is not a property of real objects – it makes little sense to ponder whether your chair is ergodic. However, if a real observable that varies over systems and time, like wealth in a population, is well modelled by a stochastic process, then we might abuse language slightly by saying "wealth is ergodic" or "wealth is non-ergodic". We really mean that the stochastic process we are using to model wealth has that property.

Ergodicity is the core idea in our treatment of economics. Now that we have defined it, we will pause to discuss why it is an important concept in science generally and in economics specifically. We will then explore it in greater mathematical depth.

3.2.1 Why is ergodicity important?

The time and ensemble averages of a stochastic process are mathematically and conceptually different operations. In general, we should not expect them to produce the same result. It is only under special conditions, namely those of ergodicity, that these two averaging procedures are interchangeable.

What are these special conditions? Put formally, ergodicity requires that a trajectory will, almost surely over long time, visit every possible value of the stochastic process, with frequency proportional to its probability density, regardless of where it starts. In simpler terms, ergodicity means that a single trajectory explores the sample space fully. If this happens, then the time average can be expressed as an expectation value under the appropriate PDF, as in (Eq. 3.19).

Each average has a distinct meaning. The ensemble average is the average of an observable over infinitely many systems at one time. To take a concrete example, consider a stochastic process whose trajectories approximate the wealths of people in a large population. The ensemble average resembles what each person would have if all the wealths were added up and divided equally. Its definition implies a mechanism – of pooling and sharing – which may or may not resemble things that happen in the real world. Where it does, the ensemble average will be a relevant average. It should be no surprise, then, that it is a central quantity in the analysis of insurance and other forms of economic *cooperation*, as we discuss in Chap. 7 and Chap. 8.

The time average is a different animal. It is the average of an observable in a single system over infinitely long time. It tells us about the behaviour of single systems or, in economic terms, of individuals. We noted in Sec. 2.5 that a stochastic process can generate different time averages for different trajectories. If so, each time average tells us only about the long-time behaviour of the system to which it corresponds. If, on the other hand, the time average of any trajectory converges almost surely to a unique value, then it carries robust information about how single systems behave over time.

Most of the time averages we study in EE will have the latter property. Our canonical example will be the time average growth rate of wealth, whose unique value provides an objective solution to the gamble problem in Chap. 6. Here an individual decision maker must decide whether or not to accept a gamble, such as a coin toss in the game in Sec. 1.1. Since they have access to only one wealth trajectory – their own – and, we assume, many such decisions ahead of them, the time average growth rate of wealth would seem the relevant average.

Indeed, in the coin game we found exactly that. The time average is the interesting quantity because it says what happens to your wealth as time passes. The ensemble average is irrelevant because you do not exist as an ensemble of many yous, pooling and sharing your wealths. Like it or not, you will experience owning your own wealth at future times; like it or not, you will never experience owning the wealth of a different realisation of yourself. For an individual, these different realisations, and therefore their average, are the stuff of fantasy, with no *a priori* relevance to decisions in the real world.

Ergodicity is a special case in which these two averages, with their different constructions and meanings, are equivalent. Knowing this fact does not absolve us of the responsibility of deciding which average, if any, is relevant to our research. Ergodicity would be a strange hobby if we were interested in neither. But, if one of the averages is relevant, then we have a trick: if we are interested in one average and know how to compute the other, ergodicity lets us replace the former by the latter.[2]

The question of when an expectation value reflects what happens over time was first raised by Boltzmann in the 1870s. Answering it was an essential step in the development of *statistical mechanics*, which began with Maxwell in the 1850s, because this step clarified under what conditions probability theory could be used in that field. Economics did not benefit from a similar questioning because its mathematical foundations were laid two centuries earlier, as part of the development of probability theory itself. This textbook is our attempt to use these insights from physicists in economics.

History: Randomness and ergodicity in physics

The 1850s were about 200 years after Fermat and Pascal introduced expectation values into the study of random systems. Following the success of Newton's laws of motion, established around the same time as the expectation value, science had become synonymous with mechanics. Mechanics had no use for randomness and probability theory, and the success of mechanics was interpreted as a sign that the world was deterministic, and that sooner or later we would understand what at the time still seemed random. At that point probability theory would become obsolete.

When Boltzmann hit upon the ingenious idea of introducing randomness into physics, to explain the laws of *thermodynamics* in terms of the underlying dynamics of large numbers of molecules, he was fighting an uphill battle. Neither molecules nor randomness were much liked in the physics community, especially in continental Europe, right up until the publication of Einstein's 1905 paper on diffusion [16]. Boltzmann had to be more careful than Fermat and

[2]Indeed, Boltzmann, who coined the term ergodicity, called the replacement of the desired average (in his case, the time average) by the computable average (in his case, the expectation value) a *Kunstgriff*, German for trick. More on him shortly.

Pascal. He had to pre-empt predictable objections from his peers, and the question of ergodicity had to be answered. The usefulness of probability theory relies heavily on expectation values but, as we have seen, they are averages over imagined future states of the universe.

Boltzmann's critics were aware of this and were not shy to voice their concerns. Under what circumstances are expectation values meaningful? Boltzmann gave two answers.

- Expectation values are meaningful when the quantity of interest really does resemble an average (or sum) over many approximately independent systems.
- Expectation values are meaningful, even if only a single system exists, when they reflect what happens over time.

Boltzmann called a physical system (like a gas in a box) "ergodic" if its possible states could be assigned probabilities, such that the expectation value of any observable with respect to those probabilities would be the same as its time average with probability one.[3]

3.2.2 Examples of ergodic and non-ergodic stochastic processes

Let's return to our definition of the ergodic property in (Eq. 3.19), which we reproduce here for convenience:

$$\lim_{\Delta t \to \infty} \frac{1}{\Delta t} \int_{t_0}^{t_0+\Delta t} x_j(s)\, ds = \int_{-\infty}^{\infty} x\, \mathcal{P}_X(x;t)\, dx, \qquad (3.21)$$

We see that the expectation value on the right-hand side is evaluated at time t and, unlike the time average on the left-hand side, can depend on time. Likewise, the time average is evaluated for trajectory j and, unlike the ensemble average, it can depend on the trajectory.

For the ergodic property to hold, $X(t)$ must belong to the class of stochastic processes for which we can define a time-independent ensemble average and a system-independent time average. It is no use if the averages change whenever we change time or system. Here we give some simple examples where the ergodic property holds. The simplest is a

[3]Initially, Boltzmann proposed the word "monodic" by combining the Greek words μόνο (unique) and 'οδός (path) to suggest that a single path, when followed for a sufficiently long time, will explore all there is to explore and reflect what happens in an ensemble. The term "ergodic" refers to the specific model Boltzmann was considering, namely of an energy ('έργον) shell over which such a path is traced.

process which generates a constant value for all time and across all systems. Since that's not very interesting, we will give an example that is almost as simple, but has variation across time and systems (and, indeed, includes the constant process as a special case).

Example: Repeated sampling

A simple and important example of an ergodic stochastic process is obtained by sampling repeatedly from a random variable Z. Suppose we generate independent realisations of Z at discrete time intervals of δt. Starting at time t_0, we define the stochastic process $X(t)$ by the rule $x(t_0 + \tau\delta t) = z_\tau$, where z_τ denotes the τth realisation of Z.

The ensemble average is trivially $\langle X(t)\rangle = \langle Z\rangle$. Following (Eq. 2.21), the time average is

$$\bar{x} = \lim_{T\to\infty} \frac{1}{T}\sum_{\tau=0}^{T-1} x(t_0 + \tau\delta t) = \lim_{T\to\infty} \frac{1}{T}\sum_{\tau=0}^{T-1} z_\tau = \langle Z\rangle\,, \tag{3.22}$$

i.e. equal to the ensemble average. This is because the temporal sample formed by repeated sampling of Z is equivalent, statistically speaking, to a spatial sample (in effect, we can switch T for N in the sum). Both averages have constant and equal value, regardless of the choice of time and system, and the ergodic property holds.

We mentioned in Sec. 3.2 that stochastic processes can exhibit transient behaviour, during which the ergodic property may not hold but after which it does. Mean reversion is an example of this.

Example: Mean reversion

Another type of an ergodic stochastic process is one which exhibits *mean reversion*. Regardless of where a trajectory starts, there is a distinguished value (the so-called mean) which the trajectory moves towards and then fluctuates around. Such processes are used to model physical observables which have an equilibrium value to which they are attracted systematically – like the position of a mass on a damped spring – but which are also subject to noise.

A simple example of a mean-reverting process is the first order autoregressive process. Here $X(t)$ is defined by the dynamics

$$x(t + \delta t) = \phi x(t) + z_t, \tag{3.23}$$

where $|\phi| < 1$ is a parameter that determines the reversion rate and

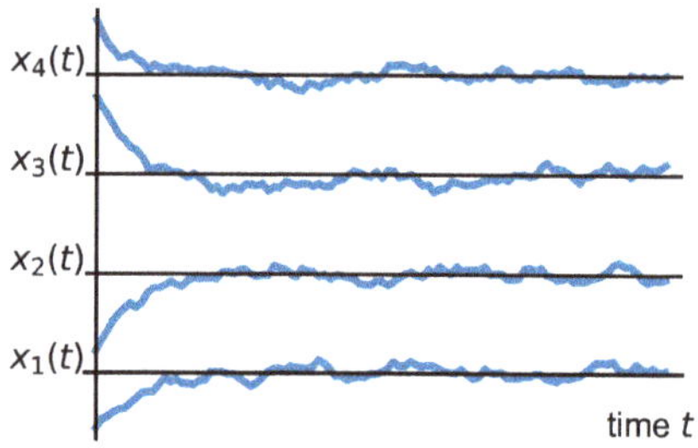

Figure 3.3: Four trajectories, $\{x_i(t)\}$ for $i = 1 \ldots 4$, of an AR(1) process generated by repeated application of (Eq. 3.23) with different initial conditions. All trajectories have a transient phase during which they move from their starting value towards $x = 0$, and after which they execute similar motion around it. **Parameters:** $\phi = 0.85$, $Z \sim \mathcal{N}(0, 0.1)$, 100 time steps.

z_t is a realisation of a stationary random variable Z with $\mathrm{E}[Z] = 0$ and finite variance. Figure 3.3 shows trajectories generated by successive application of (Eq. 3.23) with different initial conditions. All trajectories exhibit a transient phase, during which they move more or less systematically from their starting points towards the mean value, $x = 0$, and after which they fluctuate around it in a similar manner. The time average is trivially $\bar{x} = 0$. Taking the expectation value in the $t \to \infty$ limit, after the transient behaviour has been washed out, also yields $\lim_{t\to\infty} \mathrm{E}[X(t)] = 0$. The process is ergodic.

Unlike repeated sampling, our example of a mean-reverting process displays state dependence, where the value of a trajectory at the next time depends on its value at the current time. This is apparent in (Eq. 3.23), where the value of x at time $t + \delta t$ is a fraction of its value at time t plus some noise. In everyday language, we could say that each trajectory has some memory of its past. Since $|\phi| < 1$, this memory fades and the trajectory eventually "forgets about" (*i.e.* becomes statistically independent of) its previous values. The state dependence in this example is too weak to prevent full exploration of sample space and, therefore, to break ergodicity.

Example: One-and-done sampling

We now give a simple example of a non-ergodic stochastic process, based on sampling a random variable Z. Instead of sampling repeatedly to form a trajectory, we sample once and use the realisation obtained as the trajectory value for all time, *i.e.* $x_i(t) = z_i$, where z_i is the one and only realisation we make of Z in system i.

The time average is equal to the fixed value along the trajectory, $\bar{x}_i = z_i$, and depends on the system chosen. The ensemble average is simply that of the random variable being sampled, $\langle X(t) \rangle = \langle Z \rangle$.

This is constant (because Z has no time dependence) but not in general equal to the time average. Therefore, although stationary, this process is non-ergodic.

In this example, the fact that trajectories can have different time averages means that the ergodic property cannot hold. We can view this as an extreme form of state dependence, in which a trajectory never forgets – indeed remains equal to – its original value. In effect, the sample space of trajectories is partitioned into the possible realisations of Z. Once a partition is chosen, the rest of the space will never be explored.

Example: Pólya's urn

Another, less extreme, example of a non-ergodic stochastic process takes the form of a game, known as Pólya's urn. Imagine an urn containing one red and one green ball. In each round of the game, you put your hand into the urn and choose one of the balls at random. Whatever colour ball you choose, you return that ball plus one more of the same colour to the urn. We define the stochastic process $X(T)$ as the fraction of red balls to total balls in the urn after T rounds.

We will not analyse Pólya's urn in detail here, although we recommend the accessible treatment in [40] if you are interested. Instead, we will simulate some trajectories, shown in Fig. 3.4. Clearly, all trajectories start at $x_i(0) = 1/2$, but that is where the similarities end. Each trajectory seems to converge over long time to a different number between 0 and 1. Indeed, it is known analytically that each trajectory converges to the realisation of a standard uniform random variable, *i.e.*

$$\lim_{T\to\infty} x_i(T) = z_i, \tag{3.24}$$

where z_i is a realisation of Z with $\mathcal{P}_Z(z) = 1$ for $0 \leq z \leq 1$ and $\mathcal{P}_Z(z) = 0$ elsewhere. As with one-and-done sampling, the time average is the realisation $\bar{x}_i = z_i$, which varies from system to system, while the expectation value is that of the random variable, $\langle X(t)\rangle = \langle Z\rangle = 1/2$. The process is non-ergodic.

Pólya's urn exhibits weaker state dependence than one-and-done sampling. The sample space is not strictly partitioned, in the sense that it is theoretically possible to go from any one ball fraction to any other. However, the likelihood of doing so gets smaller as the urn fills up with balls, because each additional draw has less effect on the fraction. Eventually, when there are very many balls in the urn, its composition becomes essentially fixed. Although presented as a game, Pólya's urn

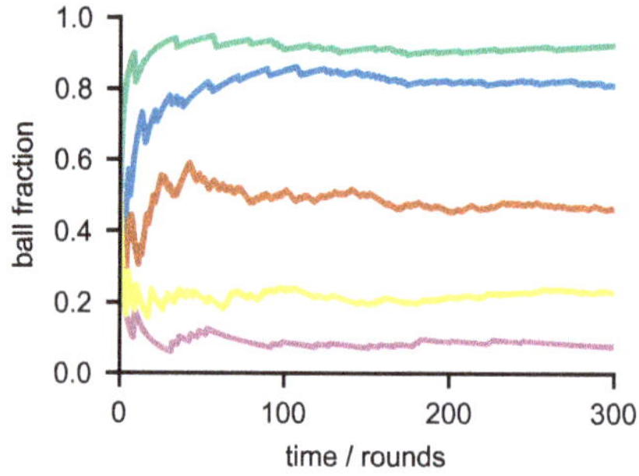

Figure 3.4: Five trajectories of the fraction of red to total balls in Pólya's urn game. All trajectories start at a ball fraction of 1/2 and converge over time to the realisation of a standard uniform random variable.

has seen use in economics, *e.g.* as a model of technological adoption in which the red and green balls represent competing products [4].

Example: The coin game

Our final example is another non-ergodic process, which we have already encountered and which is central to EE: wealth in the coin game. This is a stochastic process whose ensemble average grows exponentially with the number of rounds played, specifically $x(T) \propto 1.05^T$, but whose trajectories decay exponentially to zero almost surely. Therefore, the time average of wealth is $\bar{x} = 0$ and the process is non-ergodic. As we discussed in Sec. 1.1, the ensemble average behaves differently from a typical trajectory due to the presence in it of exceedingly improbable and exceedingly large trajectories.

Although wealth x in this model is non-ergodic, this does not mean that no ergodic observables exist that are related to x. Indeed, we will discover in Chap. 6 that it is often possible – and, more importantly, useful – to define an ergodic growth rate for a non-ergodic observable. Such growth rates are central objects in EE, since they allow us to study the long-time behaviour of single systems using the tools of probability theory.

Chapter 4

Models

4.1 Probability distributions

We have now introduced the important concepts underpinning our development of EE. With the humble random variable as our building block, we have constructed the stochastic process, of which two types of average – ensemble and time – can be defined. This led us naturally to the question of whether those two averages are equal – the ergodicity question.

We now move on to the specific random variables and stochastic processes that we will use most frequently in EE. We start by summarising two important probability distributions associated with random variables: the normal and lognormal distributions.

4.1.1 Normal distribution

A continuous random variable Z is said to have a *normal distribution* (or *Gaussian distribution*) if its sample space is $-\infty < z < \infty$ and its PDF is

$$\mathcal{P}_Z(z) = \frac{1}{\sqrt{2\pi\sigma^2}} \exp\left(-\frac{(z-\mu)^2}{2\sigma^2}\right), \tag{4.1}$$

where μ and σ are parameters that determine respectively the *mean*, $\mathrm{E}[Z] = \mu$, and the *variance*,

$$\mathrm{Var}[Z] \equiv \mathrm{E}\left[(Z - \mathrm{E}[Z])^2\right] = \sigma^2. \tag{4.2}$$

of Z. To avoid writing out (Eq. 4.1) over and over again, we indicate that Z follows a normal distribution by writing $Z \sim \mathcal{N}(\mu, \sigma^2)$, which is shorthand for "Z is normally distributed with mean μ and variance σ^2."

The transformation

$$Y = \frac{Z - \mu}{\sigma} \tag{4.3}$$

produces a new normal random variable with zero mean and unit variance, *i.e.* $Y \sim \mathcal{N}(0,1)$. In this case, we say that Y has a standard normal distribution. Practically, this means that if we can generate realisations of a standard *normal random variable*, then we can generate realisations of any normal random variable by applying the inverse transformation: $Z = \mu + \sigma Y$.

The normal distribution has some properties that make it fundamental. Indeed, whole books have been written about this distribution, so we will do our best to summarise two properties that make it important in EE.

First, we note that, for any two independent random variables, Z_1 and Z_2, the mean and variance of the sum are the sums of the means and variances:

$$\begin{aligned} \mathrm{E}\left[Z_1 + Z_2\right] &= \mathrm{E}\left[Z_1\right] + \mathrm{E}\left[Z_2\right]; \qquad (4.4) \\ \mathrm{Var}\left[Z_1 + Z_2\right] &= \mathrm{Var}\left[Z_1\right] + \mathrm{Var}\left[Z_2\right]. \qquad (4.5) \end{aligned}$$

But if Z_1 and Z_2 are independent and normally distributed, say $Z_1 \sim \mathcal{N}(\mu_1, \sigma_1^2)$ and $Z_1 \sim \mathcal{N}(\mu_2, \sigma_2^2)$, then we can go one step further and specify exactly the distribution followed by $Z_1 + Z_2$. This is simply

$$Z_1 + Z_2 \sim \mathcal{N}(\mu_1 + \mu_2, \sigma_1^2 + \sigma_2^2) \qquad (4.6)$$

i.e. the sums of normals are normal.[1]

Second, and more importantly, there is another result about sums, known as the *central limit theorem.*[2] We will discuss this in more detail in Sec. 4.2 but, essentially, it states the following. The sum of N independent random variables will, subject to some conditions on the moments of their distributions, converge under appropriate rescaling to a normal random variable as $N \to \infty$. So even the sums of non-normals look normal! This is an astonishing and powerful result. In practical terms, it says that the normal distribution will be a good model of an uncertain outcome that arises from the aggregation of many different outcomes, even when we know little about these outcomes. This makes it a universal distribution for many phenomena in science.

4.1.2 Lognormal distribution

The *lognormal distribution* is easy to define once we know about the normal distribution. A continuous random variable Z is said to be lognormally distributed if the random variable $\ln Z$ is normally distributed,

[1] The sum remains normally distributed if random variables are correlated, *i.e.* not independent, but the variance of the sum is no longer the sum of the variances.

[2] The central limit theorem was so named by Pólya because it is a limit theorem which is central, rather than a theorem about central limits.

i.e. if $\ln Z \sim \mathcal{N}(\mu, \sigma^2)$. The PDF is

$$\mathcal{P}_Z(z) = \frac{1}{z\sqrt{2\pi\sigma^2}} \exp\left(-\frac{(\ln z - \mu)^2}{2\sigma^2}\right), \tag{4.7}$$

This distribution is the subject of a wonderful book [3], sadly out-of-print but worth reading if you can find a copy. Here we will describe some of its key properties.

Since the sample space of $\ln Z$ is $-\infty < \ln z < \infty$, the sample space of Z is $0 < z < \infty$, meaning that the realisations of a lognormal random variable are guaranteed to be positive. If $\ln Z$ has expectation value μ and variance σ^2, then the corresponding statistics for Z are:

$$\mathrm{E}[Z] = \exp(\mu + \sigma^2/2); \tag{4.8}$$

$$\mathrm{Var}[Z] = \exp(2\mu + \sigma^2)[\exp(\sigma^2) - 1]. \tag{4.9}$$

The lognormal distribution is of central importance in economics. As we just discussed, the central limit theorem tells us that sums of many independent random variables are approximately normal. But what about products? Consider the random variable

$$Z_N = \prod_{i=1}^{N} Y_i, \tag{4.10}$$

where Y_i are independent random variables of unknown distribution. We can write this as a sum by taking its logarithm,

$$\ln Z_N = \sum_{i=1}^{N} \ln Y_i, \tag{4.11}$$

to which we can apply the central limit theorem (assuming the $\ln Y_i$ satisfy its conditions). This says that $\ln Z_N$ becomes normally distributed as $N \to \infty$ and, therefore, that Z_N becomes lognormally distributed. So, just as the normal distribution was a universal distribution for quantities which result from addition, so the lognormal distribution is a universal distribution for quantities which result from multiplication. Multiplication is ubiquitous in economic phenomena and, indeed, in life more generally, which makes the lognormal distribution exceedingly useful in EE. We will explore its properties more in Sec. 8.1.1.

4.2 Brownian motion

4.2.1 Random walks

In Sec. 4.2.2 we will introduce an important stochastic process, Brownian motion (BM). We will motivate this as the continuous-time limit of a more basic discrete-time stochastic process, the *random walk*.

In Sec. 3.1, we established that the discrete increments of the logarithm of wealth, x, are instances of a time-independent random variable in our game. A quantity, call it x, making such random steps over time is said to perform a random walk. Indeed, on p. 4 the blue line for a single system in Fig. 1.2 (right panel) shows a 52-step trajectory of a random walk.

Random walks come in many forms. In all of them, x changes discontinuously by an amount, δx, which is the realisation of a random variable with a stationary distribution. Each change takes places over a time interval, δt, which may be regular or which may itself be the realisation of a random variable.

We are interested in the simple case where x changes at regular intervals, *i.e.* at times $t + \delta t$, $t + 2\delta t$, and so on. For the distribution of increments, δx, we insist only that the variance,

$$\mathrm{Var}[\delta x] = \left\langle \delta x^2 \right\rangle - \left\langle \delta x \right\rangle^2 \tag{4.12}$$

is finite. Note that this means the expectation value, $\langle \delta x \rangle$, must also be finite. Increments with heavier-tailed distributions do not produce BM in the continuous-time limit.[3]

The change in x after a time $T\delta t$ is the sum of T independent increments,

$$x(t + T\delta t) - x(t) = \sum_{\tau=1}^{T} \delta x_\tau. \tag{4.13}$$

The central limit theorem (strictly speaking, the Lindeberg-Lévy version of it) tells us that this sum, itself a random variable, will become normally distributed as we add more terms and rescale appropriately. Specifically, the rescaling keeps the width of the distribution finite and removes systematic drift in the mean:

$$\lim_{T\to\infty} \overbrace{\frac{1}{\sqrt{T}}}^{\text{keep width finite}} \sum_{\tau=1}^{T} (\delta x_\tau \underbrace{- \langle \delta x \rangle}_{\text{remove systematic drift}}) \sim \mathcal{N}(0, \mathrm{Var}[\delta x]). \tag{4.14}$$

The logarithmic change in the long-time limit that was of interest to us in the analysis of the coin game in Sec. 3.1 is, therefore, normally distributed.

We can gain a partial intuition for this result from the mean,

$$\left\langle \sum_{\tau=1}^{T} \delta x_\tau \right\rangle = \sum_{\tau=1}^{T} \left\langle \delta x_\tau \right\rangle = T \left\langle \delta x \right\rangle, \tag{4.15}$$

[3] BM has continuous paths and this continuity is broken by heavy-tailed increments.

and variance,

$$\mathrm{Var}\left[\sum_{\tau=1}^{T} \delta x_\tau\right] = \sum_{\tau=1}^{T} \mathrm{Var}\left[\delta x_\tau\right] = T\mathrm{Var}[\delta x], \tag{4.16}$$

of the sum of the T independent random increments. These are easily derived and are a worthwhile exercise. They tell us the scaling of the mean and variance of the sum: both grow linearly with the number of terms, T. One way of writing the sum, then, is

$$\sum_{\tau=1}^{T} \delta x_\tau \quad \sim \quad \mathcal{D}(T\langle\delta x\rangle, T\mathrm{Var}[\delta x]) \tag{4.17}$$

$$\sim \quad T\langle\delta x\rangle + \sqrt{T}\mathcal{D}(0, \mathrm{Var}[\delta x]), \tag{4.18}$$

where $\mathcal{D}$ represents some unknown distribution with the mean and variance shown. We can rearrange this to get an identical expression for the finite sum to that in (Eq. 4.14), except that the distribution is unspecified.

So, it's fairly simple to deduce the rescaling used in (Eq. 4.14). The magic of the central limit theorem is that, in the limit $T \to \infty$, the distribution converges to a normal, *i.e.* $\mathcal{D}$ becomes $\mathcal{N}$. This is regardless of the distribution of the individual increments: we need only know that their mean and variance are finite. We won't spoil the magic here, as our main interest is in using the result, but deriving the central limit theorem (and there are many ways to do it) is another illuminating exercise for the reader.

The standard deviation (*i.e.* the "width" of the distribution) of increments in a random walk thus scales as the square-root of the number of steps taken, $\sqrt{T}$. This square-root scaling leads to many interesting results. It can make averages stable, because $\sqrt{T}/T$ converges to zero for large T, and sums unstable, because $\sqrt{T}$ diverges for large T. Consequently, we may expect that, as the size of some system or the length of some time interval increase, some properties become stable and others unstable.

Imagine simulating a single long trajectory of x and plotting it on paper.[4] The amount of time that has to be represented by a fixed length of paper increases linearly with the simulated time because the paper has a finite width to accommodate the horizontal axis. If $\langle\delta x\rangle \neq 0$ then the amount of variation in x that has to be represented by a fixed amount of paper also increases linearly with the simulated time. However, the

[4]This argument is inspired by a colloquium presented by Wendelin Werner in the mathematics department of Imperial College London in January 2012. Werner started the colloquium with a slide that showed a straight horizontal line and asked: what is this? Then answered that it was the trajectory of a random walk, with the vertical and horizontal axes scaled equally.

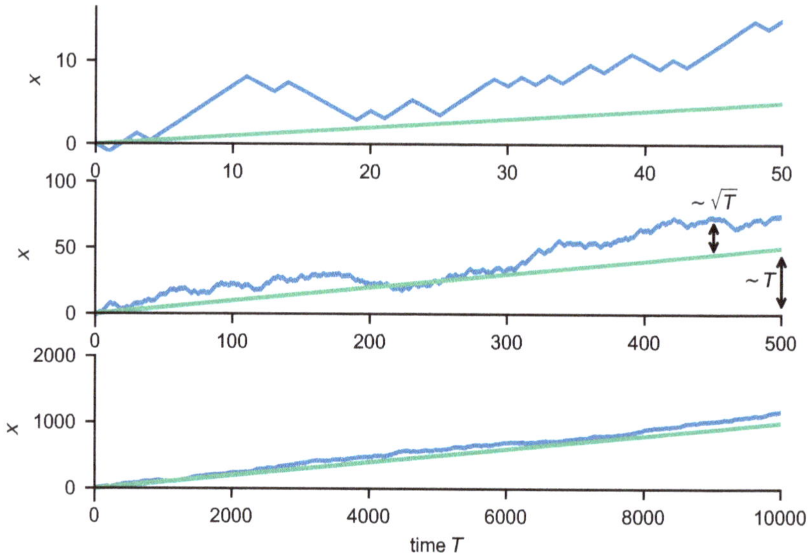

Figure 4.1: Temporal scaling in a random walk with $x(0) = 0$, $\mathrm{P}[\delta x = 1.1] = 1/2$, $\mathrm{P}[\delta x = -0.9] = 1/2$, and $\delta t = 1$ (in arbitrary units). A single trajectory (blue) and the expectation value (green) are shown in each plot. **Top:** microscale – at short times, the trajectory appears unrelated to the systematic trend. **Centre:** mesoscale – at intermediate times, the effects of both systematic growth and fluctuations are visible at similar scales. **Bottom:** macroscale – at long times, relative deviations of a typical trajectory from the expectation value are small.

departures of Δx from its expectation value $T\langle\delta x\rangle$ only increase as the square-root of T. Thus, the amount of paper-space given to these departures scales as $1/\sqrt{T}$, and for very long simulated times the trajectory will look like a straight line on paper.

Figure 4.1 illustrates these scalings for a random walk starting at $x(0) = 0$ with increments given by $\mathrm{P}[\delta x = 1.1] = 1/2$ and $\mathrm{P}[\delta x = -0.9] = 1/2$, and time step $\delta t = 1$ (all units arbitrary). As discussed, the expectation value grows linearly in time, explicitly $\langle x(T\delta t)\rangle = 0.1T$, while the standard deviation grows like the square-root of time, $\sqrt{T}$. Therefore, relative deviations of a typical trajectory from the expectation value scale like $1/\sqrt{T}$. At short times, these are so large that the trajectory appears unrelated to the systematic trend. At long times, the converse is true – a typical trajectory resembles closely the expectation value. At intermediate times, the effects of both systematic growth and fluctuations are visible at similar scales.

In the intermediate regime, fluctuations will still be visible and they will be approximately normally distributed. Here it is often easier to replace the discrete random walk model with the corresponding continuous process. This process, finally, is BM.

4.2.2 Brownian motion

We think of BM as the limit of a random walk where we shorten the duration of a step, $\delta t \to 0$, so that changes happen continuously in time and not just at discrete times. As we will see, this creates a model which is more tractable than the random walk, and this will allow us to focus on economics. How realistic it is to think of wealth changing continuously is debatable. We certainly do not measure real-world observables, such as individual wealth, continuously in time. We only ever get to glimpse them between discrete time intervals and, if we are lucky, we will collect enough glimpses to do some science. So, we are replacing the discrete-time model with a continuous-time model to use the latter to describe discrete-time glimpses in the real world. If continuity seems an unnecessary assumption to you, we don't blame you! The value in this approach is in the powerful analytical tools it will put at our disposal.

Subtracting any drift, or assuming zero drift, we know from our treatment of the random walk that the net change in x over T steps scales like $\sqrt{T}$. If the intervals are regular, *i.e.* their duration is fixed, then this means the net change scales like the square-root of the time spent walking. In BM we maintain this scaling *over all time intervals* and, in particular, over small intervals, $\delta t \to 0$. In the limit $\delta t \to 0$, the local slope of a trajectory therefore diverges, $\delta x/\delta t \to \infty$, because δx scales like $\sqrt{\delta t}$ and becomes much larger than δt. Thus, trajectories of BM are infinitely jagged, or – in mathematical terms – they are not differentiable. The way in which they become non-differentiable, through the $\sqrt{\delta t}$ factor, leaves the trajectories continuous. (This isn't the case if δx scales like δt^k, where $k < 0.5$.)

Continuity of x means that it is possible to make the difference $|x(t) - x(t + \delta t)|$ as small as we like by choosing δt small enough. Trajectories without this property contain what are appropriately called "*jumps*." Therefore, continuity means that there are no jumps. These subtleties make BM a topic of great mathematical interest, and many books have been written about it. We will pick from these books only what is immediately useful to us. To convey the universality of BM, we define it formally as follows:

DEFINITION: **Brownian motion i**

If a stochastic process has continuous paths, stationary independent increments, and is distributed according to $\mathcal{N}(\mu t, \sigma^2 t)$ then it is a Brownian motion.

The process can be defined in different ways. A particularly compact definition is this:

DEFINITION: **Brownian motion ii**

If a stochastic process is continuous, with stationary independent increments, then the process is a Brownian motion.

We quote from [21]: *"This beautiful theorem shows that Brownian motion can actually be defined by stationary independent increments and path continuity alone, with normality following as a consequence of these assumptions. This may do more than any other characterisation to explain the significance of Brownian motion for probabilistic modeling."*

Indeed, BM is not just a mathematically rich model but also – due to its emergence through the central limit theorem – a model that represents a large universality class, *i.e.* it is a good description of what happens over long times in many other models that produce random trajectories.

4.2.3 Stochastic differential equation

The power of BM lies in its simplicity and analytic tractability, involving only two parameters, μ and σ. We will often work with its representation as a stochastic differential equation (SDE):

$$dx = \mu dt + \sigma dW. \tag{4.19}$$

We had better say what this means. First, it should have quotation marks around it because all of the terms in it are infinitesimal. Really it is a shorthand for the more formal integral equation,

$$x(t) = x(t_0) + \mu \int_{t_0}^{t} ds + \sigma \int_{t_0}^{t} dW(s), \tag{4.20}$$

where each term is either a scalar quantity or a random variable. The formal study of such equations, often called *stochastic calculus*, is a huge field in its own right. We will not examine it in detail, although we will borrow some useful results from it in Sec. 4.3. Instead, we will work with the informal version, (Eq. 4.19), and we will interpret the terms in very simple ways:

- dx is a small (infinitesimal) increment in x;

- μ is a constant parameter, known as the *drift*;
- dt is a small increment in time, t;
- σ is a constant parameter, known as the *volatility*; and
- dW is the so-called *Wiener increment*, a random variable whose properties we describe below.

The name "Brownian motion" is sometimes reserved for the stochastic process generated by (Eq. 4.19) when $\mu = 0$, with "Brownian motion with drift" used for the case when $\mu \neq 0$. When $\mu = 0$ and $\sigma = 1$, then it is sometimes called "standard Brownian motion" or the "*Wiener process*."

4.2.4 Wiener process

Let's examine the random Wiener increment, dW. This is where all the action is: without it, (Eq. 4.19) would be an ordinary differential equation (ODE) with easy-to-find deterministic solutions, perfectly inadequate for modelling uncertainty across systems and over time. dW is the beating heart of many SDEs.

The Wiener increment can be defined by two properties, its distribution and its autocovariance,

$$\begin{aligned} dW &\sim \mathcal{N}(0, dt) && (4.21) \\ \langle dW_t dW_s \rangle &= \delta(t,s)dt, && (4.22) \end{aligned}$$

where the subscripts denote the starting time of each increment, *i.e.* dW_t is modelled as occurring at the end of the interval from t to $t+dt$. $\delta(t,s)$ is the *Kronecker delta*,

$$\delta(t,s) = \begin{cases} 1 & \text{if } t = s \\ 0 & \text{otherwise.} \end{cases} \tag{4.23}$$

Put very simply, the $\{dW_t\}$ are iid normal random variables with mean zero and variance dt. That's all we really need to know about the Wiener increment.

The Wiener process, $W(t)$, is assumed to start at $W(0) = 0$ and is the integral of infinitesimal Wiener increments,

$$W(t) = \int_0^t dW_s. \tag{4.24}$$

Since the integral is the limiting case of a sum over normally-distributed Wiener increments, $W(t)$ is itself normally distributed with mean zero and variance t, *i.e.*

$$W(t) \sim \mathcal{N}(0, t). \tag{4.25}$$

Its width has the same $\sqrt{t}$ scaling as the random walk.

Thus $W(t)$ is a stochastic process which, for fixed time, generates a time-dependent normal random variable. However, this does not mean we can generate a trajectory by drawing successive independent realisations from $\mathcal{N}(0,t)$. While the Wiener increments, dW_t, are independent, the Wiener process is autocorrelated. In simple terms, this is because its value at the end of a time period depends on where it started, because it must take a continuous path to travel from there. It's a standard result in stochastic calculus that the autocovariance of the values of a Wiener process at two different times is simply the earlier time, *i.e.* for $t < t'$, $\langle W(t)W(t')\rangle = t$. This is because

$$\begin{aligned}
\langle W(t)W(t')\rangle &= \langle W(t)[W(t) + W(t') - W(t)]\rangle && (4.26)\\
&= \left\langle W(t)^2\right\rangle + \langle W(t)[W(t') - W(t)]\rangle && (4.27)\\
&= t + 0, && (4.28)
\end{aligned}$$

where the final term follows by independence of increments over non-overlapping time intervals.

4.2.5 Analytical solution

Rather like an ODE, we can integrate the SDE for BM, (Eq. 4.19), say from time 0 to t, to express its solution as

$$\begin{aligned}
x(t) &= x(0) + \mu t + \sigma \int_0^t dW_s && (4.29)\\
&= x(0) + \mu t + \sigma W(t). && (4.30)
\end{aligned}$$

Fixing the time, t, yields a normal random variable,

$$x(t) \sim \mathcal{N}(x(0) + \mu t, \sigma^2 t), \tag{4.31}$$

whose location moves linearly in time and whose width grows like the square-root of time.

4.2.6 Numerical solution

BM paths can be simulated using a discretised version of (Eq. 4.19),

$$x(t + \delta t) = x(t) + \mu\delta t + \sigma\sqrt{\delta t}\xi_t, \tag{4.32}$$

where ξ_t are iid standard normal variates, $\xi_t \sim \mathcal{N}(0,1)$.

4.2.7 Ensemble average

The ensemble average of BM is obtained simply by taking the expectation value of its solution, (Eq. 4.30), to get

$$\langle x(t)\rangle = x(0) + \mu t, \tag{4.33}$$

where we have used the property $\langle W(t)\rangle = 0$. Thus $\langle x(t)\rangle$ grows linearly in time at the drift rate, μ.

We could have found the same result by constructing the distribution of a finite-ensemble average of BM trajectories using the distribution of a single trajectory in (Eq. 4.31):

$$\langle x(t)\rangle_N \sim x(t) \sim \mathcal{N}\left(x(0) + \mu t, \frac{\sigma^2 t}{N}\right) \tag{4.34}$$

The ensemble average is the $N \to \infty$ of the finite-ensemble average, which converges to $\langle x(t)\rangle = x(0) + \mu t$ with probability one for any finite time t.

4.2.8 Time average

The time average of a BM is a trickier object. Let's start by writing out the finite-time average of (Eq. 4.30) from time 0 to t:

$$\begin{aligned}
\bar{x}(0,t) &= \frac{1}{t}\int_0^t x(s)ds && (4.35)\\
&= \frac{1}{t}\int_0^t \left(x(0) + \mu s + \sigma W(s)\right) ds && (4.36)\\
&= x(0) + \frac{\mu t}{2} + \frac{\sigma}{t}\int_0^t W(s)ds. && (4.37)
\end{aligned}$$

Note that we have dropped the trajectory index, as we don't need it in this computation.

The final term contains the finite-time average of the Wiener process,

$$\bar{W}(0,t) \equiv \frac{1}{t}\int_0^t W(s)ds. \tag{4.38}$$

The Wiener process is known to be recurrent: with probability one it returns to zero arbitrarily many times in the long-time limit. We might guess, therefore, that $\bar{W}(0,t)$ will converge to zero with probability one as $t \to \infty$. We would be wrong. Yes the process has no drift, and yes it returns to zero infinitely many times, but its time average is not a delta function at zero. Instead, $\bar{W}(0,t)$ turns out to be a random variable, normally distributed with variance that grows linearly in time, specifically

$$\bar{W}(0,t) \sim \mathcal{N}(0, t/3). \tag{4.39}$$

Figure 4.2: A trajectory of the finite-time average of the Wiener process. The time average does not converge to a number, but is instead distributed as $\mathcal{N}(0, t/3)$ for all times. The finite-time average arises from integrating a trajectory of the Wiener process. Integration is a smoothing operation, so finite-time average trajectories are smoother than those of the underlying process.

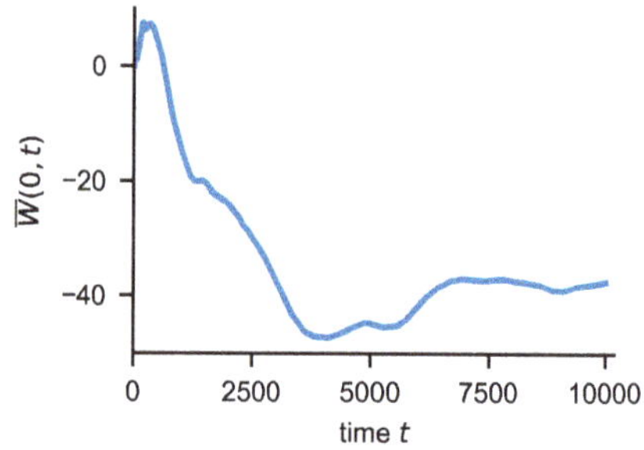

Averaging over time, in this case, does not remove the randomness.

The proof of (Eq. 4.39) is technical and we will not reproduce it here, but we can check whether it is plausible by simulation. Figure 4.2 shows a sample trajectory of the finite-time average of a Wiener process. In the literature this process is called "*random acceleration process*" [13].

Plugging (Eq. 4.39) back into (Eq. 4.37) gives us the distribution of the finite-time average of BM,

$$\bar{x}(0,t) \sim \mathcal{N}\left(x(0) + \frac{\mu t}{2}, \frac{\sigma^2 t}{3}\right). \tag{4.40}$$

The time average, the $t \to \infty$ of (Eq. 4.40), diverges unless $\mu = 0$, but even with $\mu = 0$ the limit is a random variable with diverging variance – something whose density is zero everywhere.

4.2.9 Non-ergodicity

Comparing the ensemble average in (Eq. 4.33) and the time average just derived shows that the ergodic property does not hold for BM. In no meaningful sense do the two quantities converge to the same scalar in the relevant limits. We find it a frequently misunderstood point that BM, whose increments are ergodic, is a non-ergodic stochastic process. However, that doesn't make BM unmanageable or unpredictable – we know the distribution of BM, and indeed of its finite-ensemble average and finite-time average, at any moment in time and for any number of systems.

4.3 Itô calculus

Our next target stochastic process will be the continuous-time analogue of the coin game in Sec. 1.1. This is known as geometric Brownian motion (GBM) and we will present it in the next section.

Before we do that, we will introduce a final tool, known as *Itô calculus*, which will simplify our analysis of GBM enormously. As usual, we will focus on what we need in our applications, rather than complete rigour – a full treatment of Itô calculus would be a textbook in its own right! Itô's key insight was that the non-differentiability of so-called Itô processes leads to a new form of calculus. In particular, a new chain rule is needed.

An Itô stochastic process is generated by an SDE of the form

$$dx = a(x,t)dt + b(x,t)dW, \tag{4.41}$$

where $a(x,t)$ and $b(x,t)$ are coefficient functions. If we are interested in the behaviour of some other quantity that is a function of x and t, say $f(x,t)$, then f obeys the SDE,

$$df = \left(\frac{\partial f}{\partial t} + a(x,t)\frac{\partial f}{\partial x} + \frac{1}{2}b(x,t)^2\frac{\partial^2 f}{\partial x^2}\right)dt + b(x,t)\frac{\partial f}{\partial x}dW. \tag{4.42}$$

This result is known as *Itô's formula*.

In EE, we are interested in functions of x alone, *i.e.* in time-independent transformations of an observable, such as $\ln x$. The partial time derivative in (Eq. 4.42) vanishes, leaving us with

$$df = \left(a(x,t)\frac{\partial f}{\partial x} + \frac{1}{2}b(x,t)^2\frac{\partial^2 f}{\partial x^2}\right)dt + b(x,t)\frac{\partial f}{\partial x}dW. \tag{4.43}$$

We will confine our attention to such cases.

Many derivations of Itô's formula are available. Intuitive derivations, such as [22], use the scaling of the variance of the Wiener process. More formal derivations, along the lines of [21], rely on integrals. We provide an informal derivation here, with three basic steps, which we find easier than learning (Eq. 4.43) by heart. The steps are:

- Taylor expand the total derivative, df, in terms of dt, dx, and dx^2;
- substitute for dx using the known SDE for x;
- replace $dW^2 = dt$ and keep only $O(dW)$ and $O(dt)$ terms.

The key insight remains that the variance of the Wiener increment has linear (*i.e.* random walk) scaling in time. Replacing dW^2 by dt in the final step incorporates this insight. Itô showed how to do this formally for integral equations, for which SDEs are shorthand representations.

Let's follow these steps for general $f(x)$. Taylor expanding for df, we get

$$df = \cancel{\frac{\partial f}{\partial t}}dt + \frac{\partial f}{\partial x}dx + \frac{1}{2}\frac{\partial^2 f}{\partial x^2}dx^2. \tag{4.44}$$

Substituting (Eq. 4.41) for dx gives us

$$df = \frac{\partial f}{\partial x}(a\,dt + b\,dW) + \frac{1}{2}\frac{\partial^2 f}{\partial x^2}(a^2 dt^2 + 2ab\,dt\,dW + b^2 dW^2), \quad (4.45)$$

where we have suppressed the x and t dependence of $a(x,t)$ and $b(x,t)$ for compactness. Finally, we replace dW^2 by dt and throw away terms which tend to zero faster than dt. This gives

$$\begin{aligned} df &= \frac{\partial f}{\partial x}(a\,dt + b\,dW) + \frac{1}{2}\frac{\partial^2 f}{\partial x^2}(a^2 \cancel{dt^2} + 2ab\,\cancel{dt\,dW} + b^2 dt) + \cancel{O(dt^2)} \\ &= \left(a\frac{\partial f}{\partial x} + \frac{b^2}{2}\frac{\partial^2 f}{\partial x^2}\right) + b\frac{\partial f}{\partial x}dW, \end{aligned} \quad (4.46)$$

which reproduces Itô's formula in (Eq. 4.43). With this method in our toolbox, we are ready to tackle GBM.

4.4 Geometric Brownian motion

GBM is straightforwardly defined.

> DEFINITION: **Geometric Brownian motion**
>
> If the logarithm of an observable performs BM, then the observable itself performs GBM.

In Sec. 4.2, the observable x performs BM. If instead $\ln x$ performs BM, then x performs GBM. The change of variable from x to $\ln x$ is trivial to state, but it has interesting consequences. It implies, for instance, that

- $x(t)$ is lognormally distributed;
- increments in x are neither stationary nor independent;
- $x(t)$ cannot change sign;
- the most likely value of x (the mode) does not coincide with the expectation value of x.

These and other properties of the lognormal distribution will be discussed in detail in Chap. 8.

4.4.1 Stochastic differential equation

Our definition, coupled with the SDE for BM in (Eq. 4.19), means that GBM obeys

$$d\ln x = \alpha dt + \beta dW \quad (4.47)$$

where α and β are constant parameters.

This is an equation for infinitesimal differences in the transformed variable, $\ln x$. It is a perfectly valid way of writing an SDE, but it would help our intuition to see an equation for the differences in x itself, since this is the variable that is actually performing GBM. Let's use Itô's formula to derive this.

Suppose x obeys the Itô SDE in (Eq. 4.41), which we repeat here:

$$dx = a(x,t)dt + b(x,t)dW. \tag{4.48}$$

We want the corresponding SDE for $f(x) = \ln x$, which we know must be identical to (Eq. 4.47). Let's follow the procedure we learned in Sec. 4.3. First we Taylor expand for df up to order dx^2, noting there is no time-dependence, to get

$$d\ln x = \frac{1}{x}dx - \frac{1}{2x^2}dx^2. \tag{4.49}$$

Then we substitute in the SDE for dx to get

$$d\ln x = \frac{1}{x}\left(a(x,t)dt + b(x,t)dW\right) - \frac{1}{2x^2}\left(a(x,t)dt + b(x,t)dW\right)^2. \tag{4.50}$$

Finally, we replace $dW^2 = dt$, consolidate terms in dt and dW, and neglect higher-order terms to get

$$d\ln x = \left[\frac{a(x,t)}{x} - \frac{1}{2}\left(\frac{b(x,t)}{x}\right)^2\right]dt + \frac{b(x,t)}{x}dW. \tag{4.51}$$

This must be identical to (Eq. 4.47). We achieve this by setting $b(x,t) = \beta x$ and $a(x,t) = (\alpha + \beta^2/2)x$.

For future notational simplicity, we will define parameters $\sigma = \beta$ and $\mu = \alpha + \beta^2/2$. This sleight of hand allows us to write the governing SDE for x in the compact form,

$$dx = x(\mu dt + \sigma dW), \tag{4.52}$$

with the corresponding SDE for $\ln x$ becoming

$$d\ln x = \left(\mu - \frac{\sigma^2}{2}\right)dt + \sigma dW. \tag{4.53}$$

These will be our canonical SDEs for GBM for all future applications. Note the contribution of $-\sigma^2/2$ to the drift parameter when moving from linear to logarithmic variable – this is known as the *Itô correction.* More on this later.

The SDE for the untransformed variable, x, is interesting. It implies that, over each short time increment, x changes by a random multiple of its current value. This is consistent with the allusions we have made previously to GBM being the continuous-time version of the coin game in Sec. 1.1, where the change in wealth during each round is a random multiple of the wealth at the start of the round.

4.4.2 Analytical solution

Once we have the SDE for $\ln x$, we can integrate it from time 0 to t, as we did for BM in (Eq. 4.30). This gives a stochastic process,

$$\ln x(t) = \ln x(0) + \left(\mu - \frac{\sigma^2}{2}\right) t + \sigma W(t), \tag{4.54}$$

which, for fixed t, is a normally-distributed random variable,

$$\ln x(t) \sim \mathcal{N}\left(\ln x(0) + \left(\mu - \frac{\sigma^2}{2}\right) t, \sigma^2 t\right). \tag{4.55}$$

Thus $x(t)$ is lognormally distributed.

Exponentiating (Eq. 4.54) yields a solution for $x(t)$,

$$x(t) = x(0) \exp\left[\left(\mu - \frac{\sigma^2}{2}\right) t + \sigma W(t)\right]. \tag{4.56}$$

which shows that $x(t)$ follows noisy exponential growth. If we write $x(t) = x(0)\exp(g(t)t)$, we can express the noise as manifesting itself through a random exponential growth rate,

$$g(t) = \mu - \frac{\sigma^2}{2} + \frac{\sigma W(t)}{t}. \tag{4.57}$$

4.4.3 Numerical solution

Since GBM in x can be expressed as BM in $\ln x$, we can follow the discretisation method in Sec. 4.2.6 to simulate trajectories for $\ln x$. The discretised form of (Eq. 4.53) is

$$\ln x(t + \delta t) = \ln x(t) + \left(\mu - \frac{\sigma^2}{2}\right) \delta t + \sigma\sqrt{\delta t}\xi_t, \tag{4.58}$$

where $\xi_t \sim \mathcal{N}(0, 1)$ are instances of a standard normal variable. BM trajectories generated in this way can be exponentiated to produce trajectories of the corresponding GBM in x.

Alternatively, we could have discretised the SDE for x, (Eq. 4.52), directly, calculating changes in x as random multiples of x. We don't recommend this approach. If care is not taken, it is possible to generate large negative random multipliers that cause x to turn from positive to negative, which cannot happen in the GBM model. This pitfall is avoided in the approach suggested above.

GBM on logarithmic vertical scales looks like BM on linear vertical scales. Figure 1.2 is, in fact, an example of a very coarse discretisation of GBM. But it's useful to look at a more finely discretised trajectory of GBM on linear scales to develop an intuition for this important process. We are now able to simulate this – an example trajectory is shown in Fig. 4.3.

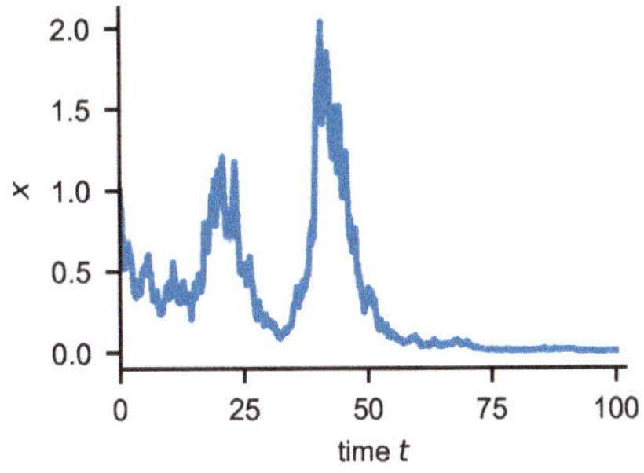

Figure 4.3: Single trajectory of a GBM. What happens to the trajectory tomorrow depends strongly on where it is today. Unlike in BM, it is difficult to recover from a low value of x, and trajectories are likely to get stuck near zero (indeed, certain in the long run when $\mu - \sigma^2/2 < 0$). Occasional excursions are characterised by large fluctuations. **Parameters:** $\mu = 0.05$ and $\sigma^2 = 2\mu$ per unit time, corresponding to zero long-run growth rate.

4.4.4 Ensemble average

There are many ways to compute the ensemble average of GBM. An easy way is to take expectation values of both sides of (Eq. 4.52) to get the ODE,[5]

$$\begin{aligned} \langle dx \rangle &= \langle x\mu dt \rangle + \langle x\sigma dW \rangle & (4.59) \\ \Rightarrow \quad d\langle x \rangle &= \langle x \rangle \mu dt, & (4.60) \end{aligned}$$

where we have used the linearity of the expectation operator and the property that $\langle dW \rangle = 0$. Assuming the initial condition, $x(0)$, is the same for all trajectories, this has solution

$$\langle x(t) \rangle = x(0)\exp(\mu t). \tag{4.61}$$

Thus $\langle x(t) \rangle$ grows exponentially at a constant rate equal to the drift parameter, μ, in (Eq. 4.52).

4.4.5 Time average

Consider a single trajectory of the solution in (Eq. 4.56) from time 0 to t. Recall this is exponential growth at a noisy rate,

$$g(t) = \mu - \frac{\sigma^2}{2} + \frac{\sigma W(t)}{t}. \tag{4.62}$$

We are interested in the behaviour of this trajectory over long time. We know that $W(t)$ scales like $\sqrt{t}$, so the final term in the growth rate scales

[5]This is a simple case of a general method [26, Chapter 4] to turn a SDE for x into an ODE for its kth moment, $\langle x^k \rangle$. One uses Itô's formula to find the SDE for x^k and then takes expectation values of both sides. Stochastic terms vanish by the zero-mean property of the Wiener increment, leaving an ODE. Here we do it for $k = 1$, so we already know the SDE.

like $1/\sqrt{t}$ and vanishes almost surely in the $t \to \infty$ limit. This leaves an exponential growth rate of $\mu - \sigma^2/2$.

This observation is sufficient for the applications in this book. For completeness, we could compute the time average of a single trajectory of GBM,

$$\bar{x} = \lim_{t\to\infty} \frac{1}{t} \int_0^t x(s)ds, \tag{4.63}$$

and compare it to the ensemble average. However, this is even trickier than the corresponding calculation for BM in Sec. 4.2.8. For brevity, we will skip it.

4.4.6 Non-ergodicity

We have found that, for non-zero σ – *i.e.* for any amount of noise in (Eq. 4.52) – the long-run exponential growth rate of a single trajectory, $\mu - \sigma^2/2$, is less than that of the ensemble average over all trajectories, μ. Indeed, the difference is exactly the Itô correction we found in Sec. 4.4.1. Therefore, in GBM, a single trajectory grows more slowly (or decays more quickly) over long time than the ensemble average, and the ergodic property cannot hold.

This difference in growth rates is consistent with our findings in the coin game in Sec. 1.1 and Sec. 3.1, where we found that playing a single game for many rounds caused wealth to decay, while averaging over many parallel instances of the game led to growing wealth.

The basic message of the game is that we may obtain different values for growth rates, depending on how we average: an expectation value is one average; a time average is quite another. Although phrased in different words, this key insight has appeared in the literature as far back as 1870 [69], and then again in 1944 [23]. And in 1956 [25], and in 1966 [67], and in 1991 [14], and at many other times! And yet we believe this basic insight remains underappreciated in economics, where it is undoubtedly relevant. Because people experience their wealth over time (which may be described by GBM) and have no access to the ensemble of other possible trajectories, they quite reasonably behave closer to optimising the growth rate of a single trajectory through time than of the average over parallel trajectories. We will explore the consequences of this in the next part of this book.

Part II

Individuals

Preview of Part II

Having introduced the necessary mathematical tools in Part I, we will now get our teeth into EE proper, starting with a model of individual behaviour: disregarding what others may be doing, how might we choose among a set of different options? As we said right at the beginning of this book, the model we will explore in depth is one where people choose what makes them wealthiest in the long run. This may sound like a trivially naïve model which will produce nothing but atomistic greed, but it is not. The reason it generates interesting behaviour is its focus on time, on the long run. It rejects short-term, multiverse, one-shot thinking. Every set of options is interpreted as representing a type of situation, and every decision is interpreted as part of a consistent behavioural protocol.

We will build this model systematically, starting in Chap. 5 with decisions in the absence of risk and uncertainty. Because our model is dynamic and includes time, we can explore discounting, and we find that commonly observed behavioural patterns are reproduced.

Next, in Chap. 6, we introduce a systematic way of randomising the processes used in Chap. 5. This allows us to explore human behaviour in risky situations, and again we find that the model produces common behavioural patterns such as risk aversion. We also understand under what circumstances risk-seeking behaviour is optimal, and we relate the EE formalism to the classic economics model that is expected-utility theory.

Finally, in Chap. 7, we explore a few example applications of the model. Choosing a famous behavioural puzzle, we show how the 300-year-old St. Petersburg paradox is resolved. Next, we discuss a high-powered experiment whose outcomes attest to the predictive power of the model. Specifically, this experiment found human subjects intuitively and quickly to adjust their behavioural patterns in order to optimise long-time wealth growth when dynamic conditions were changed. We close the chapter, and Part II, with a hint of what comes next as we resolve another famous puzzle: why might people buy insurance if doing so decreases their expected wealth? The answer: despite a decrease in expected wealth, an insurance policy can increase the time-average growth rate of wealth. This will lead us naturally on to Part III where we discuss collectives of individuals and the collective phenomena that emerge by maximising personal long-time growth in a connected world.

Chapter 5

Decisions in a riskless world

5.1 Models and science fiction

We will do decision theory by using mathematical models, and since this can be done in many ways we will be explicit about how we choose to do it. We will define a wealth process – a model of how wealth changes with time – and a decision criterion. The wealth process and the decision criterion may or may not remind you of the real world. We will not worry too much about the accuracy of these reminiscences. Instead we will "shut up and calculate" – we will let the mathematical model create its world. Writing down a mathematical model is like laying out the premise for a science-fiction novel. We may decide that people can download their consciousness onto a computer, that medicine has advanced to eliminate ageing and death – these are premises we are at liberty to invent. Once we have written them down we begin to explore the world that results from those premises. A decision criterion is really a model of human behaviour – what makes us who we are if not our decisions? It therefore implies a long list of specific behaviours that will be observed in a given model world. For example, some criteria will lead to cooperation, others will not, some will lead to the existence of insurance contracts, others will not, *etc.* We will explore the worlds created by the different models. Once we have done so we invite you to judge which model you find most useful for your understanding of the world. Of course, having spent many years thinking about these issues we have come to our own conclusions, and we will put them forward because we believe them to be helpful.

To keep the discussion to a manageable volume we will only consider a setup that corresponds to making purely financial decisions. We may bet on a horse or take out personal liability insurance. This chapter will not tell you whom you should marry or even whose textbooks you should read.

5.2 The decision axiom

A "decision theory" is a model of human behaviour. We will write down such a model phrased as the following simple axiom:

Decision axiom

People optimise the growth rate of their wealth.

Without discussing why people might do this, let's step into the world created by this axiom. To do that, we need to be crystal clear about what a growth rate is, so we'll discuss that first, in Sec. 5.3. Typically, decisions involve an uncertain future: we have to decide on a course of action now although we don't know with certainty what will happen to us in the future under any of our choices. We will work our way towards this setup systematically, beginning with trivial decisions where neither time nor uncertainty matters in Sec. 5.4.1, next introducing time in Sec. 5.4.2 (where we will shed light on what's called "discounting"). In the next chapter, Chap. 6, we will introduce uncertainty (where we will shed light on what's called "expected utility theory").

5.3 Growth rates

When we say that $\mathsf{x}(t)$ is a *growth process*, we mean that it is a monotonic function of t. If you're thinking about randomness – don't, we'll come to that later. For now, we will just work with a deterministic function $\mathsf{x}(t)$ – we even use an unusual font to indicate that this is a deterministic function.

You may know that the rate of change of $\mathsf{x}(t)$ is also called the *additive growth rate*, or linear growth rate,

$$g_{\mathrm{a}} = \frac{\mathsf{x}(t+\Delta t) - \mathsf{x}(t)}{\Delta t}, \tag{5.1}$$

and that the rate of change of the logarithm of $\mathsf{x}(t)$ is called the *multiplicative growth rate*, or exponential growth rate,

$$g_{\mathrm{m}} = \frac{\ln \mathsf{x}(t+\Delta t) - \ln \mathsf{x}(t)}{\Delta t}. \tag{5.2}$$

Why are both "growth rates" – they're different objects, what is it that makes them both growth rates? By the end of this section, the answer to this question should be clear.

For a given process, there exists an appropriate growth rate, g, which solves the following problem for us: how do we characterise how fast x grows? A *growth rate* is a mathematical object of the form

$$g = \frac{v(\mathsf{x}(t+\Delta t)) - v(\mathsf{x}(t))}{\Delta t}, \tag{5.3}$$

where $v(\mathsf{x})$ is a monotonically increasing function of wealth x. Comparing to (Eq. 5.1) and (Eq. 5.2), we find that $v(\mathsf{x}) = \mathsf{x}$ corresponds to the additive growth rate and $v(\mathsf{x}) = \ln \mathsf{x}$ to the multiplicative growth rate. The transformation $\mathsf{x} \to v(\mathsf{x})$ ensures temporal stability of g.

How does this work, and what does it mean? Specifically,

1. why the transformation?
2. how do we know which transformation to use?

We will start with the mathematically simple case of the additive growth rate (Eq. 5.1) and discuss its properties by applying it to additive growth. Next we will ask under what conditions the exponential growth rate (Eq. 5.2) is appropriate, and that will lead us to the *general growth rate* (Eq. 5.3).

5.3.1 Additive growth rate

If I want to know how fast $\mathsf{x}(t)$ grows, the most obvious thing to compute is its rate of change – that's the additive growth rate (Eq. 5.1). This tells me by how much x grows in the interval $[t, t+\Delta t]$. If $\mathsf{x}(t)$ is linear in t, so that

$$\mathsf{x}(t) = \mathsf{x}(0) + \gamma t, \tag{5.4}$$

where γ is a constant, then this is a very informative quantity. We'll now state carefully why it is informative in this case. That may seem pedantic at this point, but it will become useful when we generalise in Sec. 5.3.2 and Sec. 5.3.3.

The additive growth rate (Eq. 5.1) is informative of how fast x grows under *additive dynamics* (Eq. 5.4) because in this case the t-dependence drops out: we can measure g_{a} whenever we want, and we'll always get the same value, $g_{\mathrm{a}} = \gamma$, Fig. 5.1. Not to get too philosophical about it, but this kind of time-translation invariance is a key concept in science: the search for laws is the search for universal structure – especially for time-translation invariant structure, for something "timeless."

Let's re-write the linear dynamic (Eq. 5.4) in differential form

$$d\mathsf{x} = \gamma dt. \tag{5.5}$$

Because γ depends neither on t nor on x, we can re-write this as

$$d\mathsf{x} = d(\gamma t). \tag{5.6}$$

Figure 5.1: Wealth in an additive growth process: the additive growth rate, $\Delta \mathsf{x}/\Delta t$, always takes the same value, γ, irrespective of when we measure it. That's because in any time interval, Δt, the increase in x, namely $\Delta \mathsf{x}$, is identical.

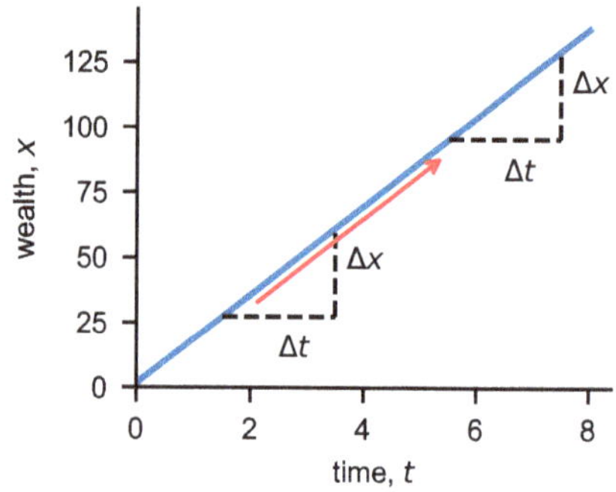

This way of writing it tells us that the growth rate γ is really a sort of clock speed. There's no difference between rescaling t and rescaling γ (by the same factor).

We make a mental note: *the growth rate is a clock speed.* But what kind of clock speed are we talking about? What's a clock speed anyway?

Or: what's a clock? A *clock* is a process that does something repeatedly at regular intervals measured on another clock. Since this definition is circular, a standard clock was agreed in 1967. By convention, after 9,192,631,770 cycles of the radiation produced by the transition between two levels of the *Caesium-133* atom we say "one second has elapsed." That's just something we've agreed on. It lets us measure time by counting repetitions of any other thing that does something regularly, like the Earth completing one full rotation around its axis ("one day").

When we say "the growth rate of the process is γ," we mean that x advances by γ units on the process-scale (meaning in x) in one standard time unit (in finance we often choose one year as the unit, *i.e.* the Earth completing an orbit of the Sun). So it's a conversion factor between the time scales of a standard clock and the process clock.

Of course, a clock is no good if it speeds up or slows down. For processes other than additive growth, we have to be quite careful before we can use them as clocks, *i.e.* before we can state their growth rates.

5.3.2 Multiplicative growth rate

Now what if x is not an additive process but a multiplicative process? In this case, we have

$$d\mathsf{x} = \gamma \mathsf{x} dt, \tag{5.7}$$

with solution

$$\mathsf{x}(t) = \mathsf{x}(0) \exp(\gamma t). \tag{5.8}$$

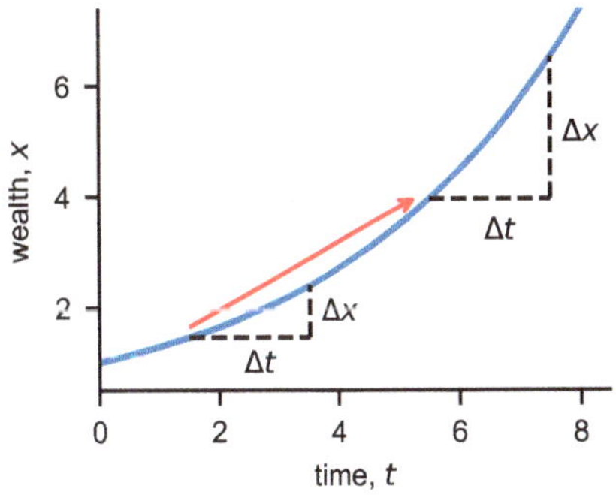

Figure 5.2: Wealth in a multiplicative process (Eq. 5.8). Unlike in Fig. 5.1, here the additive growth rate, $\Delta x/\Delta t$, depends on when we measure it. It is not an invariant quantity for this process.

The additive growth rate is a problematic measure of the speed of this process because it is not stable in time. Writing it out,

$$g_{\mathrm{a}} = \frac{x_0 \exp(\gamma(t + \Delta t)) - x_0 \exp(\gamma t)}{\Delta t}, \tag{5.9}$$

we find that the additive growth rate measured in a multiplicative process depends on the initial value x_0, the time t at which we start measuring, and also on Δt, how long we measure, see Fig. 5.2. If we were to use (Eq. 5.1) to characterise the growth described by (Eq. 5.8), we would find lots of contradictions. Some people would say the growth is faster, others slower, simply because they measured it at different times or for different periods. Thus the additive growth rate does not extract the clock speed, γ, from multiplicative growth: there's a mismatch between the process and the functional form of the rate.

If we want to extract the clock speed of this process, we need to bring the right-hand side of (Eq. 5.7) into the form of (Eq. 5.6). The change which occurs over an interval Δt of whatever is on the left-hand side divided by Δt will then extract γ for us, and it is guaranteed to be constant in time.

Rearranging (Eq. 5.7) accordingly gives

$$\frac{dx}{x} = \gamma dt, \tag{5.10}$$

which we re-write as

$$d \ln x = \gamma dt, \tag{5.11}$$

and we find that the functional form of the growth rate which extracts the clock speed, γ, in this instance is the rate of change of the logarithm of x,

$$g_{\mathrm{m}} = \frac{\Delta \ln x}{\Delta t}. \tag{5.12}$$

as in (Eq. 5.2).

5.3.3 General growth rate

Finally let's be more ambitious and posit a general process, $\mathsf{x}(t)$, of which we assume only that it grows according to a dynamic that can be written down as a separable differential equation.

How do we define a growth rate now?

Well, as in Sec. 5.3.2, we insist that the thing we're measuring will be a clock speed, *i.e.* a time-independent rescaling of time. We enforce this by writing down the dynamic in differential form, containing time rescaling factor, γ. Then we'll work backwards and solve for the functional form of g which will extract this factor for us.

Our general separable differential equation is

$$d\mathsf{x} = f(\mathsf{x})d(\gamma t) \tag{5.13}$$

(for linear growth, like in (Eq. 5.4), $f(\mathsf{x})$ would just be $f(\mathsf{x}) = 1$, and for exponential growth, (Eq. 5.8), it would be $f(\mathsf{x}) = \mathsf{x}$, but we're leaving it general). We separate variables in (Eq. 5.13) and integrate the differential equation

$$\int_{\mathsf{x}(t)}^{\mathsf{x}(t+\Delta t)} \frac{1}{f(\mathsf{x})} d\mathsf{x} = \gamma \Delta t, \tag{5.14}$$

and we've got what we want, namely the functional form of g:

$$g = \frac{\int_{\mathsf{x}(t)}^{\mathsf{x}(t+\Delta t)} \frac{1}{f(\mathsf{x})} d\mathsf{x}}{\Delta t} = \gamma. \tag{5.15}$$

This doesn't quite look like our stated aim: the general expression for a growth rate, (Eq. 5.3). But we get there, by simplifying (Eq. 5.15) and denoting the indefinite integral by v, so that

$$\int_{\mathsf{x}(t)}^{\mathsf{x}(t+\Delta t)} \frac{1}{f(\mathsf{x})} d\mathsf{x} = v(\mathsf{x}(t+\Delta t)) - v(\mathsf{x}(t)) = \Delta v. \tag{5.16}$$

Equation (5.3) now follows exactly by substituting (Eq. 5.16) in (Eq. 5.15). This answers the second question of Sec. 5.3: "how do we know which transformation to use?"

For a general process $d\mathsf{x}$, the appropriate growth rate is

$$g = \frac{\Delta v(\mathsf{x})}{\Delta t}. \tag{5.17}$$

The key conceptual message from this section is this: any growth process defines an appropriate functional form of a growth rate. If we measure a process with the wrong form of growth rate, we obtain something that's not stable in time. Measurements will be irreproducible or inconsistent, depending on arbitrary circumstances, *e.g.* the time we started measuring and how long we measured for.

The key formal result is this: (Eq. 5.3) tells us there is a specific transformation of wealth that is required to state meaningfully how fast wealth grows. Equation (5.16) tells us what that transformation is.

The transformation is a linearisation. At the moment we could call it the constancy transformation because it appropriately removes time dependence and ensures constancy of the growth rate. But we will call it the *ergodicity transformation*. The reason for this will become clear later when we generalise to random growth processes.

In the economics literature, the closest thing to the ergodicity transformation is called the utility function – a term we will mostly avoid because (like expectation) it comes with unhelpful connotations.

5.4 Decisions in a deterministic world

Having clarified what a growth rate is, we can now apply our decision axiom to different situations: act so as to maximise the growth rate of your wealth. In other words, we can explore the world generated by this axiom. We will build from the ground up. First, in Sec. 5.4.1, we will consider two simultaneous payments of different magnitude – which one will be chosen by the model human who obeys our axiom? This is a sanity check: does the model human choose the bigger payment? Next, in Sec. 5.4.2 we add time – what if the model human chooses between two payments of different magnitudes that will occur at different times? This is already a far more complex situation, where the decision criterion requires knowledge of the dynamic. It will shed light on what's called "discounting."

In Chap. 6, we will add fluctuations, noise, uncertainty: what if the model human doesn't know the magnitude (or time) of the payments with certainty? But for now everything will be perfectly known.

5.4.1 Different magnitudes

I'm off to the bank to withdraw some money for you. I offer to give you either

(1) \$10 when I get back or

(2) \$25 when I get back.

You tell me what you prefer.

Let's see what our decision axiom says you'll do. Remember there's no uncertainty. I'm not lying to you and no-one will rob me on my way back from the bank.

I haven't told you how long it will take me to get back from the bank, so we have to keep that general. We'll call that time interval Δt. Since Δt is the same under options (1) and (2), we don't actually need to know its value to compare the growth rates for the two options. Nor do we need the functional form of the growth rate. In this simple case, we can work with a general $v(\mathsf{x})$ in (Eq. 5.3), and any growth rate should give us the same decision. Let's see. Under option (1) we have

$$g^{(1)} = \frac{v(\mathsf{x} + \$10) - v(\mathsf{x})}{\Delta t}, \tag{5.18}$$

and under option (2) we have

$$g^{(2)} = \frac{v(\mathsf{x} + \$25) - v(\mathsf{x})}{\Delta t}. \tag{5.19}$$

To find out which growth rate is larger, we subtract $g^{(1)}$ from $g^{(2)}$

$$g^{(2)} - g^{(1)} = \frac{v(\mathsf{x} + \$25) - v(\mathsf{x}) - (v(\mathsf{x} + \$10) - v(\mathsf{x}))}{\Delta t} \tag{5.20}$$

$$= \frac{v(\mathsf{x} + \$25) - v(\mathsf{x} + \$10)}{\Delta t}. \tag{5.21}$$

Since $v(\mathsf{x})$ is monotonically increasing, this difference in growth rates is positive, *i.e.* $g^{(2)} > g^{(1)}$. Any proper growth rate will be greater under option (2) and our model humans will always go for option (2). That's good because we would have chosen option (2) if we were you, and our model reproduces this intuitive result.

More generally, and concisely, our model says: of two guaranteed payments of different sizes at the same time, choose the larger.

5.4.2 Different magnitudes and times: discounting

Let's make the decision a little harder. What if we offer you the same amounts as before, but now at different times? For example, suppose it is 1st July. Do you prefer to receive:

(1) \$10 on 1st August; or

(2) \$25 on 1st September?

Again, we will compute the two growth rates corresponding to options (1) and (2), and then choose the bigger one. That's how we have been programmed to behave in the world that our axiom is creating. Unlike in the previous case, the functional form of the growth rate will now be important, because the intervals between decision and payment are different.

Discounting under additive dynamics

The behaviour generated by growth-rate maximisation under additive dynamics is both interesting and easily derived. But before we jump in, it seems appropriate to remember that we're exploring a model world and to ask very briefly under what kind of circumstances this model world will resemble the real world. The moment we add time to model, many questions about the *context* of the decision come up. Why might you receive \$10 on 1st August? Do you have to do something in return until then that will keep you from doing other profitable and/or fun things? Is this a rate of pay?

The problem statement doesn't answer these questions, and if the situation is literally that of a stranger approaching us in the street out of the blue and asking which payment we prefer as a one-time event, computing growth-rates, additive or otherwise, may not be our first concern. Maybe your first question would be: why would the stranger want to make these payments to me? What's the deal here? The answer would inform your choices in building a model of the impact of these payments on your wealth.

With these words of warning out of the way, let's specify one particular context, however unlikely that may be, which makes the additive growth rate relevant and then get on with the mathematics: if the payments are repeated and specify a stream of many identical payments at regular intervals, and if nothing is expected from you in return, then the implied additive growth rate will be a pretty good criterion to assess the two options.

Using the additive growth rate as the decision criterion, (Eq. 5.1), which payment do the model humans choose? We've got all the parameters, so this is just a matter of substitution

$$g_{\text{a}}{}^{(1)} = \frac{\mathsf{x} + \$10 - \mathsf{x}}{1 \text{ month}} = \$120 \text{ p.a.}, \tag{5.22}$$

and

$$g_{\text{a}}{}^{(2)} = \frac{\mathsf{x} + \$25 - \mathsf{x}}{2 \text{ months}} = \$150 \text{ p.a..} \tag{5.23}$$

The result is clear: the decision axiom, using this growth rate, produces model humans that prefer payment (2). The additive growth rate has a unique feature: initial wealth, x cancels out. I didn't need to know your initial wealth to compute the rate! Only under additive dynamics does initial wealth not enter into the computation of the growth rate, and growth rates can be computed with knowledge of only the payouts and waiting times.

But perhaps the setup is more interesting than it seems at first glance. In the economics literature, decision-making based on additive growth

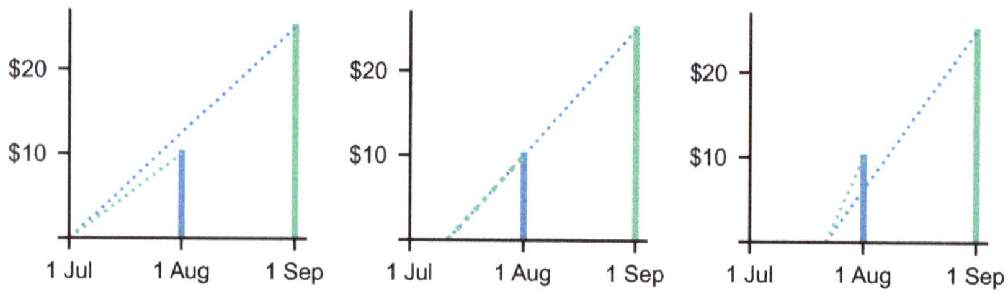

Figure 5.3: Slopes with linear vertical scales are *additive* growth rates. **Left:** at the beginning option (2) yields the highest additive growth rate. **Centre:** after 1/3 of a month, the options are equally good. **Right:** after 2/3 of a month, preference reversal has taken place, and option (1) now yields the highest growth rate. As the first payment approaches, the associated growth rate diverges.

rates is called "*hyperbolic discounting*" because this case is mathematically equivalent to discounting payments in the future with the hyperbolic function $\frac{1}{\Delta t}$.

An interesting feature of optimising additive growth rates is what's called *preference reversal*. In our example, let's keep the payment dates the same but move the decision date forward in time, *i.e.* instead of being asked to choose on 1st July, we are asked at a later date in July. Under these conditions, there comes a time, precisely after a third of a month (around 11th July), when option (2) is no longer preferred, see Fig. 5.3.

You may wonder why someone might model wealth as an additive process. Here is one possibility: if wealth is mostly affected by income and expenses then an additive dynamic may be a good description. Imagine you have a monthly salary of $1,000, and you spend $900 every month on all your expenses. So long as any investment income, like interest payments *etc.*, is negligible, your wealth will follow (Eq. 5.4) with $\gamma = \$100$ per month.

Discounting under multiplicative dynamics

Evaluating the two payments via the multiplicative growth rate is similarly easy, and it also brings about an interesting behavioural pattern. But let's once more ask under what circumstances you might want to turn to multiplicative-growth rate optimisation to decide which payment to take.

Here is one possible answer: if the payments are actually interest payments, transferred to you in return for locking up your liquid wealth x for the relevant time intervals, then the multiplicative growth rate would be an interest rate. Especially if you have the option to leave your money invested at this rate indefinitely, you may wish to use this

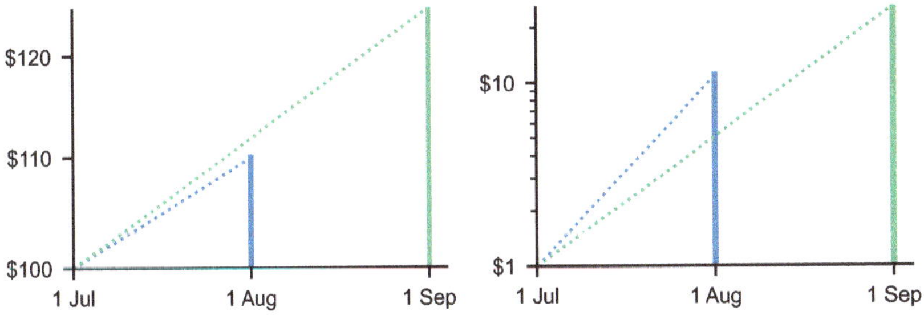

Figure 5.4: Slopes with logarithmic vertical scales. **Left:** if you have a lot of money (here \$100), exponential growth-rate optimisation tells you to be patient and choose the later, larger, payment of \$25. **Right:** if you have little money (here \$1), the same criterion – exponential growth-rate optimisation – tells you to get the cash as fast as possible, and choose the earlier, smaller, payment of \$10.

criterion.

So what about the exponential growth rate, with $v(\mathsf{x}) = \ln \mathsf{x}$ in (Eq. 5.3)? We now have growth rates

$$g_{\mathrm{m}}{}^{(1)} = \frac{\ln(\mathsf{x} + \$10) - \ln(\mathsf{x})}{1 \text{ month}}, \tag{5.24}$$

and

$$g_{\mathrm{m}}{}^{(2)} = \frac{\ln(\mathsf{x} + \$25) - \ln(\mathsf{x})}{2 \text{ months}}. \tag{5.25}$$

Curiously, which is greater depends on your initial wealth in our model world. If your wealth is \$100, then $g_{\mathrm{m}}{}^{(1)} \approx 114\%$ p.a., $g_{\mathrm{m}}{}^{(2)} \approx 134\%$ p.a., and you will choose option (2), shown in Fig. 5.4 (left panel).

But if your initial wealth is \$1, then $g_{\mathrm{m}}{}^{(1)} \approx 2,877\%$ p.a., $g_{\mathrm{m}}{}^{(2)} \approx 1,955\%$ p.a., and you'll choose option (1), Fig. 5.4 (right panel).

Notice how the poorer decision maker seems to be less patient, in spite of using the exact same decision axiom. Using $v(\mathsf{x}) = \ln(\mathsf{x})$ in (Eq. 5.3) is related to what's called "*exponential discounting*" in the economics literature [1]. The word "exponential" is there because we're discounting under *multiplicative dynamics* (which means exponential growth), and the logarithm is the inverse function of the exponential, which we need to define the appropriate growth rate, see (Eq. 5.17).

Multiplicative processes have the property that how much you gain tomorrow is proportional to how much you currently have. Increases in wealth are proportional to wealth – this multiplicative property is virtually ubiquitous in nature. You can imagine many reasons why it applies to wealth. Not only can wealth be invested in interest-paying bonds; it can also be invested in oneself: I may pay for a roof over my head, which transforms my life and earning potential from that of someone living on the streets to that of someone with a home address. Similarly, I can invest in my health and education. In nature, multiplicativity and exponential growth occur whenever something lives. That's because the most successful definitions we have of life insist on self-reproduction, and that implies multiplicative growth.

In this slightly more complex though still fully deterministic case, which option is preferable depends not only on the options available but also on the circumstances of the decision maker. Both my current wealth and the way (I believe) it is evolving as a dynamical process influence my preferences.

Perhaps the most significant message is the richness of this problem. We apply nothing but a very simple axiom, and yet it forces us to choose how we model the dynamics of our wealth. In reality, this may depend strongly on many hard-to-specify circumstances. For example, payments are not just offered at some point in time, but usually in return for something – work or assets. Depending on the specific exchange, an additive, multiplicative, or more general model will be appropriate. Such models are explored in greater detail in [1].

Importantly, we need not resort to psychology to generate a host of behaviours, such as preference reversal as time passes or *impatience* of poorer individuals.

Chapter 6

Decisions in a risky world

6.1 An axiom for risky decisions

In the previous chapter we saw some interesting types of behaviour that occur in the model world generated by our decision axiom. We were able to relate these to phenomena that already have names in the more complex model worlds of classical economics, for instance "discounting" and "preference reversal."

In the present section we will introduce randomness to our model, which will resemble situations where a decision maker is not completely sure about what the consequences of any decision will be. We will do this in a way that's natural from the perspective of growth rate optimisation, and it will lead us to discover precisely what the meanings are in our new framework of concepts in classical economics, such as gambles and utility functions.

We clearly have to do something about our axiom: with randomness the growth rates that are the basis of decisions in our model will also be random. We get around that problem by interpreting "growth rate" in the axiom as "time-average growth rate" when there's randomness involved. Finding these time averages will be simple: the growth rate that's time-invariant for a given deterministic growth process is ergodic when we introduce randomness. Its time average can therefore be computed as its expectation value, which makes this a local (in time) operation.

Decision axiom *with randomness*

People optimise the *time-average* growth rate of their wealth.

6.2 Building the risky world

We begin by introducing *noise* into the wealth dynamic. This has to be done carefully because we want the significance of the noise to stay the same as time passes. That doesn't necessarily mean that the amplitude of the noise – the absolute size of the typical *perturbation* – will stay the same. But we don't want to have to adjust the perturbation by hand, either – we're looking for a systematic way of perturbing the process that automatically takes into account the way in which $x(t)$ changes with time.

Without further ado, here's the solution: introduce a constant-amplitude perturbation to something about the process that is otherwise unchanging. Of course – you've guessed it – the growth rate fits the bill. We will choose a "benign" perturbation – Gaussian with zero mean. Nonetheless, in general – namely unless $x(t)$ is additive – the perturbation will change the expectation value $\langle x(t)\rangle$, that is, in general we will have

$$\langle x(t)\rangle \neq \mathsf{x}(t) \tag{6.1}$$

and we will explore the consequences of this inequality.

We will follow the familiar structure, and first try out this recipe for additive dynamics, $v(x) = x$, then for multiplicative dynamics, $v(x) = \ln x$, and finally for general dynamics.

6.2.1 Perturbed additive dynamics

We expect additive dynamics to be a trivial case because the additive growth rate is just the rate of change, and the ergodicity transformation is the identity, $v(x) = x$. We start from deterministic additive growth, written in differential form,

$$g_{\mathrm{a}} = \frac{d\mathsf{x}}{dt} = \gamma, \tag{6.2}$$

then rearrange and add the perturbation. This makes sure that the dynamic significance of the perturbation doesn't change over time: the constant growth rate becomes the ergodic growth rate. Specifically, our perturbation is the increment in a Wiener process multiplied by a constant scale factor, σ:

$$d\mathsf{x} = \gamma dt \quad \longrightarrow \quad dx = \gamma dt + \sigma dW(t). \tag{6.3}$$

We integrate (Eq. 6.3) from time 0 to t (setting $x(0) = 0$ for simplicity):

$$x(t) = \int_0^t (\gamma ds + \sigma dW(s)) \tag{6.4}$$

$$= \gamma t + \sigma W(t). \tag{6.5}$$

Because of additivity, in this special case we expect $\mathsf{x}(t) = \langle x(t) \rangle$, meaning (Eq. 6.1) is not true here. So let's check by taking expectations:

$$\begin{aligned} \langle x(t) \rangle &= \langle \gamma t + \sigma W(t) \rangle && (6.6) \\ &= \gamma t. && (6.7) \end{aligned}$$

Comparing to the deterministic x in (Eq. 5.4), we confirm that the perturbation in this case does not change the expectation value of the process.

To recap: first, the noise in this dynamic has constant dynamic significance because it is a constant-amplitude perturbation applied to something that is unchanging in time in the deterministic case. Second, the expectation value of this dynamic is identical to the unperturbed, deterministic, case ($\sigma = 0$).

6.2.2 Perturbed multiplicative dynamics

Multiplicative dynamics will be less trivial but shouldn't be too hard. The multiplicative growth rate is just the rate of change of the logarithm, meaning the ergodicity transformation is the logarithm, $v(\mathsf{x}) = \ln \mathsf{x}$. We start from deterministic multiplicative growth, written in differential form

$$g_{\mathrm{m}} = \frac{d \ln \mathsf{x}}{dt} = \gamma \qquad (6.8)$$

then, as before, rearrange and add the perturbation to the ergodic growth rate. Again this ensures that the dynamic significance of the perturbation doesn't change over time. Like in the additive case, we perturb by adding a scaled (by σ) Wiener increment:

$$d \ln \mathsf{x} = \gamma dt \quad \longrightarrow \quad d \ln x = \gamma dt + \sigma dW(t). \qquad (6.9)$$

Just as we did to arrive at (Eq. 6.5), we have to integrate a BM with drift to find the solution of this SDE. Because we're working in the transformed variable, $v(x) = \ln x$, this is a recurring theme: whatever the process $x(t)$, once it has gone through the appropriate transformation, we will end up at BM with drift. Integrating (Eq. 6.9) from time 0 to t (setting $\ln x(0) = 0$ for simplicity), we get

$$\begin{aligned} \ln x(t) &= \int_0^t (\gamma ds + \sigma dW(s)) && (6.10) \\ &= \gamma t + \sigma W(t). && (6.11) \end{aligned}$$

Unlike for additive dynamics, the ergodicity transformation is no longer the identity, but the logarithm. To find the actual solution we therefore have to invert the logarithm (apply $v^{(-1)}(\cdot) = \exp(\cdot)$),

$$x(t) = \exp\left(\gamma t + \sigma W(t)\right). \qquad (6.12)$$

Multiplicative dynamics are not additive, meaning there is a mismatch between the additive expectation value and the multiplicative effects of time. The expectation value of an exponentiated Wiener noise is boosted by the fluctuations: the expectation value is linear, but the exponential generates disproportionately large contributions for positive values of $W(t)$. We leave it as an exercise to compute the expectation value $\langle x(t)\rangle$ (hint: $x(t)$ is log-normally distributed) and state only the well-known result here:

$$\langle x(t)\rangle = \langle \exp(\gamma t + \sigma W(t))\rangle \tag{6.13}$$

$$= \exp\left[\left(\gamma + \frac{\sigma^2}{2}\right)t\right]. \tag{6.14}$$

Comparing to the deterministic x in (Eq. 5.8), we see that in this case, as in most cases, the perturbed and unperturbed process do not share the same expectation value, and (Eq. 6.1) applies. It is worth stressing that (Eq. 6.14) shouldn't be misinterpreted in everyday language as "increasing the fluctuations in a multiplicative process boosts expectations." This would be misleading for two reasons: first, we introduced the perturbation in a specific way which ensures that the time-average growth rate is independent of σ; for instance, the parametrisation of GBM in (Eq. 4.52) does not have this feature. Second, we must bear in mind that the expected value is an average over the ensemble and has little significance when we're concerned with a single realisation or a finite number of realisations.

6.2.3 Perturbed general dynamics

The simplest, and probably most important, models to describe real-life wealth are additive, $v(x) = x$, and multiplicative, $v(x) = \ln x$. But it helps to think of those two cases as examples of something more general. In this section, we will re-do what we did for additive and multiplicative dynamics but keep things more general – within reason, $x(t)$ may now follow any dynamic you like. To confirm we're really just generalising, you can go through the following steps and verify that Sec. 6.2.1 and Sec. 6.2.2 are special cases.

We find it intuitive to start with a deterministic process and add an appropriate perturbation. However, because this approach doesn't always produce the smoothest mathematics, we will return to the problem in Sec. 6.6 from a slightly different angle. That will allow us to use Itô calculus and lead to a deeper analysis, but first things first.

The starting point is now a general deterministic growth rate,

$$g = \frac{dv(\mathsf{x})}{dt} = \gamma. \tag{6.15}$$

We re-arrange this and add the perturbation to get

$$dv(\mathsf{x}) = \gamma dt \quad \longrightarrow \quad dv(x) = \gamma dt + \sigma dW(t). \tag{6.16}$$

As before, the perturbation is guaranteed to have constant dynamic significance because it is applied to the otherwise unchanging growth rate. That's how v is defined: it's the transformation of x that grows linearly in time (so that $g = \frac{dv}{dt}$ is constant, taking the value γ in the absence of perturbations). We integrate (Eq. 6.16) from time 0 to t (assuming $v(0) = 0$ for simplicity),

$$v\left(x(t)\right) = \int_0^t \left(\gamma ds + \sigma dW(s)\right) \tag{6.17}$$

$$= \gamma t + \sigma W(t), \tag{6.18}$$

and then apply the inverse function $v^{(-1)}$ to get

$$x(t) = v^{(-1)}\left(\gamma t + \sigma W(t)\right). \tag{6.19}$$

Equation (6.19) can be read as x being a non-linear function, $v^{(-1)}$, of a symmetrically perturbed time, $\gamma t + \sigma W(t)$. Whether this perturbation boosts or suppresses the expected value is determined by the well-known *Jensen's inequality*.

Jensen's inequality

$$f(\langle x \rangle) \leq \langle f(x) \rangle \tag{6.20}$$

for any convex function $f(x)$.

If $v^{(-1)}$ is convex, as in multiplicative dynamics, then Jensen's inequality tells us that the expectation value of the perturbed function (Eq. 6.19) is greater than the unperturbed case. This means that at any time

$$\langle x(t) \rangle > \mathsf{x}(t), \tag{6.21}$$

in agreement with (Eq. 6.14). It can be shown that $v^{(-1)}$ is convex whenever v itself is concave (to prove this v has to be monotonically increasing, which is true by construction in our case). If v is convex, then Jensen's inequality points the other way, and the expected value $\langle x \rangle$ is reduced by the symmetric perturbation we've introduced.

6.3 The appropriate growth rate is ergodic

Equation (5.3) defines deterministic dynamics by specifying a growth rate. Knowledge of the growth rate is thus knowledge of the dynamic. In

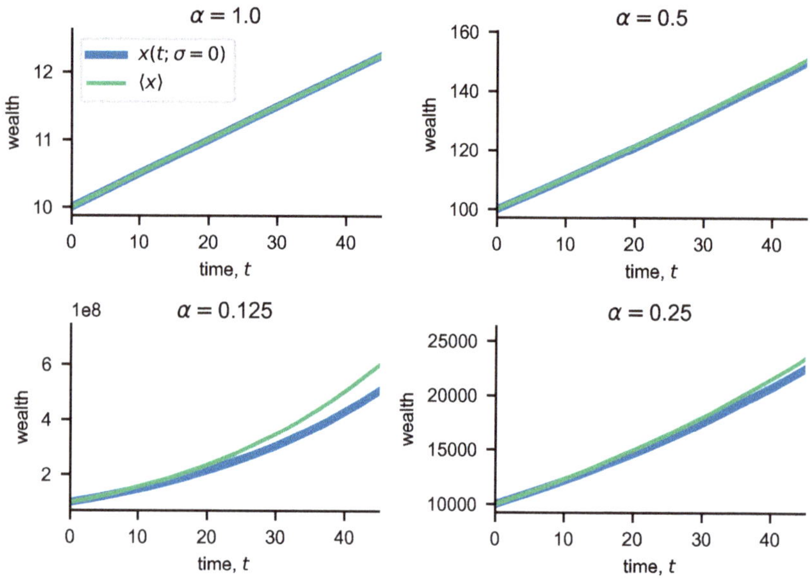

Figure 6.1: Zero-noise trajectories (blue) and ensemble averages (green) for dynamics with increasingly concave $v(x) = x^\alpha$ (with α decreasing from 1 to 0.125, from top left clockwise). As the concavity of $v(x)$ increases, the ensemble average becomes increasingly misleading: it is greater than the noiseless growth rate, which explains what economists call "risk aversion."

the deterministic case, we defined growth rates by insisting that they not change over time. In the risky, or noisy, case, of course growth rates do change over time but – crucially – the appropriately defined growth rate changes only because of the noise and nothing else – it fluctuates from one time interval to another, but it does not systematically increase or decrease. Specifically, the way we constructed noisy dynamics, starting from the growth rate, guarantees that the noisy growth rates are ergodic: their expectation values are also their long-time averages. We will now prove this result. We will prove it only for the general case because that's easily done, and it implies the veracity of the statement for any special case.

Proof. To avoid problems with differentiating the non-differentiable Wiener process, we begin with the expectation value of gdt:

$$\langle gdt\rangle = \langle dv\rangle \tag{6.22}$$
$$= \langle \gamma dt + \sigma dW(t)\rangle \tag{6.23}$$
$$= \gamma dt. \tag{6.24}$$

Since dt is deterministic, we can take it outside the expectation operator and divide both sides by it, showing that the expectation value of g is

$$\langle g\rangle = \gamma. \tag{6.25}$$

Next, we compute the time average of g. By the definition of time averages, that's

$$\overline{g} = \lim_{\Delta t\to\infty} \frac{\Delta v}{\Delta t} \tag{6.26}$$
$$= \lim_{\Delta t\to\infty} \frac{\int_t^{t+\Delta t} dv}{\Delta t} \tag{6.27}$$
$$= \lim_{\Delta t\to\infty} \frac{\int_t^{t+\Delta t} (\gamma dt + \sigma dW(t))}{\Delta t} \tag{6.28}$$
$$= \gamma + \lim_{\Delta t\to\infty} \frac{\sigma W(\Delta t)}{\Delta t} \tag{6.29}$$
$$= \gamma, \tag{6.30}$$

where the last line follows with probability one from the scaling properties of the Wiener process.

Comparing (Eq. 6.25) and (Eq. 6.30), we conclude that the expectation value and time average of g are identical for general dynamics, and hence that the growth rate, appropriately defined for a given process, is an ergodic observable. □

The result shows that the two averages are identical, irrespective of whether (Eq. 6.1) applies or not. So, while the expectation value of x usually does not reflect what actually happens over time in a single system, the expectation value of the growth rate g is *guaranteed* to reflect what happens over time in a single system.

We cannot overstate the importance of this fact: *the appropriate growth rate for a stochastic wealth process is an ergodic observable.* Economic theory, historically, is based on expectation values, and they are often taken of non-ergodic wealth where they do not reflect what happens to individuals over time. This is simply because when the foundations of economic theory were laid, expectation values had been invented as tools of analysis, whereas time averages had not. It leads to numerous puzzles in economics.

With this key result under our belt, we can fully appreciate why we used the term "ergodicity transformation" instead of constancy transformation on p. 65. In the stochastic case, which is more general, $v(x)$ allows us to recover ergodicity from a non-ergodic wealth process, though not constancy. Similarly, in the stochastic case we compute time-average growth rates rather than just growth rates because the growth rate observed over a finite time in a given realisation is random, and without taking the time average we could easily be misled by fluctuations and choose a slowly growing process.

The use of expectation values is indiscriminate in much of classical economic theory. In contrast to this, our confirmation of the *ergodicity of growth rates* explicitly allows us to use their expectation values even in cases where we're actually interested in time averages. This, and its science-historical significance, will be worked out in detail in Sec. 6.5.

6.4 Long-term decision algorithm

We're now in a position to specify how humans in our model will make decisions under uncertainty. In Chap. 5 we worked out precisely how a growth rate must be defined for a given deterministic dynamic. In Sec. 6.2 we used our knowledge of such growth rates to generate consistently perturbed dynamics.

It is possible to write down dynamics that don't allow the definition of a growth rate. It is also possible to perturb a dynamic in an inconsistent way. But in this book, all deterministic dynamics will have proper growth rates, and all stochastic dynamics are obtained from deterministic dynamics in the way we have described.

Given these constraints on the processes we consider, we can specify the algorithm our model humans will follow when making decisions under risk. Specifically, we consider a choice between two wealth processes whose dynamics are structurally the same (*i.e.* both are additive, both multiplicative, or both something else) but have different parameters.

Long-term decision algorithm

To choose long-term optimally between wealth processes, x_1 and x_2,

- determine the ergodicity transformation $v(x)$.
- compute the time-average growth rates $\overline{g}_1$ and $\overline{g}_2$ either directly by averaging over time or by invoking the ergodic property and averaging over the ensemble; and
- choose the process with faster growth.

You can see why we wanted to keep the dynamics the same. If we did not, *e.g.* if we considered a choice between an additive wealth processes and a multiplicative wealth process, then we would get stuck at step 3 trying to compare growth rates of different forms and different dimensions – apples and oranges. In effect, we are treating wealth dynamics as the "rules of the game" in which choices are made. They constitute a description of the model world in which our model humans live and act. Different dynamics will resemble more or less closely the real economic environments of real people.

6.5 Relation to earlier economic theories

In the previous section we presented the EE model of decision-making that is to maximise the time-average growth rate of wealth.

In the present section, we will detail precisely how that model is related to models that were developed earlier, specifically at a time before the ergodicity question had been asked. This section is thus about history: how did we model human decision making under risk before we knew we had to find appropriate ergodic growth rates?

The story is fascinating. Despite the absence of appropriate tools and concepts, early researchers invented ingenious mathematical representations of human behaviour. With not very much work, it is possible to tweak these old models, at least in special cases, to coincide with EE.

The roadmap for this section is as follows. We will first introduce the concept of a *gamble*. This is a random wealth change realised over some finite time – in essence, a little piece of a stochastic wealth process. Next, we will describe the *gamble problem*, namely the problem of choosing between different gambles (or between a gamble and doing nothing). To connect to EE, we point out how different ways of repeating a gamble generate different wealth dynamics, similar to the types considered in Sec. 6.2. Finally, we will present the classical solution to the gamble problem, known today as expected utility theory (EUT), in which a nonlinear transformation called the utility function, $u(x)$, is applied to monetary wealth. This will be summarised in the EUT decision algorithm.

6.5.1 Gamble – random number and duration

One fundamental building block of mathematical decision theory is the gamble. This is a mathematical object that resembles situations in real life where we face decisions with uncertain financial consequences. An example is buying a lottery ticket. We define the gamble mathematically as follows.

DEFINITION: **Gamble**

A gamble is a pair of a random variable, Q, called the *profit* and a time interval, δt, called the *duration*. Q takes one of K possible monetary values, $\{q_1, \ldots, q_K\}$, associated with probabilities, $\{p_1, \ldots, p_K\}$.

We interpret the profit as the net change in the gambler's wealth. It can be positive, associated with a monetary gain, or negative, associated with a loss. We order the profit realisations so that $q_1 < \ldots < q_K$.

We think of the duration as the time elapsed from the decision to accept the gamble to the realisation of the profit or, in a sequence of gambles, as the time between consecutive gambles.

In mainstream economics, the duration of a gamble is rarely discussed. It does not feature in classical decision theories such as EUT. However, it is crucial information, as a trivial example shows. Suppose you can choose between two gambles. One pays \$1 with probability 1 and takes one second to complete; the other also pays \$1 also with probability 1 but takes one year to complete. Clearly the former is more attractive.[1] In EE, we are interested in how wealth evolves over time, so it should come as no surprise that the duration of the gamble is a necessary ingredient in our analysis.

The following situations may be modelled as gambles:

Example: Betting on a fair coin

Imagine betting \$10 on the toss of a fair coin. Tails you lose \$10,

[1] More realistically, any gambler knows that betting on the winner of a football match is a very different proposition from betting on the winner of the league, even if the odds are similar. Unless it is the last day of the season, the latter bet takes much longer to resolve than the former.

heads you win \$10. We would model this with the following profits and probabilities:

$$q_1 = -\$10, \qquad p_1 = 1/2; \tag{6.31}$$
$$q_2 = +\$10, \qquad p_2 = 1/2. \tag{6.32}$$

The duration could be the time between flipping the coin and receiving the profit or if, say, we take part in one coin toss every day, we could set $\delta t = 1$ day.

Example: Playing the lottery

We can also imagine a gamble akin to a lottery, where we pay an amount, F, for a ticket which will win the jackpot, B, with probability, p. The corresponding profit realisations and probabilities are:

$$q_1 = -F, \qquad p_1 = 1 - p; \tag{6.33}$$
$$q_2 = B - F, \qquad p_2 = p. \tag{6.34}$$

Note that we deduct the ticket price F in the realisation q_2 to make it the net change in wealth caused by winning the jackpot. The duration might be $\delta t = 1$ week.

Example: The null gamble

It is useful to introduce the *null gamble*, in which a profit of zero is received with certainty: $q_1 = \$0$, $p_1 = 1$. This represents the "no bet" or "do nothing" option, which we use as a reference point. By comparing a specific gamble with the null gamble, we can determine whether or not the specific gamble is worth taking.

Typically, the duration of the null gamble is set equal to that of the specific gamble with which it is being compared.

The gamble we have presented is discrete, in that the profit, Q, is a random variable with a countable (and usually we assume small) number of possible values. The extension to continuous random variables is straightforward and is used to model real situations in which the number of possible outcomes is large, *e.g.* the change in a stock price over a day.

This presents a natural connection to the continuous wealth processes we use in EE. Given a wealth dynamic, $dx(t)$, the net change in wealth

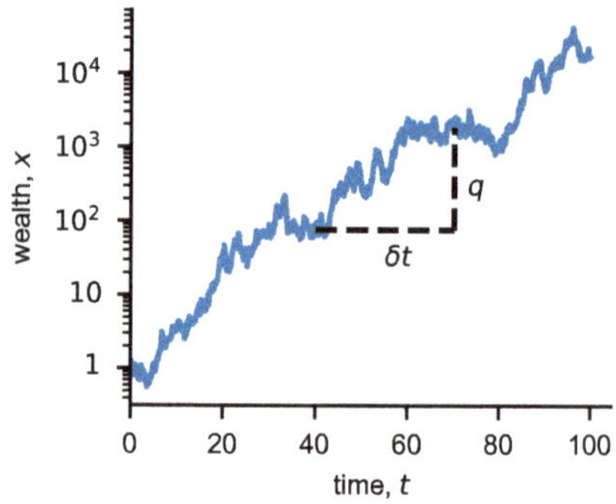

Figure 6.2: A stochastic wealth process is made up of random changes in wealth. Each such change can be viewed as a gamble. Here is one that results in realisation q and is of duration δt.

from time t to $t + \delta t$ is a gamble with profit

$$Q = x(t+\delta t) - x(t) \tag{6.35}$$

$$= \int_t^{t+\delta t} dx(t), \tag{6.36}$$

and duration δt, see Fig. 6.2.

Suppose now that you have to choose between two options that you've modelled as two gambles (possibly including the null gamble). Which should you choose, and why? This is the *gamble problem*, the central question of decision theory, and the basis for much of mainstream economics.

DEFINITION: **The gamble problem**

The gamble problem is the problem of choosing between two gambles.

We stress here that the gamble alone is not enough information to answer this question. The value of a gamble – clearly – depends on more information than is contained in the profit realisations, probabilities, and duration. Crucially, it depends on:

1. How the gamble affects our future. For instance, if we go bankrupt as a result, can we recover from that?

2. Our circumstances. When you're very rich you can afford to take risks that you can't afford when you're poor.

3. Our personality. Some people are more willing to take financial risks than others. Some like the thrill of gambling, others find it unpleasant.

EE focuses on points 1 and 2. Defining the ergodic growth rate and computing its time average requires knowledge of the wealth dynamics that arise when the gamble is repeated over time. Moreover, in the specific case of multiplicative dynamics and more generally, this growth rate depends on the individual's wealth, $x(t)$, at the start of the gamble. Mainstream economics, specifically EUT, focuses on points 2 and 3 instead: the utility function takes an individual's wealth as its argument and its shape is treated as encoding the individual's psychological attitude to risk.

Although the gamble problem is underspecified by gambles alone, the gamble is a useful conceptual unit because it specifies that part of the model of evolving wealth that is independent of individual circumstances (and, indeed, psychology). Thus it splits an easily observable part of the problem from information that's much harder to obtain. We can all buy a lottery ticket with publicly disclosed prizes, probabilities, and duration. For some of us that will be attractive, for others it won't, for a variety of reasons.

6.5.2 Repeated gamble: towards a wealth process

We already know one touch point between EE and the classic gamble setup: we know how to construct a gamble as the random variable corresponding to the net change in wealth following a stochastic process, (Eq. 6.36). EE specifies how to evaluate a wealth process, and if it's justifiable to identify the gamble with the process, then we know how to evaluate the gamble under EE.

We will now strengthen this connection by showing what it might mean to identify the gamble and the process. To do this we will take a gamble and construct from it a wealth process. That means we have to extend the gamble over an arbitrarily long time. A principled way of doing that (one that keeps extra assumptions to a minimum and clearly visible) is to imagine the gamble is being repeated over and over again.

Crucially, *the mode of repetition is not specified in the gamble itself.* It is the only additional assumption we have to make to arrive at a wealth process and unlock the power of EE. We shall focus on two modes: *additive* and *multiplicative* repetition, which correspond to additive and multiplicative dynamics. Thus *the same gamble can correspond to different dynamics.*

Additive repetition

Additive dynamics are the simplest dynamics, in that the wealth increment has no wealth-dependence. We simply generate a realisation of the random profit and add it to the previous wealth.

DEFINITION: **Additive repetition**

If a gamble is repeated additively, then a newly generated realisation of the random profit, Q, is *added* to $x(t)$ in each round. We define the change in wealth occurring over a single round as

$$\delta x(t) \equiv x(t + \delta t) - x(t). \tag{6.37}$$

In the additive case, we have

$$\delta x(t) = Q. \tag{6.38}$$

Under additive repetition, δx is a stationary random variable, meaning the ergodicity transformation is the identity, $v(x) = x$, and we're in the case of additive dynamics. Starting at time, t_0, the wealth after T rounds is

$$x(t_0 + T\delta t) = x(t_0) + \sum_{\tau=1}^{T} q(\tau), \tag{6.39}$$

where $q(\tau)$ is the realisation of Q in round τ. This is an evolution equation for wealth following a noisy additive dynamic. Note that $x(t_0 + T\delta t)$ is itself a random variable.

The additive growth rate is ergodic, and its expectation value

$$\left\langle \frac{\delta x}{\delta t} \right\rangle \tag{6.40}$$

is the time-average growth rate under this mode of repetition.

Example: Additive repetition of a \$10 bet

We return to our first example of a gamble: a \$ 10 bet on a coin toss. Under additive repetition, successive bets will always be \$10, regardless of how rich or poor you become. Suppose your starting wealth is $x(t_0) = \$100$. Then, following (Eq. 6.39), your wealth after T rounds will be

$$\begin{aligned} x(t_0 + T\delta t) &= \$100 + \$10 n_{\text{heads}} - \$10(T - n_{\text{heads}}) && (6.41) \\ &= \$[100 + 10(2n_{\text{heads}} - T)], && (6.42) \end{aligned}$$

where $0 \leq n_{\text{heads}} \leq T$ is the number of winning tosses.

Note that we have assumed your wealth is allowed to go negative. We could imagine instead that this is not allowed and that a special rule applies if your wealth reaches zero, for instance remaining zero for all time thereafter. This complicates the analysis considerably, since some or all of the wealth trajectories will hit the absorbing barrier at $x = \$0$ and remain there. But complicated or not, when this sort of ruin is an important consideration, then a simple additive process which dips in and out of negative wealth is not a good wealth model.

Multiplicative repetition

An alternative is multiplicative repetition. In the example above, let us imagine that the first \$10 bet were viewed not as a bet of fixed monetary size, but as a fixed fraction (10%) of the starting wealth (\$100). Under multiplicative repetition, each successive bet is for the same fraction of wealth which, in general, will be a different monetary amount.

The formalism is as follows.

DEFINITION: **Multiplicative repetition**

If a gamble is repeated multiplicatively, then the profit, Q, is expressed as a random multiplier of the initial wealth,

$$R \equiv \frac{x(t_0) + Q}{x(t_0)}. \tag{6.43}$$

This multiplier is itself a random variable and multiplicative repetition means drawing a new realisation of it every δt and multiplying wealth $x(t)$ accordingly. Under multiplicative repetition, $\delta \ln x$ is a stationary random variable, the ergodicity transformation is $v(x) = \ln x$, and we're in the case of multiplicative dynamics.

Starting at time t_0, the wealth after T rounds is

$$x(t_0 + T\delta t) = x(t_0) \prod_{\tau=1}^{T} r(\tau), \tag{6.44}$$

where $r(\tau)$ is the realisation of R in round τ. The exponential growth rate is ergodic, and its expectation value

$$\left\langle \frac{\delta \ln x}{\delta t} \right\rangle \tag{6.45}$$

is the time-average growth rate under this mode of repetition.

Example: Multiplicative repetition

The \$10 bet on a coin toss is now re-expressed as a bet of a fixed fraction of wealth at the start of each round. Following (Eq. 6.43), the random multiplier, R, has two possible realisations:

$$r_1 = \frac{\$100 - \$10}{\$100} = 0.9, \qquad p_1 = 1/2; \tag{6.46}$$

$$r_2 = \frac{\$100 + \$10}{\$100} = 1.1, \qquad p_2 = 1/2. \tag{6.47}$$

The wealth after T rounds is, therefore,

$$x(t_0 + T\delta t) = \$100\ (1.1)^{n_{\text{heads}}}\ (0.9)^{T-n_{\text{heads}}}, \tag{6.48}$$

where $0 \leq n_{\text{heads}} \leq T$ is the number of winning tosses.

There is no question of bankruptcy in this model, since we can lose no more than 10% of our wealth in each round (although, in decaying wealth trajectories, we may lose resemblance with reality, where money is not infinitely divisible and minimum monetary amounts exist).

We have defined a gamble and clarified how it is related to EE. It can be derived from a wealth dynamic; conversely a wealth dynamic can be constructed from a gamble provided we know how to repeat the gamble. But early decision theory didn't use the concepts of repetition, time averages, or ergodicity transformations. In the next section we will present how the gamble problem was addressed before the advent of EE, and precisely how this earlier treatment is related to ours.

6.5.3 Expected wealth and expected utility

In EE, we solve the gamble problem by maximising the time (or, equivalently, ensemble) average of the ergodic growth rate for the wealth process, of which we consider the gamble to represent an increment.

This is not how economists treat the gamble problem. It's instructive to mention two earlier maximands for gamble evaluation: the expected wealth change, invented around 1654; and the expected utility change, invented around 1738. These criteria can be mapped, under certain conditions, to maximands in EE. In later extensions of EUT, including prospect theory in the 1970s and cumulative prospect theory in the 1990s, it is unclear how to ascribe physical meaning to the resulting models.

Expected-value theory

The first gamble evaluation criterion, which emerged in the early days of probability theory in the 17th century, was to maximise the expected change in wealth. We will call this expected-value theory (EVT). A model human behaves according to these instructions:

EVT decision algorithm

1. Specify $Q^{(m)}$ for the gambles offered;
2. Determine the expected change in wealth arising from each gamble,
$$\langle \delta x \rangle^{(m)} = \left\langle Q^{(m)} \right\rangle ; \tag{6.49}$$
3. Choose the gamble, m^*, with the largest $\langle \delta x \rangle^{(m)}$.

The history of this criterion is linked to finding what was perceived as a *fair value* of an uncertain prospect. Say we're playing a game of chance, for some amount of money in a pot, maybe we're rolling dice, best out of three. If you're currently ahead, say after two throws, and someone wants to take over your position, it may be fair to sell your position for the expectation value of your winnings. One reason this criterion makes some sense is conservation: the sum of the expected winnings of all players is precisely the pot, so buying all players out of their positions is equivalent to buying the pot, as perhaps it should be.

Connecting this back to EE: does the expected value of wealth grow faster or more slowly than individual wealth in the long-time limit? This question goes to the heart of EVT: if we make decisions based on expected wealth, will we be overly optimistic or pessimistic? And will time-optimal behaviour be *risk-averse* or *risk-seeking*?

To answer this question, we make use of the ergodicity of the growth rate. Its expected value tells us how fast individual wealth grows over time, whereas applying the growth rate to expected wealth tells us, well how fast expected wealth grows. Under what conditions, then, is EVT systematically overly optimistic so that risk-averse behaviour is optimal, in other words when is $\frac{\Delta v(\langle x \rangle)}{\Delta t} \geq \left\langle \frac{\Delta v(x)}{\Delta t} \right\rangle$?

The answer is easy to find. We assume starting with wealth $x(t)$ and consider the growth rate going forward,

$$\frac{\Delta v(\langle x \rangle)}{\Delta t} \geq \left\langle \frac{\Delta v(x)}{\Delta t} \right\rangle \tag{6.50}$$

$$\Leftrightarrow v(\langle x(t+\Delta t) \rangle) - v(\langle x(t) \rangle) \geq \langle v(x(t+\Delta t)) \rangle - \langle v(x(t)) \rangle \tag{6.51}$$

$$\Leftrightarrow v(\langle x(t+\Delta t) \rangle) \geq \langle v(x(t+\Delta t)) \rangle \tag{6.52}$$

where the final step follows from the fact that our starting wealth, $x(t)$ is a known number, not a random variable, and hence $v(\langle x(t) \rangle) = \langle v(x(t)) \rangle = v(x(t))$. By Jensen's inequality, (Eq. 6.52) holds whenever

$v(x)$ is concave, as is the case for multiplicative dynamics. We find that EVT leads to inappropriately optimistic decisions when dynamics are multiplicative. More sloppily, any tweak to additive dynamics in the direction of multiplicativity will mean that acting according to EVT is not in our long-term interest. We should be more risk averse.

Conversely, of course, if $v(x)$ is convex then it will be time-optimal to take even greater risks than EVT suggests.

With this, it is also easy to see under what conditions an EE agent would evaluate a gamble by computing $\langle \delta x \rangle$. The answer is: under additive dynamics, where the ergodicity transformation is linear, $v(x) = x$ – neither concave nor convex. The EE maximand is then $\langle g_{\text{a}} \rangle = \frac{\langle \delta x \rangle}{\delta t}$. Apart from the δt in the denominator (which cancels if we assume all gambles offered have the same duration), this is EVT. We conclude that EVT is equivalent to EE under the assumption of additive wealth dynamics, one of the simplest wealth models we can write down.

There's a good reason why additive dynamics may have been assumed in the early developments. Taylor expanding the time average of the general ergodic growth rate (which we may write as an ensemble average because of ergodicity) about $\delta x = 0$, we find

$$\overline{g} = \frac{\langle \delta v(x) \rangle}{\delta t} \tag{6.53}$$

$$= \frac{1}{\delta t} \left\langle \left[\frac{dv}{dx} \delta x + \frac{1}{2} \frac{d^2 v}{dx^2} \delta x^2 + \cdots \right] \right\rangle \tag{6.54}$$

$$= \frac{1}{\delta t} \left[\frac{dv}{dx} \langle \delta x \rangle + \frac{1}{2} \frac{d^2 v}{dx^2} \langle \delta x^2 \rangle + \cdots \right] \tag{6.55}$$

The last line follows from the fact that the derivatives of v are known functions, evaluated at the known wealth x before the gamble takes place. In other words, they are just constants and can be taken out of the expectation operator, $\langle \cdot \rangle$. If δx is small, keeping only the first term in the expansion is often a valid approximation, in which case we will call the dynamic "linearisable." The expression becomes

$$\overline{g} \approx \frac{\langle \delta x \rangle}{\delta t} \frac{dv}{dx}, \tag{6.56}$$

which is proportional to the expected wealth change, $\langle \delta x \rangle$. Since we have assumed $v(x)$ is monotonic increasing, we have $\frac{dv}{dx} > 0$. In behavioural terms, multiplying a maximand by a positive constant preserves the ranking of any set of gambles. Therefore, maximising $\overline{g}$ yields the same behaviour as maximising $\langle \delta x \rangle$.

Summary: the first formal decision theory is expected wealth change maximisation. EVT is equivalent to EE under additive dynamics, and additive dynamics are equivalent to any linearisable dynamic in the limit of small wealth changes.

Expected-utility theory

In the language of economics, EVT treats humans as "*risk neutral*," *i.e.* they have no preference between gambles whose expected changes in wealth are identical (over the same time interval). For example, they are indifferent between keeping what they have (the null gamble) and tossing a fair coin for \$1,000.

At least since 1713 [39, p. 402], this has been known to be a flawed model. Nicolas Bernoulli pointed out that gambles can be constructed – at least in theory – whose expected wealth change does not exist. What then, would this criterion mean? Moreover, EVT does not always accord well with observed behaviour. For instance, anyone who buys an *insurance contract* prefers the certain loss of the insurance fee to a random loss of smaller expectation value. Such a person does not maximise their expected wealth change and yet insurance contracts have been signed since Phoenician times.

In 1738, Daniel Bernoulli [9] put forward a new model of human behaviour that addressed some of the empirical failures of EVT[2]. Bernoulli wrote [9, p. 24] "that a gain of one thousand ducats is more significant to a pauper than to a rich man." Similarly, we might add that an inveterate gambler has a different attitude to risking \$100 on the spin of a roulette wheel than a prudent saver, their wealths being equal.

After correspondence with Cramer, Bernoulli devised what is now known as EUT to model these considerations. He observed that money may not translate linearly into usefulness and assigned to an individual an idiosyncratic *utility function*, $u(x)$, that maps wealth, x, into usefulness, u. He claimed that this was the quantity whose expected change, $\langle \delta u(x) \rangle$, is maximised in a choice between gambles.

This is the axiom of EUT. It leads to another decision algorithm:

EUT decision algorithm

1. Specify $Q^{(m)}$ for the gambles offered;
2. Specify the individual's idiosyncratic utility function, $u(x)$, which maps wealth to utility;
3. Determine the change of expected utility arising from each gamble,
$$\langle \delta u \rangle = \left\langle u\left(x + Q^{(m)}\right)\right\rangle - u(x); \tag{6.57}$$
4. Choose the gamble, m^*, with the largest $\langle \delta u \rangle^{(m)}$.

[2]Bernoulli's original paper contains an error. The theory as we present it here is a corrected version that can be found in [27], see also [46] for a discussion of the error.

Let's ask the same question for EUT as we did for EVT: under what conditions would EE maximise the quantity in (Eq. 6.57)? The utility function $u(x)$ is defined as the object whose expected changes are maximised by a person. Under EE, people are modelled as maximising the expected rate of change of the ergodicity transformation, $v(x)$.

Mapping: EUT $\Leftrightarrow$ EE

We conclude that EUT is equivalent to EE for gambles of equal duration *if the utility function, $u(x)$, coincides with the ergodicity transformation, $v(x)$.*

Bernoulli did not just write down a general function $u(x)$. He argued for the logarithm as a plausible candidate for this function. People, he suggested, tend to behave as if they were maximising expected changes in the logarithm of wealth. Exactly why that was the case, he did not know.[3] We do. Using the logarithm as the ergodicity transformation, *i.e.* equating $u = v$, we can rephrase Bernoulli's claim as saying that people maximise the time-average growth rate of wealth under multiplicative dynamics. Suddenly this is a plausible claim – we have already identified multiplicative dynamics as a fundamental model of wealth, resembling many real situations.

This is quite an astonishing mapping, which we believe is not coincidental. In the 18th century, researchers discovered elements of the mathematical structure of EE. They did this by careful observation alone, since the appropriate mathematical tools had yet to be invented. As mathematical concepts were immature at the time, a nomenclature emerged ("utility," "risk preferences," and so on) that seems quaint and imprecise from today's perspective. That is unsurprising – no research field starts life fully formed. However, this nomenclature placed a strong emphasis on individual human psychology as the primary driver of human decisions, and no emphasis on dynamics and other structural environmental considerations. These priorities are not consigned to history: they remain prominent in mainstream behavioural models to this day.

Summary: historically, the second formal decision theory is expected utility maximisation. EUT is equivalent to EE if the utility function is the ergodicity transformation. Each dynamic thus has a corresponding growth-optimal utility function. The special case treated by Bernoulli in detail – logarithmic utility – is equivalent to EE under multiplicative dynamics. EVT is a special case of EUT, namely using a linear utility function (corresponding to EE under additive dynamics).

[3] He speculated [9, p. 27] that an infinitesimal increase in wealth should lead to an infinitesimal utility increase which is proportional to the wealth change and inversely proportional to the existing wealth. In symbols, *i.e.* $du \propto dx/x$, integration of which yields the logarithm.

6.6 From ergodicity transformation to wealth process and back

In this section we will use Itô calculus to consolidate and extend our results. In addition to what we already know (converting ergodicity transformations into wealth processes), we will arrive at a recipe for going the other way: converting wealth processes, dx, into ergodicity transformations, $v(x)$. This is an important part of the connection to EUT: give us the growth process, and we will tell you which utility function will outperform all others in the long run.

Furthermore, we will arrive at a set of conditions for these mappings to be possible. We illustrate the procedure with one example for each direction: we derive the growth process that corresponds to a square-root ergodicity transformation; and we derive the utility function (which will be exponential) that corresponds to a curious-looking dynamic. In other words, we go beyond linear and logarithmic ergodicity transformations.

6.6.1 Itô setup

We have seen that specifying a process $x(t)$ is equivalent to specifying an ergodicity transformation $v(x)$. When we mapped one onto the other, we had to invert v. This tells us one restriction: v has to be invertible. In this section, we will do the mapping again, but using Itô calculus, which will allows us to say more about the restrictions on v and x.

We will also revisit the inequality between expected wealth and the corresponding unperturbed wealth, (Eq. 6.21), and discover an ageing phenomenon – a dependence on t of the magnitude of this inequality.

We start with the self-imposed restriction that the wealth dynamic be an Itô process, which you may remember from (Eq. 4.41) in Sec. 4.3. We restrict ourselves further to coefficient functions $a_x(x)$ and $b_x(x)$ that have no explicit t-dependence, *i.e.* wealth follows

$$dx = a_x(x)dt + b_x(x)dW. \tag{6.58}$$

Put simply, we consider here models in which the "rules of the game" for wealth don't change over time.

In this framework, we can implement additive dynamics by setting $a_x = \mu$ and $b_x = \sigma$ as constants to obtain BM with drift, (Eq. 6.3). Or we can choose multiplicative dynamics by setting $a_x = \mu x$ and $b_x = \sigma x$ as linear functions of wealth to get GBM, (Eq. 6.9). Thus, Itô processes of the type in (Eq. 6.58) include the important models we have studied already, as well as many others.

Our aim is to find pairs of wealth dynamics, dx, and their corresponding ergodicity transformations, $v(x)$. By "corresponding" we mean that with x generated by dx, increments dv are ergodic. This means we're after a connection between an Itô process, x, and a function of an Itô process, $v(x)$. That's exactly what Itô's formula is for. By construction, v follows a BM with drift, *i.e.* an Itô process whose coefficient functions, a_v and b_v, are constant:

$$\begin{aligned} dv &= a_v dt + b_v dW & (6.59)\\ &= \gamma dt + \sigma dW. & (6.60)\end{aligned}$$

Since we have already used γ and σ to denote the constant drift and volatility of the Itô process for v, we will stick with them instead of switching to general notation, a_v and b_v.

First we will go from transformation to dynamics. In the language of classical economics, we assume that we know a person's "utility function" (*i.e.* their psychological risk preferences) and ask: under what dynamics would their decisions be growth optimal? Or, in the language we use here: in which model world would our model humans maximise $\left\langle \frac{dv(x)}{\delta t} \right\rangle$?

Next we will go from dynamics to transformation, which may seem a little more natural.

6.6.2 From ergodicity transformation to wealth process

We will now take an ergodicity transformation as given and construct the *corresponding wealth process.* In other words, take some function $v(x)$ and assume that its increments are ergodic. This generates a wealth dynamic x under which we behave optimally in the long run if we maximise $\langle \Delta v(x) \rangle$. This is an interesting exercise because it provides an interpretation of EUT. If we observe someone make choices which are consistent with EUT and a utility function u, then we know that person behaves long-time optimally if u is the ergodicity transformation. In other words, we can translate an ostensibly individualist-psychological fact "this person has utility function u" in dynamical terms. It tells us of observed behaviour in what context the behaviour is optimal.

When we thought about how to perturb a general growth process, in Sec. 6.2.3, we wrote $x(v)$ as the inverse of $v(x)$, *i.e.* $x = v^{(-1)}(v(x))$, (Eq. 6.19). Since we know the SDE obeyed by v, (Eq. 6.60), we can use Itô's formula, (Eq. 4.43), to find the SDE obeyed by $x(v)$. We get

$$dx = \left(\gamma x' + \frac{1}{2}\sigma^2 x''\right) dt + \sigma x' dW, \qquad (6.61)$$

where, to reduce clutter, we have adopted Lagrange notation to indicate the first and second derivatives of x with respect to v, *i.e.* $x' \equiv dx/dv$ and $x'' \equiv dx'/dv$.[4]

[4] By construction, $v(x)$ and, therefore, $x(v)$ have no explicit time-dependence, meaning we can ignore the partial time-derivative, $\partial x/\partial t$, that appears in Itô's formula. We need to consider only the v-derivatives of x here.

We want to express dx in the form of (Eq. 6.58), which means identifying $a_x(x)$ and $b_x(x)$ with the coefficients of dt and dW in (Eq. 6.61):

$$a_x(x) = \gamma x' + \frac{1}{2}\sigma^2 x''; \quad (6.62)$$

$$b_x(x) = \sigma x'. \quad (6.63)$$

We have thus shown that

EUT has a dynamic interpretation

Given a utility function, $v(x)$, a class of corresponding wealth processes dx can be obtained such that the rate of change (*i.e.* the additive growth rate) in expected utility is the time-average growth rate of wealth.

Optimising the expected changes of the ergodicity transformation, $\langle \Delta v \rangle$, is equivalent to optimising time-average wealth growth for the corresponding wealth process, $\overline{g}(x)$.

We note that not all utility functions can be put through our mechanism to generate a corresponding wealth dynamic. For instance, problems can arise when $v(x)$ is not invertible, or when $x(v)$ is not differentiable. In such cases it may be impossible to interpret EUT dynamically.

However, assuming that all steps can be carried out, in the language of EUT, a utility function is an encoding of a wealth dynamic. Under that dynamic, behaving according to EUT with the given utility function is optimal over time. The dynamic arises as utility – or rather: transformed wealth, v – performs BM with drift, and wealth itself is obtained from the inverse ergodicity transformation, $x(t) = v^{(-1)}(v(t))$.

Equation (6.61), creates the now familiar pairs of ergodicity transformations (utility functions) $v(x)$ and dynamics dx. Below we state the two familiar examples and work out a third one to illustrate the generality and ease of using Itô calculus.

Examples

- The linear ergodicity transformation (utility function) corresponds to additive wealth dynamics (BM with drift),

$$v(x) = x \quad \leftrightarrow \quad dx = \gamma dt + \sigma dW, \quad (6.64)$$

  as is easily verified by substituting $x(v) = v$ in (Eq. 6.61).

- The logarithmic ergodicity transformation (utility function) corresponds to multiplicative wealth dynamics (GBM),

$$v(x) = \ln(x) \quad \leftrightarrow \quad dx = x\left[\left(\gamma + \frac{1}{2}\sigma^2\right) dt + \sigma dW\right]. \quad (6.65)$$

- To demonstrate the generality of our procedure, we carry it out for another special case that is historically important. The first utility function ever to be suggested was the square-root function $u(x) = x^{1/2}$, by Cramer in a 1728 letter to Daniel Bernoulli, partially reproduced in [9]. What would be the dynamic under which it is optimal to behave according to this utility function? In other words, what dx corresponds to the ergodicity transformation $v(x) = x^{1/2}$, with inverse $x(v) = v^2$? This case will display ageing – a new phenomenon that we haven't encountered yet. So we'll go through it slowly.

  In the next three lines we:

  – restate (Eq. 6.61) ;
  – substitute $x' = 2v$ and $x'' = 2$; and
  – substitute $v = x^{1/2}$ to express the SDE is in terms of x only.

$$\begin{aligned} dx &= \left(\gamma x' + \frac{1}{2}\sigma^2 x''\right) dt + \sigma x' dW & (6.66) \\ &= (2\gamma v + \sigma^2)dt + 2\sigma v dW & (6.67) \\ &= (2\gamma x^{1/2} + \sigma^2)dt + 2\sigma x^{1/2} dW. & (6.68) \end{aligned}$$

We have thus established the third mapping in our collection:

$$v(x) = x^{1/2} \quad \leftrightarrow \quad dx = (2\gamma x^{1/2} + \sigma^2)dt + 2\sigma x^{1/2} dW. \qquad (6.69)$$

The new phenomenon we've mentioned – *ageing* – is observed when we compare the time average growth rate and that of the expectation value. By construction, the time-average growth rate is $\overline{g} = \left\langle \frac{\Delta v}{\Delta t} \right\rangle = \gamma$.

To compare this to the growth rate of the expectation value, we compute $\langle x \rangle$ as follows. We take the expectation value of (Eq. 6.67),

$$\begin{aligned} \langle dx \rangle &= (2\gamma \langle v \rangle + \sigma^2)dt & (6.70) \\ &= (2\gamma \langle \gamma t + \sigma W(t) \rangle + \sigma^2)dt & (6.71) \\ &= (2\gamma^2 t + \sigma^2)dt, & (6.72) \end{aligned}$$

which we integrate to get,

$$\langle x(t) \rangle = \gamma^2 t^2 + \sigma^2 t + \langle x(0) \rangle . \qquad (6.73)$$

Therefore,

$$v(\langle x(t) \rangle) = \left[\gamma^2 t^2 + \sigma^2 t + \langle x(0) \rangle\right]^{1/2}, \qquad (6.74)$$

and we obtain the growth rate of $\langle x \rangle$ as,

$$g_{\langle\rangle} = \frac{dv(\langle x \rangle)}{dt} = \frac{1}{2}\left(2\gamma^2 t + \sigma^2\right)\left[\gamma^2 t^2 + \sigma^2 t + \langle x(0) \rangle\right]^{-1/2}. \quad (6.75)$$

The first thing to notice here is that the expectation-value growth rate, appropriately defined, is not constant but depends on when we measure it! This is what is meant by "ageing:" the system, the dynamic itself, changes with time.

The second thing to notice is the asymptotic value. In the long run, the growth rate of the expectation value under the Cramer dynamic converges to the ergodic growth rate,

$$\lim_{t\to\infty} \frac{dv(\langle x \rangle)}{dt} = \gamma. \quad (6.76)$$

It's quite subtle. While Jensen's inequality still holds,

$$\frac{dv(\langle x \rangle)}{dt} > \frac{d\,\langle v(x) \rangle}{dt}, \quad (6.77)$$

the magnitude of this inequality vanishes in the long-time limit. We leave the discussion of the Cramer dynamic here. It shows that EE is full of open and interesting avenues. Try out your own dynamics, and discover new phenomena!

6.6.3 From wealth process to ergodicity transformation

We now ask how to invert the procedure in (Eq. 6.61), *i.e.* how to find the ergodicity transformation $v(x)$ for specified wealth dynamics, dx. Where this is possible, optimisation over time can be represented by optimisation of expected utility changes, and as we have seen, this can be analytically appealing. Starting with a wealth process is interesting because wealth dynamics are much easier to observe than utility functions, and we can reason about them mechanistically. For instance, if your income is dominated by a monthly salary, then your wealth will have a strong additive component.

We ask whether a given dynamic can be mapped into a $v(x)$ that follows BM with drift, (Eq. 6.60). And, if it can, we show how to do it.

In Sec. 6.6.1, we restricted ourselves to an Itô process for x, (Eq. 6.58), with coefficients $a_x(x)$ and $b_x(x)$ which are functions of x only. We want to know whether this is equivalent to v following BM with drift, (Eq. 6.60), for some function $v(x)$. You have probably already guessed that we will use Itô's formula to find an SDE for v that is equivalent to the known SDE for x. The tricky part – the part that gives us constraints

– is that the coefficients of this SDE for v, namely γ and σ, must be constant, since we insist that v follows BM with drift.

Let's start by reminding ourselves of the SDE for x, (Eq. 6.58), which we now assume that we know:

$$dx = a_x(x)dt + b_x(x)dW. \tag{6.78}$$

Next we use Itô's formula to write down the equivalent SDE for $v(x)$,

$$dv = \left(a_x(x)v' + \frac{1}{2}b_x(x)^2 v''\right) dt + b_x(x)v'dW, \tag{6.79}$$

where we have again used Lagrange notation to indicate first and second derivatives (this time of v with respect to x). For this to be BM with drift, $dv = \gamma dt + \sigma dW$, the following two equations must be satisfied:

$$a_x(x)v' + \frac{1}{2}b_x(x)^2 v'' = \gamma; \tag{6.80}$$

$$b_x(x)v' = \sigma. \tag{6.81}$$

It follows from (Eq. 6.81) that

$$v' = \frac{\sigma}{b_x(x)} \tag{6.82}$$

and

$$v'' = -\frac{\sigma {b_x}'(x)}{b_x(x)^2}, \tag{6.83}$$

which we can substitute into (Eq. 6.80) and rearrange to find an equation for $a_x(x)$ in terms of $b_x(x)$:

$$a_x(x) = b_x(x)\left(\frac{\gamma}{\sigma} + \frac{1}{2}{b_x}'(x)\right). \tag{6.84}$$

This equation is a consistency check on the wealth dynamics. The Itô process for x can be mapped to a BM with drift *via* an ergodicity transformation, $v(x)$, if and only if the coefficient functions $a_x(x)$ and $b_x(x)$ satisfy (Eq. 6.84). We do not need to find the ergodicity transformation explicitly to know whether or not it *exists*. We just need to plug $a_x(x)$ and $b_x(x)$ into (Eq. 6.84).

If the ergodicity transformation does exist, then the most straightforward way to find it is to integrate (Eq. 6.82) to get

$$v(x) = \int^x \frac{\sigma}{b_x(s)} ds + C, \tag{6.85}$$

where s is a dummy variable and C is a constant of integration.

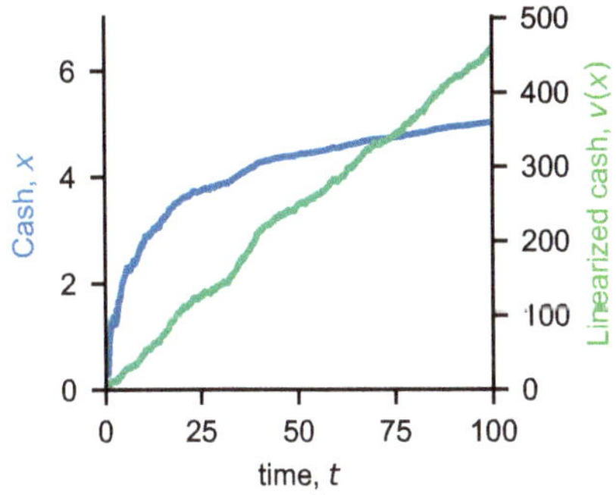

Figure 6.3: **Blue:** typical trajectory $x(t)$ of the wealth dynamic (Eq. 6.86), with parameter values $\gamma = 1/2$ and $\sigma = 1$. **Green:** the corresponding BM with drift $v(t)$, obtained according to (Eq. 6.90) as $v(t) = \exp[x(t)]$. Note that the fluctuations in $x(t)$ become smaller for larger wealth.

We have assumed here that the wealth dynamics are known, namely that we know the drift coefficient $a_x(x)$ and noise coefficient $b_x(x)$ in the Itô process for x, (Eq. 6.58). We can say whether there exists an ergodicity transformation $v(x)$ that is consistent with them and, if so, what it is. More generally, whichever two out of the three objects – drift coefficient, noise coefficient, and ergodicity transformation – we know, we can say whether the third object exists such that $v(x)$ is, indeed, an ergodicity transformation (*i.e.* that v executes BM with drift).

These arguments may seem a little esoteric when first encountered, using bits and pieces from different fields of mathematics. But they constitute the actual physical story behind the fascinating history of decision theory. To prevent the discussion from getting too dry, let's illustrate the procedure with an example.

Example: a curious-looking dynamic

We will work with the following wealth dynamics:

$$dx = e^{-x}\left(\frac{\gamma}{\sigma} - \frac{1}{2}e^{-x}\right)dt + e^{-x}dW. \tag{6.86}$$

A typical trajectory of (Eq. 6.86) is shown in Fig. 6.3.

We will: check whether an ergodicity transformation exists for it; find that it does; construct it explicitly; and then discuss some of its properties.

Check consistency: In (Eq. 6.86), we have

$$a_x(x) = e^{-x}\left(\frac{\gamma}{\sigma} - \frac{1}{2}e^{-x}\right) \tag{6.87}$$

and

$$b_x(x) = e^{-x}. \tag{6.88}$$

Substituting these into (Eq. 6.84) shows that the consistency condition is satisfied by the dynamic in (Eq. 6.86). Therefore, a function $v(x)$ exists such that v executes BM with drift.

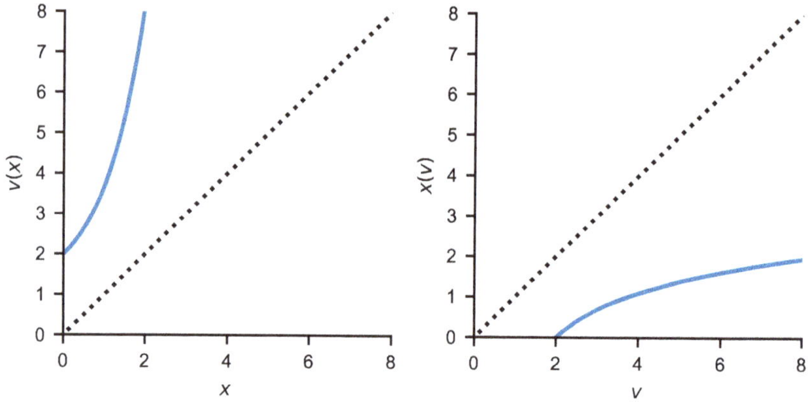

Figure 6.4: The exponential ergodicity transformation (or utility) $v(x)$, (Eq. 6.90) with $\sigma = 1$ and $C = 1$, is monotonic and unbounded and therefore invertible. **Left:** $v(x)$. **Right:** inverse $x(v)$.

Construct the ergodicity transformation: Having confirmed the existence of an ergodicity transformation, we construct it by performing the integration in (Eq. 6.85),

$$v(x) = \int^x \sigma e^s ds + C \tag{6.89}$$

$$= \sigma e^x + C, \tag{6.90}$$

which we plot in Fig. 6.4.

Discussion: This exponential ergodicity transformation is convex. From the perspective of EUT (where the ergodicity transformation is called a utility function), an individual behaving optimally according to this function would be labelled "risk-seeking." This behaviour would commonly be observed under the dynamic (Eq. 6.86) because Jensen's inequality in (Eq. 6.21) now points the other way from what we had in all previous examples: the expectation value of x *understates* what typically happens to a single trajectory over time.

Another new phenomenon: under the dynamic (Eq. 6.86), optimal behaviour is "*risk-seeking,*" in the sense that it will lead to faster wealth growth than risk-averse behaviour. This dynamic has the feature that fluctuations in wealth become smaller as wealth grows. High wealth is therefore *sticky*, and a risk-seeking individual will quickly fluctuate out of low wealth and into higher wealth, where it will tend to stay.

Once more, we see the conceptual difference to mainstream economics and EUT: from the perspective of EE what's optimal is determined by the dynamic, not by the individual. Of course the individual may choose not to behave optimally.

Chapter 7

Decisions in the real world

7.1 The St. Petersburg paradox

In Chap. 6 we established an important behavioural model of EE, including its formal relationship with EUT. From here on we will forge ahead and try out some applications. By applications we mean both theoretical applications of our new conceptual toolkit, which will allow us to solve or elicit new aspects of theoretical problems, and empirical applications, where we analyse data collected in the lab or in the wild. We will start with the early unsystematic observations surrounding the *St. Petersburg paradox*, an early thought experiment involving a hypothetical lottery that led to the development of EUT.

We present the St. Petersburg paradox from the perspective of EE. This will bring some historical and cultural colour to the discussion. Moreover, it will shed light on how EUT came to be, and how and why EE is fundamentally different. Often a deep understanding of a scientific discipline comes from knowing the history of how it developed.

The motivating problem was suggested by Nicolas Bernoulli in 1713 in his correspondence with Montmort [39]. It involves a hypothetical lottery for which the expected profit diverges for any finite ticket price. EVT would predict, therefore, that people pay any price to enter the lottery. However, it seems that researchers in the early 18th century conducted rudimentary informal experiments, presenting the gamble to friends and strangers and asking them how much they were willing to wager. In other words, EVT was tested empirically. And it failed unequivocally: nobody wanted to wager more than a few ducats (the currency of the day). This is the first well-documented example of the *inadequacy of EVT* as a model of human decision-making. It was the primary motivation for Daniel Bernoulli's and Cramer's development of EUT [9].

7.1.1 The St. Petersburg lottery

A player of the *St. Petersburg lottery* pays a fee F in exchange for a random monetary prize. In the original presentation, realisations of the prize were imagined as outcomes of a coin game with the following rules. The prize starts at \$1 (originally 1 ducat). A fair coin is tossed: if tails, the prize is collected; if heads, the prize is doubled and the procedure is repeated. Thus the possible prizes are \$1, \$2, \$4, \$8, and so on.

We will not dwell on this coin game, which is just an 18th century random number generator for selecting profit realisations. Instead we work with a compact definition of the lottery as a gamble, whose random profit Q has realisations and probabilities,

$$q_j = \$2^{j-1} - F, \tag{7.1}$$

$$p_j = 2^{-j}, \tag{7.2}$$

for $j \in \mathbb{N}^+$, *i.e.* the set of all positive integers. Note that the profit is obtained by subtracting the fee from the prize to get the net change in wealth. The vast majority of realised profits are small, and can be negative, but occasionally an extremely large profit (corresponding to a long unbroken sequence of heads in the coin game) is made.

Neither the duration nor the wealth dynamics are specified in the classical presentation of the gamble. Indeed, neither is required to analyse it under EVT and EUT. We will assume the lottery takes a fixed amount of time Δt to play, and we will make some assumptions about the wealth dynamics when we come to tackle the problem using EE.

We already mentioned a mathematical property of this gamble, namely that the expected profit diverges. Let us check this with a simple calculation:

$$\langle Q \rangle = \sum_{j=1}^{\infty} p_j q_j \tag{7.3}$$

$$= \sum_{j=1}^{\infty} 2^{-j}\,\$2^{j-1} - \sum_{j=1}^{\infty} p_j F \tag{7.4}$$

$$= \$\sum_{j=1}^{\infty} \tfrac{1}{2} - F. \tag{7.5}$$

The first term *diverges positively* and so, for any finite F, the expected profit $\langle Q \rangle$ also diverges positively.[1]

[1] Remember that whenever you see $\sum_{j=1}^{\infty} a_j$, it is shorthand for the more formal limit $\lim_{N\to\infty} \sum_{j=1}^{N} a_j$. If in doubt, write it out.

7.1.2 Expected-value theory – a paradox

The question of whether a player should accept this gamble was posed when EVT was the only model in town. Following the criterion we presented in (Eq. 6.49), researchers at the time computed (or, more strictly, could not compute) the expected wealth change, $\langle \Delta x \rangle = \langle Q \rangle$, of the lottery. A model player enters the lottery if it yields an expected wealth change greater than the zero change of the null gamble. The idea, therefore, was to compute the expected profit as a function of the fee, $\langle Q(F) \rangle$, and then to find the fee, $F^{\max}$, at which $\langle Q(F^{\max}) \rangle = 0$. The player accepts the gamble when the fee is lower than $F^{\max}$ and declines it when the fee is higher.

Since $\langle Q(F) \rangle$ diverges positively for all finite F, there is no fee $F^{\max}$ above which a player should decline the gamble. Thus, the apparently valid application of the accepted behavioural model produced no answer to the question: what is the most one should pay to play this lottery? This was considered paradoxical because it was known that real people, when asked the same question, did produce answers, usually modest (and definitely finite) monetary amounts.

We can view this failure of EVT as both *empirical* and *theoretical.* Empirically, if we interpret the diverging change in expected wealth for all fees as a prediction that real people will pay very high fees, then observations of low maximum fees show the model as unrealistic. Theoretically, the non-existence of a maximum fee is a red flag alerting us to a problem with the model or the problem to which it is applied. This quantity diverges under EVT– a good place to remember that *infinity as a model output is an error message.*

It is a pity that this deliberately provocative and unrealistic lottery played such an important role in the development of classical decision theory. The coin game of Sec. 1.1 shows that it is quite unnecessary to invent a gamble with a diverging change in expected wealth to expose the unrealism of EVT. Moreover, the infinities in the St. Petersburg lottery create confusion and permit objections on the grounds that the lottery is physically impossible and could never be offered. Such objections do little to advance decision theory: they address problems only with the gamble and not with the behavioural model. Nevertheless, the paradox is an indelible part of economic history and an active topic of debate [45]. We describe next an early attempt to resolve it, which led ultimately to the development of EUT, the bedrock of modern-day decision theory.

7.1.3 Expected-utility theory – a resolution

The implausible conclusion that there is no price at which the St. Petersburg lottery should be declined exposed the weakness of judging a gamble by its effect on expected wealth. Daniel Bernoulli suggested to resolve the paradox by adopting EUT. His choice of utility function was the logarithm, $u(x) = \ln x$.

Instead of the change in expected wealth, we follow the criterion in (Eq. 6.57) and calculate the change in expected utility,

$$\begin{aligned} \langle \Delta \ln x \rangle &= \langle \ln(x+Q) - \ln x \rangle & (7.6) \\ &= \sum_{j=1}^{\infty} p_j \left(\ln(x+q_j) - \ln x \right) & (7.7) \\ &= \sum_{j=1}^{\infty} 2^{-j} \ln \left(\frac{x + \$2^{j-1} - F}{x} \right), & (7.8) \end{aligned}$$

where x is the player's wealth at the start of the lottery.

The sum in (Eq. 7.8) converges to a finite value provided the player's wealth remains positive after the lottery, even if the smallest prize is won.[2] Expressing this no-bankruptcy condition as a condition on the fee, $\langle \Delta \ln x \rangle$ exists when the fee is less than the player's wealth plus the smallest prize, *i.e.* $F < x + \$1$. The change in expected utility may be positive or negative, depending on the values of F and x, but, unlike the change in expected wealth, it exists and can be compared to zero (the utility change of the null gamble) to determine a maximum fee, $F^{\max}$.

EUT resolves the St. Petersburg paradox in the sense that, for some choices of utility function, it creates model worlds in which prices exist at which players decline to buy lottery tickets. Specifically, it creates such a world when the utility function is logarithmic – but not, as we know from the failure of EVT, when it is linear. As we described in Sec. 6.5.3, Bernoulli argued for both his framework and his choice of utility function in somewhat plausible terms. Yet, his framework left questions unanswered, most notably: what determines the form of the utility function? EE answers this question by embedding the gamble in wealth dynamics.

7.1.4 Ergodicity economics – enter dynamics

We resolve the St. Petersburg paradox here using EE. We do this by specifying the player's wealth dynamics. Our choice of dynamics is a judgement we base on observed reality: we might look at the circumstances of a person – for example wealth, how it is invested, whether there is income from a job, and so on – and conclude something like "this person's wealth evolves roughly multiplicatively". Unlike utility functions, treated in mainstream decision theory as encoding psycholog-

[2] If the player's wealth were allowed to reach zero, then the first term in the sum would diverge negatively. Provided this cannot happen, convergence of the sum can be shown by applying d'Alembert's ratio test.

ical risk preferences, wealth dynamics are something about which we can *reason mechanistically*.

Having specified the dynamics, we compute the ergodic growth rate corresponding to participation in the lottery and find the fee $F^{\max}$ at which this growth rate is zero, *i.e.* at which playing the lottery yields the same growth rate as not playing it. Our model player accepts the gamble at any fee lower than this. Since dynamics are generally non-additive, EE, unlike EVT, does not run aground. For realistic dynamics, we find that maximum fees both exist and are consistent with fees that real people are willing to pay.

Multiplicative dynamics

Without further ado, here's a solution. We will not say it is "the" solution because it depends on the choice of dynamics. We will assume multiplicative wealth dynamics, for which we know the ergodic growth rate is $\Delta \ln x/\Delta t$. The dynamics are not specified in the classical presentation of the paradox, but neither is a utility function or anything else that would allow a resolution. The problem as stated is *underspecified*: we resolve this by specifying how wealth evolves when the gamble is repeated; mainstream economics resolves this by specifying the player's attitude to risk.

We compute the time average of the growth rate. We do this by invoking ergodicity and computing its expectation value:

$$\overline{g} = \left\langle \frac{\Delta \ln x}{\Delta t} \right\rangle = \frac{1}{\Delta t} \left\langle \ln \left(\frac{x + Q(F)}{x} \right) \right\rangle . \tag{7.9}$$

$\overline{g}$ exists under the same no-bankruptcy condition, $F < x + \$1$, that we met in Sec. 7.1.3 (the existence condition for $\langle \Delta \ln x \rangle$). It can be positive or negative, depending on F and x. $F^{\max}$ is the fee at which $\overline{g} = 0$. Thus, in our model world, where players maximise time-average growth rates under multiplicative wealth dynamics, the St. Petersburg lottery does not create a paradox.

Equation (7.9) tells us that $\overline{g}$ and, therefore, $F^{\max}$ depend on x, the player's wealth at the start of the lottery. Although we cannot write a closed-form expression for $F^{\max}$, we can find it numerically. In Fig. 7.1 we plot $F^{\max}$ as a function of the player's wealth. The model predicts that a richer player will pay more to enter the lottery than a poorer player, although never arbitrarily more.

What do multiplicative wealth dynamics mean in terms of how we imagine the lottery being repeated? Recall from (Eq. 6.43) that each round of the gamble multiplies the player's wealth by a realisation of the random variable,

$$R = \frac{x(t_0) + Q(F)}{x(t_0)}, \tag{7.10}$$

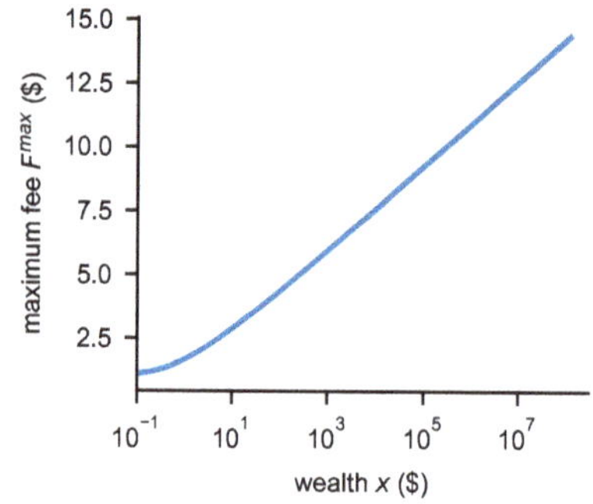

Figure 7.1: Maximum fee $F^{\max}$ which a player is willing to pay *vs.* the player's wealth x, according to growth maximisation, assuming multiplicative dynamics. For a given wealth x, this is the value of F for which $\bar{g}$ in (Eq. 7.9) is zero. This resolves the 300-year old paradox because, for any finite x, a finite $F^{\max}$ exists. Adapted from [45].

where $x(t_0)$ is the player's wealth at the start of the first round. Playing in this way, you would pay a fixed fraction of your wealth to enter the lottery and receive a profit in proportion to this stake, where F and $x(t_0)$ are parameters which determine the betting odds. In other words, the lottery – its fee and its prizes – is assumed to scale with the player's wealth. Example trajectories of repeated lotteries under multiplicative dynamics are shown in Fig. 7.2.

Treatments of the St. Petersburg lottery based on multiplicative repetition have appeared sporadically in the literature, starting with Whitworth in 1870 [69, App. IV].[3] It is related to the famous Kelly Criterion [25], although Kelly did not explicitly treat the St. Petersburg game.[4] It relates tangentially to Itô's lemma [23] and appears as an exercise in a well-known text on information theory [14, Ex. 6.17]. A full and rigorous resolution of the paradox, including the epistemological significance of the shift from ensemble to time averages, was published in [45].

[3]Whitworth was dismissive of EUT: "The result at which we have arrived is not to be classed with the arbitrary methods which have been again and again propounded to evade the difficulty of the Petersburg problem." He continued: "Formulae have often been proposed, which have possessed the one virtue of presenting a finite result... but they have often had no intelligible basis to rest upon, or... sufficient care has not been taken to draw a distinguishing line between the significance of the result obtained, and the different result arrived at when the mathematical expectation is calculated." Alas, he placed these revolutionary remarks in an appendix of a probability textbook.

[4]Kelly was similarly unimpressed with the dominant formalism. In his treatment of decision theory, which he developed from the perspective of information theory and which is identical to EE under multiplicative dynamics, he remarked that the utility function is "too general to shed any light".

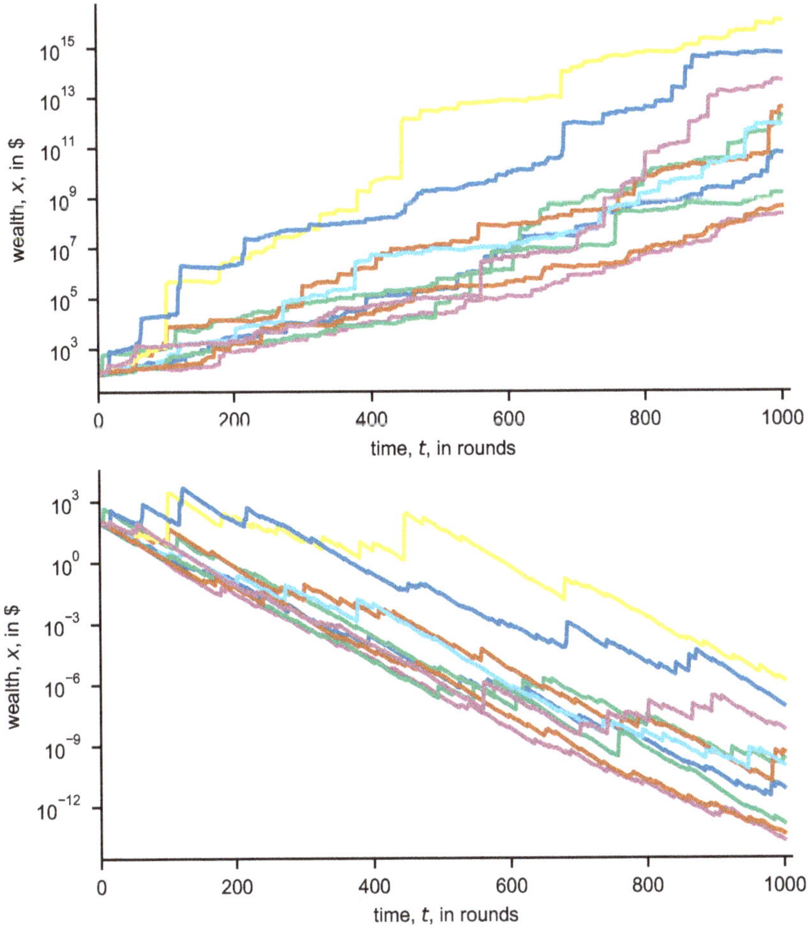

Figure 7.2: Wealth trajectories for the repeated St. Petersburg lottery under multiplicative dynamics with starting wealth $x(0) = \$100$. Ten trajectories are plotted over 1,000 rounds. **Top:** ticket price, $F = \$2$. **Bottom:** ticket price, $F = \$7$. The prize realisations are identical in both cases but the different fees make the game long-term profitable or long-term detrimental when multiplicatively repeated.

Additive dynamics

What about other dynamics? In particular, what about additive dynamics, for which the ergodic growth rate is $\Delta x/\Delta t$? Maximising the time-average growth rate under additive dynamics is equivalent to maximising $\langle \Delta x \rangle$, *i.e.* to EVT. Therefore, EE must also arrive at the conclusion that there exists no fee at which the lottery should be declined. How do we escape the paradox?

Our answer highlights the advantage of building mechanistic models, in this case of wealth dynamics. An ergodicity economist would say that a model player enters the St. Petersburg lottery at any price *if it can be repeated additively.* The qualification in italics is important. The corresponding prediction would be that real people will pay very high prices to play such a lottery if their wealth dynamics look roughly additive.

We should anticipate such a prediction being realistic only if the dynamics are realistic, and herein lies the problem. Additive wealth dynamics are generally rather *unrealistic*: they imply things like returns on investments being unrelated to the investment size, and people being able to assume unlimited debt. Knowing that such dynamics are seldom observed in reality, we do not cry "paradox!" when real people fail to corroborate our prediction.

If a player can keep making St. Petersburg bets of fixed size, going into debt if necessary, then their wealth will grow eventually because of the exceedingly large and rare profit realisations. We can see this in the wealth trajectories in Fig. 7.3, where we have simulated repeated fixed-fee lotteries under additive dynamics, *i.e.* a realisation of Q is added to each player's wealth at each round.

The trajectories in Fig. 7.2 and Fig. 7.3 are based on the same sequences of prize realisations but with different wealth dynamics. Comparing the two figures shows us visually what we have already understood analytically: that what appears favourable in EVT, corresponding to additive dynamics, results in the decay of wealth under more realistic dynamics.

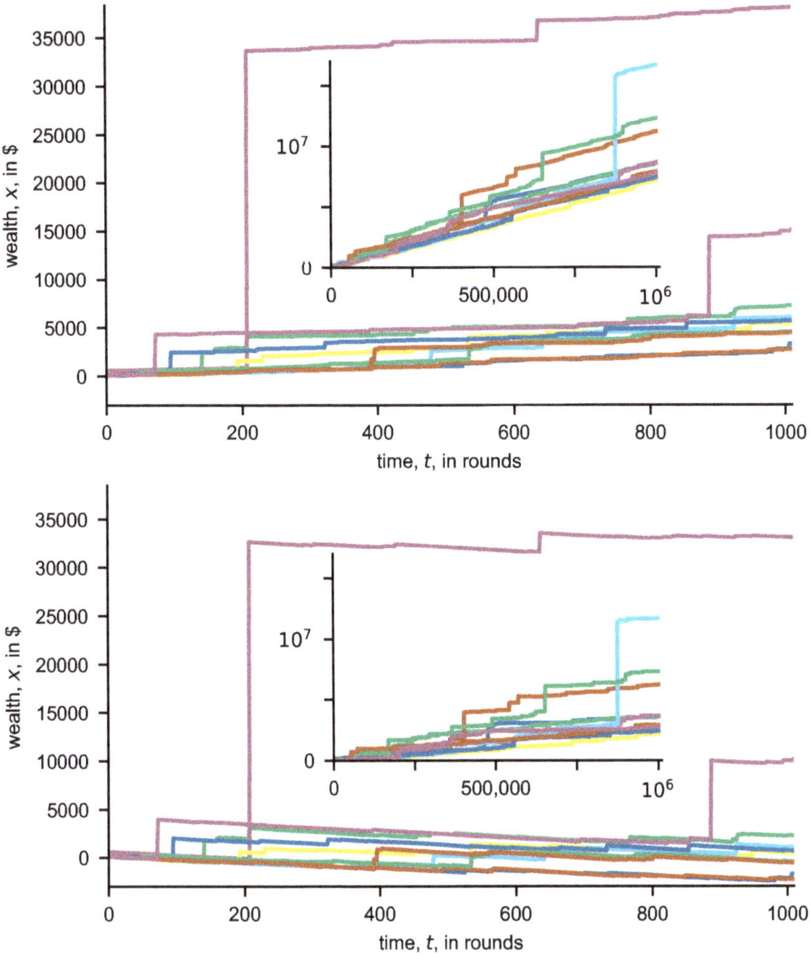

Figure 7.3: Wealth trajectories for the repeated St. Petersburg lottery under additive dynamics. As in the multiplicative setting in Fig. 7.2, the starting wealth is $x(0) = \$100$, and we once more use the same realisations of the gambles as in the multiplicative case. Ten trajectories are shown, in the main panels over one thousand rounds. To highlight long-term trends, the insets show one million rounds. Top: ticket price, $F = \$2$. Bottom: ticket price, $F = \$7$.

7.2 The Copenhagen experiment

At the end of Chap. 6, we arrived at a mapping between EUT and EE. The fact that such a mapping is possible is fascinating: careful thinking leads to almost identical mathematical expressions, whether we operate in the conceptual universe of 1738 or in that of post-1870 statistical physics. Since the difference is first and foremost conceptual, it is fair to ask whether EE is just another way of looking at the subject without fundamentally different or new results. That alone would be a wonderful achievement, but as Rota put it when speaking about exterior algebra [57, p.48]: "[It] is not meant to prove old facts, it is meant to disclose a new world."

Do the differences between concepts allow an experiment, at least in principle, that would tell us something radically new? More specifically, since we can map EE and EUT under certain conditions, can an experiment be designed that has discriminating power between the two mapped models?

A group of neuroscientists at the Danish Research Centre for Magnetic Resonance in Copenhagen asked precisely this question, and we have collaborated with them to design an experiment that fits the bill.

The experiment is inspired by the discussion in [52], where we had worked out in detail the correspondences of linear utility to additive dynamics, and logarithmic utility to multiplicative dynamics. What if the dynamics of wealth could be controlled? With two artificial environments – one additive, one multiplicative – do people adjust their behaviour to be growth-optimal in each?

At least in principle this question can be answered: for each condition, observe choices and infer from them the ergodicity transformation (or utility function) whose expected rate of change is being optimised. Compare: is the known ergodicity transformation for a given environment predictive of the real observed choices made in that environment?

A positive result – people changing their utility functions in response to the dynamics – would challenge EUT. In the worldview of EUT, the utility function encodes a personality. Supposedly, it's a psychological or even neurological property of a human being, and not something that can change over the course of a few hours (the duration of the experiment).

A negative result – people not changing utility functions – would challenge EE. In the worldview of EE, the term "utility function" is a label for the ergodicity transformation that sits in the functional form of the relevant growth rate. This transformation is different for these two dynamics, as we've seen. And the postulate of the EE model we've been exploring is that people behave so as to optimise the rate of change of the expected ergodicity transformation (*i.e.* the time-average ergodic growth rate). If they keep using the same transformation, irrespective of dynamics, then this postulate would not describe real behaviour, at least not in this experiment.

As we discuss the experiment, we have to keep its limitations in mind. Of course, the experiment may be flawed in ways we don't yet understand, we could have a bug in the code to analyse the observations, or the results could be a statistical fluke. Such experiments would challenge neither EUT nor EE; they would just be invalid.

The experiment is described in detail in [64]. Here we will only outline the setup. 58 participants attended two sessions each. We'll describe the protocol for a single individual, whom we'll call Alice. In the first session, Alice is exposed to an additive wealth environment. That means, she is endowed with a starting wealth of 1,000 points and then makes 160 choices, each between a pair of gambles of the *additive* form "would you rather toss a fair coin for

a) winning 20 points or losing 10 points;

or

b) for winning 100 points or losing 70 points?"

In the second session Alice is exposed to a multiplicative environment. Again, she starts with 1000 points, and again she makes 160 choices, each between a pair of gambles – but this time of the *multiplicative* form "would you rather toss a fair coin for

a) winning 30% of current wealth, $x(t)$, or losing 20% of current wealth;

or

b) winning 100% or losing 70%?"

The choices are consequential: game points are eventually converted into a real payment, of up to a few hundred dollars. Alice's choices are recorded, and from them the ergodicity transformation (or utility function) is inferred that best describes them.

Let's work through a single observation – a single choice made by Alice – to understand the data analysis. Let's say Alice's current wealth is $x(t) = 200$ points. Imagine we observe that Alice chooses the 50/50 gamble of winning 20 points or losing 10 (for future wealth 220 or 190); and rejects the alternative gamble of winning 100 or losing 70 (for future wealth 300 or 130). What does this tell us about Alice's beliefs about the ergodicity transformation?

We're testing EE and EUT. In both theories, the decision criterion is the expectation value of a change in some function of wealth. So the question is really: for what kind of $v(x)$ would Alice make the observed choice, assuming that the time-average ergodic growth rate (or expected utility) is being optimised?

The time-average ergodic growth rate (or rate of change of expected utility) is

$$g = \frac{\langle \Delta v(x) \rangle}{\Delta t}. \tag{7.11}$$

We have to restrict the space of $v(x)$ in an intelligent way for the observations to tell us something meaningful. The restriction has to allow the two cases predicted by EE: linear ergodicity transformation (utility function) for additive dynamics and logarithmic ergodicity transformation for multiplicative dynamics. We chose to restrict $v(x)$ to a family of functions known in economics as *isoelastic utility functions* (and in physics as q-logarithms), namely to

$$v(x;\eta) = \frac{x^{1-\eta}-1}{1-\eta}. \tag{7.12}$$

The parameter η controls the concavity of $v(x;\eta)$, with the special value $\eta = 0$ corresponding to linear $v(x)$, and $\eta = 1$ corresponding to logarithmic $v(x)$.[5]

With the restriction to this family of ergodicity transformations, and assuming that Alice is maximising the time-average growth rate, we can phrase the decision made by Alice in terms of her beliefs about the dynamic, here parameterised by η. Assuming that the example choice above was made in agreement with EE, we have

$$\frac{\frac{1}{2}[v(220)+v(190)]-v(200)}{\Delta t} > \frac{\frac{1}{2}[v(300)+v(130)]-v(200)}{\Delta t}. \tag{7.13}$$

To check when this inequality is satisfied, we subtract the right-hand side and simplify, to arrive at the condition

$$[v(\$220)+v(\$190)]-[v(\$300)+v(\$130)] > 0. \tag{7.14}$$

Figure 7.4 shows the left-hand side of (Eq. 7.14) as a function of η. We see that for any $\eta > 0.59$ the inequality is satisfied, and we refer to the location of this zero crossing as the critical value η_c. Assuming that Alice is maximising (Eq. 7.11), we conclude from this one observation that she believes $\eta > 0.59$. For example, this is consistent with Alice believing that the dynamics are multiplicative ($\eta = 1$).

Each participant made 160 observed gambling choices in each condition. Each choice produces a similar statement – a bound on η. The location of the bound is given by the gamble pair on offer and current wealth, and the choice made determines whether it is an upper bound or a lower bound. Perhaps the next observation would show that Alice believes $\eta < 1.2$, which would bracket her belief about the value of η into $0.59 < \eta < 1.2$.

[5] By application of l'Hôpital's rule in the limit $\eta \to 1$.

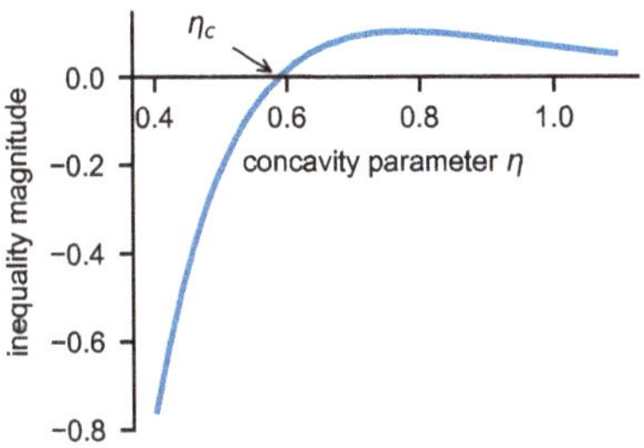

Figure 7.4: left-hand side of (Eq. 7.14). The inequality in (Eq. 7.14) is satisfied for any $\eta > \eta_c = 0.59$, wherefore Alice's choice indicates that an ergodicity transformation with $\eta > 0.59$ is being optimised. For instance, this observation is consistent with a logarithmic ergodicity transformation ($\eta = 1$).

Of course, inconsistencies in Alice's behaviour may be observed, *e.g.* of the type $\eta > 0.59$ and $\eta < 0.5$. We deal with these using a *logistic regression*: give all of Alice's observed upper bounds the value 1 and all her lower bounds the value zero. Put them on a graph and fit a logistic curve, Fig. 7.5. The curve is a fit to the proportion of times Alice chooses the risky gamble when offered a gamble pair at a given η_c value, Fig. 7.5. The point where Alice is indifferent, *i.e.* where she chooses low risk as often as high risk is interpreted as Alice's estimate of η (or, in utility terms, it is interpreted as her level of risk aversion), η_{Alice}. This happens at the inflection point of the fitted logistic curve.

Repeating this procedure for all 58 individuals under each condition produces overall group estimates of $\eta_{\text{additive}} = 0.1 \pm 0.2$ (95% confidence interval) under additive conditions and of $\eta_{\text{multiplicative}} = 1.1 \pm 0.4$ under multiplicative conditions, see [64] for details. This is in close agreement with the values predicted by the ergodicity transformations of the EE model: linear $v(x)$, meaning $\eta = 0$, for additive conditions; and logarithmic $v(x)$, meaning $\eta = 1$, for multiplicative conditions.

Given the limitations of the experiment – for instance people had a training phase of only about half an hour to get used to a given dynamic environment – the EE predictions don't look so bad. Experiments, unlike mathematics, never give black-and-white answers but we have grown more confident as we have challenged and replicated the experiment over the years. The EUT model is challenged by these findings. EUT suggests stable utility functions which depend only on the individual, not on the dynamics under which the individual operates. EUT performs poorly in the experiment – it cannot capture the observed dependence on dynamics of best-fit utility functions, which really seem to be the relevant ergodicity transformations.

7.3 Insurance

The *insurance contract* is an important and ubiquitous type of economic transaction, which can be modelled as a gamble. Its significance is two-

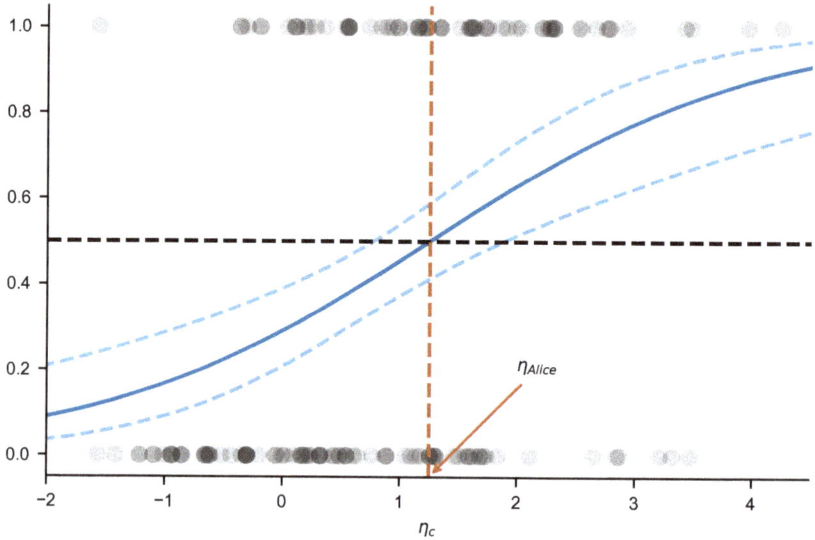

Figure 7.5: Logistic fit of the proportion of times Alice chose the risky gamble out of a gamble pair versus the critical value of the pair, η_c (solid blue: best fit, dashed blue: standard-error envelop). Grey circles at vertical value 1 indicate an observed choice implying an upper bound, grey circles at vertical value 0 indicate a lower bound. 160 choices are shown, revealing that Alice would have behaved close to time-optimally in a dynamic whose ergodicity transformation is (Eq. 7.12) with $\eta_{\text{Alice}} \approx 1.2$ – a little more risk averse than a multiplicative optimiser.

fold: insurance contracts transfer risk from one party to another, and this – the transfer, or sharing, of risk – is a key driver of the emergence of social structure at all levels of evolution, see Sec. 9.1. More mundanely, insurance is an important thing to understand because the selling and buying of insurance contracts (derivatives) constitutes a large fraction of global trade. Perhaps – a tantalising hypothesis – these two facts are not unrelated.

However, classically insurance poses a puzzle [47, 48]. In EVT, insurance contracts shouldn't exist, because buying insurance would only be rational at a price at which it would be irrational to sell. More specifically:

1. To be viable, an insurer must charge an *insurance premium* of at least the expectation value of any claims that may be made against it, called the "net premium" [24, p. 1].

2. The insurance buyer therefore has to be willing to pay more than the expectation value of any claims (the net premium), so that an insurance contract may be successfully signed.

3. Under EVT it is irrational to pay more than the net premium, and therefore insurance contracts should not exist.

In this picture, an insurance contract can only ever be beneficial to one party. It has the anti-symmetric property that the expectation value of one party's gain is the expectation value of the other party's loss.

The puzzle is that insurance contracts are observed to exist. Why? Classical resolutions appeal to utility theory (*i.e.* psychology) and *asymmetric information* (*i.e.* ignorance or deception). However, EE naturally predicts contracts with a range of prices that increase the time-average growth rate for both buyer and seller. This is rather an important point. It means that insurance contracts can be mutually beneficial – a theme we will return to in Sec. 9.1. We will also see that these voluntary contracts lead to a flow of cash from poor to rich – another theme we will return to, in Sec. 9.2.

We illustrate how this all works with an example drawn from maritime trade, in which the use of insurance has a very long history.[6] A similar example, involving a St. Petersburg merchant called Caius, was used by Bernoulli [9] in the paper containing his solution to the St. Petersburg paradox.

[6] Contracts between Babylonian traders and lenders were recorded around 1750 BC in the Code of Hammurabi. Chinese traders practised diversification by spreading cargoes across multiple vessels even earlier than this, in the third millennium BC.

7.4 A shipping insurance contract

We imagine Caius to be a shipowner sending cargo from St. Petersburg to Amsterdam, with the following parameters:

- owner's wealth, $x_{\text{own}} = \$100,000$;
- gain on safe arrival of cargo, $G = \$5,500$;
- probability ship will be lost, $p = 0.05$;
- replacement cost of the ship (insured loss), $L = \$50,000$; and
- voyage time, $\delta t = 1$ month.

An insurer with wealth $x_{\text{ins}} = \$1,000,000$ proposes to insure the voyage for a fee, $F = \$3,125$. If the ship is lost, the insurer pays the owner L to make him good on the loss of his ship.

The insurer's wealth is considerably larger than Caius's. At the time of Bernoulli's writing, St. Petersburg was ruled by Empress Anna Ioannovna, who extracted heavy taxes and was very wealthy indeed, so let's say the insurer is called Anna.

We phrase the decision the owner is facing as a choice between two gambles.

Definition The owner's gambles

Sending the ship uninsured corresponds to gamble

$$Q_{\text{owner}}^{\text{uninsured}} = \{(-L, p), (G, 1-p)\}. \tag{7.15}$$

Sending the ship fully insured corresponds to gamble

$$Q_{\text{owner}}^{\text{insured}} = \{(-F, p), (G-F, 1-p)\}. \tag{7.16}$$

We also model the insurer's decision whether to offer the contract as a choice between two gambles.

Definition The insurer's gambles

Not insuring the ship corresponds to the null gamble

$$Q_{\text{insurer}}^{\text{uninsured}} = \{(0, 1)\}. \tag{7.17}$$

Insuring the ship corresponds to gamble

$$Q_{\text{insurer}}^{\text{insured}} = \{(F-L, p), (F, 1-p)\}. \tag{7.18}$$

To establish the puzzle, we ask in EVT whether the owner should sign the contract, and whether the insurer should have proposed it.

Insurance under EVT

In EVT, decision makers maximise the rate of change of the expectation values of their wealths, according to (Eq. 6.49). Under this paradigm, Caius the owner judges gamble $Q_{\text{owner}}^{\text{uninsured}}$ by its expectation value

$$\left\langle Q_{\text{owner}}^{\text{uninsured}} \right\rangle = (1-p)G + p(-L) \tag{7.19}$$

$$= \$2,725, \tag{7.20}$$

and gamble $Q_{\text{owner}}^{\text{insured}}$ by

$$\left\langle Q_{\text{owner}}^{\text{insured}} \right\rangle = (1-p)(G-F) + p(-F) \tag{7.21}$$

$$= \$2,100. \tag{7.22}$$

The difference, $\delta \langle Q_{\text{owner}} \rangle$, between the expected values with and without a signed contract is the expected loss minus the fee,

$$\delta \langle Q_{\text{owner}} \rangle = pL - F. \tag{7.23}$$

The sign of this difference indicates whether the insurance contract is beneficial to the owner, Caius. In the example this is not the case, $\delta \langle Q_{\text{owner}} \rangle = -\$625$.

Anna the insurer evaluates the gambles $Q_{\text{insurer}}^{\text{uninsured}}$ and $Q_{\text{insurer}}^{\text{insured}}$ similarly, with the result

$$\left\langle Q_{\text{insurer}}^{\text{uninsured}} \right\rangle = \$0 \tag{7.24}$$

and

$$\left\langle Q_{\text{insurer}}^{\text{insured}} \right\rangle = p(-L+F) + (1-p)F \tag{7.25}$$

$$= +\$625. \tag{7.26}$$

Again we compute the difference, the net benefit to the insurer that arises from signing the contract, as

$$\delta \langle Q_{\text{insurer}} \rangle = F - pL. \tag{7.27}$$

In the example this is $\delta \langle Q_{\text{insurer}} \rangle = +\$625$, meaning that in the world of EVT Anna the insurer will offer the contract.

But because only one party (the insurer) is willing to sign, no contract will come into existence. We could think that we got the price wrong, and the contract would be signed if offered at a different fee. But this is not the case. Looking at (Eq. 7.23) and (Eq. 7.27) we notice the anti-symmetric relationship between the two expressions,

$$\delta \langle Q_{\text{owner}} \rangle = -\delta \langle Q_{\text{insurer}} \rangle \tag{7.28}$$

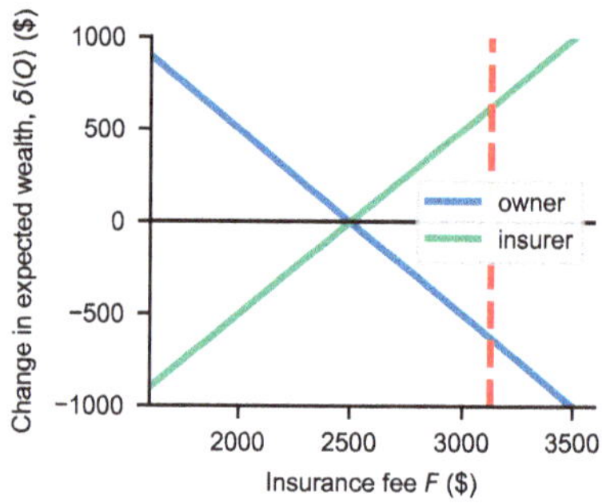

Figure 7.6: Change in expected wealth for Caius the shipowner (blue) and Anna the insurer (green) as a function of the insurance fee, F. The red vertical line indicates the proposed insurance fee.

By symmetry, there can be no fee at which both expressions are positive. If one is positive, the other must be negative. The only point where this isn't the case is when both sides are exactly zero. Hence there are no circumstances in the world created by EVT under which both parties have an incentive to sign; there is merely one specific price at which neither party has a reason not to sign. Insurance contracts cannot exist in this model world.

Fundamental insurance puzzle

In the model world created by EVT, *no price exists* at which two parties will sign an insurance contract.

One party winning at the expense of the other makes insurance an unsavoury business in EVT. This is further illustrated in Fig. 7.6, which shows the change in expected wealth for both parties as a function of the fee, F. There is no price at which the decision variable is positive for both parties. The best they can do is to pick the price at which neither of them cares whether they sign or not.

In this picture, the existence of insurance contracts requires some asymmetry between the contracting parties, such as:

- different psychological attitudes to bearing risk;
- different access to information about the voyage;
- different assessments of the riskiness of the voyage;
- one party to deceive or coerce the other into a bad decision.

It is difficult to believe that this is truly the basis for a market of the size and reach of the insurance market.

7.4.1 Ergodicity economics solution

EE resolves the insurance puzzle under many different types of dynamics – so long as the ergodicity transformation is concave. For simplicity we will assume multiplicative dynamics, pausing to reflect on the difference from additive dynamics. Assuming a multiplicative wealth dynamic models the ship owner as sending out a ship and a cargo whose values are proportional to his wealth at the start of each voyage. A rich owner who has had many successful voyages will send out more cargo, a larger ship, or perhaps a flotilla, while an owner to whom the sea has been a cruel mistress will send out a small vessel until his luck changes. Modelling wealth with an additive dynamic, the ship owner would send out the same amount of cargo on each journey, irrespective of his wealth. Shipping companies the size of Mediterranean Shipping Company or Maersk would be inconceivable under additive dynamics, where returns on successful investments are not reinvested.

Under multiplicative dynamics, the two parties seek to maximise

$$\overline{g}_{\mathrm{m}} = \lim_{\Delta t \to \infty} \frac{\Delta v(x)}{\Delta t} = \frac{\langle \delta \ln x \rangle}{\delta t}, \tag{7.29}$$

where we have used the ergodic property of $\Delta v(x) = \Delta \ln x$.

Using the same parameters as before, the time-average growth rate of Caius's wealth without insurance is

$$\overline{g}_{\mathrm{m}\,\mathrm{owner}}^{\mathrm{uninsured}} = \frac{[(1-p)\ln(x_{\mathrm{own}} + G) + p\ln(x_{\mathrm{own}} - L)] - \ln(x_{\mathrm{own}})}{\delta t} \tag{7.30}$$

or 1.6% per month. His time-average growth rate with insurance is

$$\overline{g}_{\mathrm{m}\,\mathrm{owner}}^{\mathrm{insured}} = \frac{[(1-p)\ln(x_{\mathrm{own}} + G - F) + p\ln(x_{\mathrm{own}} - F)] - \ln(x_{\mathrm{own}})}{\delta t} \tag{7.31}$$

or 2.1% per month. This gives a net benefit for the ship owner of

$$\delta \overline{g}_{\mathrm{m}\,\mathrm{owner}} \approx +0.5\% \text{ per month.} \tag{7.32}$$

The time paradigm thus creates a world where the owner will sign the contract.

What about Anna the insurer? Without insurance, Anna plays the null gamble, and

$$\overline{g}_{\mathrm{m}\,\mathrm{insurer}}^{\mathrm{uninsured}} = \frac{0}{\delta t} \tag{7.33}$$

or 0% per month. Her time-average growth rate with insurance is

$$\overline{g}_{\mathrm{m}\,\mathrm{insurer}}^{\mathrm{uninsured}} = \frac{[(1-p)\ln(x_{\mathrm{ins}} + F) + p\ln(x_{\mathrm{ins}} + F - L)] - \ln(x_{\mathrm{ins}})}{\delta t} \tag{7.34}$$

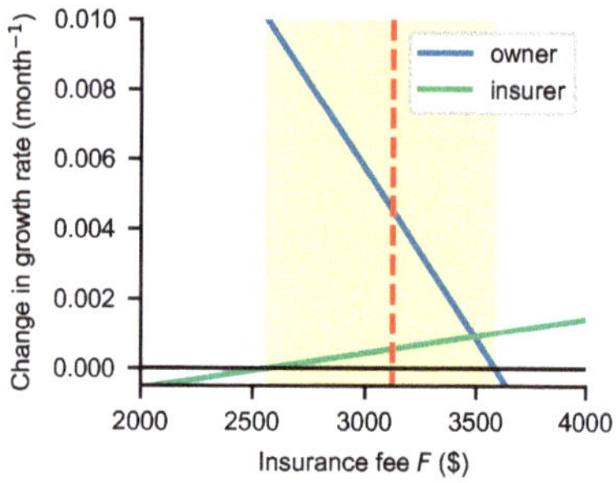

Figure 7.7: Change in the time-average growth rate of wealth, $\delta\overline{g}_{\mathrm{m}}$, as a function of the insurance fee, F. **Blue:** for Caius the shipowner. **Green:** for Anna the insurer. The mutually beneficial fee range is marked by the beige background.

or 0.06% per month. The net benefit to the insurer is therefore also

$$\delta\overline{g}_{\mathrm{m}\,\mathrm{insurer}} \approx 0.06\% \text{ per month.} \tag{7.35}$$

Unlike EVT, EE with the assumption of multiplicative repetition creates a world where an insurance contract can exist – there exists a range of fees F at which both parties gain from signing the contract!

We view this as the fundamental resolution of the insurance puzzle.

Fundamental resolution of the insurance puzzle:

An insurance contract will be signed by both parties if doing so increases the time-average ergodic growth rate of both the seller's wealth and the buyer's wealth.

It requires no appeal to arbitrary utility functions or asymmetric circumstances, rather it arises naturally from the model of human decision-making that we have set out. Fig. 7.7 shows the *mutually beneficial range of insurance premia* predicted by our model.

Figure 7.8 illustrates the dynamical real-world meaning of these findings by showing the wealth of two shipowners, both subject to the multiplicative dynamics with our example parameters. Because insurance at these fees boosts long-time growth, the wealth of the shipowner with insurance outgrows that of the uninsured shipowner.

Generalising, the message of EE is that business happens when both parties gain. In the world created by this model, any agreement, any contract, any commercial interaction comes into existence because it is mutually beneficial.

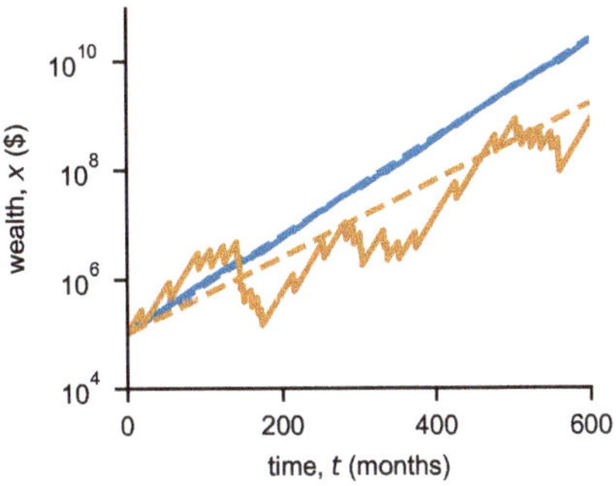

Figure 7.8: Wealth of two ship owners under multiplicative dynamics, over fifty years using our example parameters. **Blue:** this owner buys insurance at a fee of $F = 0.03125 \times x_{\text{own}}$. **Yellow:** this owner chooses not to buy insurance. As time goes by, the insured owner systematically outperforms the uninsured owner. Identical noise realisations were used for both owners.

7.4.2 The classical solution of the insurance puzzle

The classical solution of the insurance puzzle is identical to the classical solution of the St. Petersburg paradox. Wealth is replaced by a non-linear utility function of wealth, which breaks the symmetry of EVT which we saw in (Eq. 7.28). While it is always true that $\delta \langle Q_{\text{owner}} \rangle = -\delta \langle Q_{\text{insurer}} \rangle$ the expected future values of non-linear utility functions don't share this anti-symmetry. A difference in the decision makers' wealths is sufficient, though often different utility functions are assumed for owner and insurer, which is a model that can create pretty much any behaviour. The downside of a model with this ability is, of course, that it makes no predictions – nothing is ruled out, so the model cannot be falsified. Popper would mark it as not science.

Part III

Populations

Preview of Part III

In Part II we developed a model of individual behaviour – time-average growth rate optimisation – which assumed knowledge of the stochastic process governing individual wealth. In this part, we use our model individual as a building block to create model populations, societies, and markets – a primitive model economy, if you will.

We start in Chap. 8 with a model population whose members do not interact. Given the stochastic process that describes individual wealth, we explore what happens when each individual follows an independent trajectory. Viewing the stochastic process as a family of time-dependent random variables tells us how wealth is distributed at each point in time and, therefore, how the distribution evolves. We use multiplicative wealth dynamics to present our approach, and find that inequality grows inexorably. We quantify how through the definition of two key growth rates and an inequality measure, which emerge naturally from our analysis and can be generalised to other wealth processes. We also gain an understanding of when and how results for finite populations differ from those for the infinite ensemble.

In Chap. 9, we add interactions to our population of noisy multipliers. It turns out that growth optimisation at the individual level creates emergent behaviour – cooperation, or more precisely, the sharing and pooling of resources. The effect of cooperation on the time-average growth rate of wealth (or other resources) explains why we see socio-economic structure, from the formation of firms to nation states with taxation and redistribution. To explore this further, we build a model of wealth evolution with a reallocation mechanism resembling tax, which produces realistic wealth distributions. We find conditions under which the resulting stochastic process is ergodic, and ask whether these conditions hold in the real world using US wealth data.

Finally, in Chap. 10, we apply our behavioural model to a simple portfolio selection problem in a market of two assets: one risky, the other riskless. We ask how a growth-optimal investor should allocate money between the two assets, phrased in terms of leverage. We contrast the classical approach, which requires the investor's risk preferences, with our approach, in which an objectively optimal leverage exists that maximises the time-average growth rate. We explore what this optimal leverage means for financial markets. We argue that, if all market participants aim for the same optimal leverage, strong and quantifiable constraints are placed on the price fluctuations that emerge from their trading. This leads to a theory of noise in stock prices, resolves the equity premium puzzle, provides a framework for setting interest rates, and suggests a method for fraud detection. We make testable predictions, which we confirm using data from the US stock markets, Bitcoin, and the Madoff Ponzi scheme.

Chapter 8

People

8.1 Each one alone

We have seen that risk aversion constitutes optimal behaviour for an individual whose wealth follows GBM, provided time scales are long enough for systematic trends to be significant. In this chapter we will continue to explore GBM, but now in the context of a population. By "explore" we mean that we will let the model generate its world: if each individual in a population has wealth that follows an independent trajectory of GBM, what kind of economy emerges?

This simple model of a population will be the ground on which we build more complex and realistic models in Chap. 9. There, our individuals will interact and we will see that cooperation and the formation of social structure also constitute optimal behaviour under multiplicative growth.

The trajectories of GBM tell us what is likely to happen to an individual over long time, while the PDF of the random variable, $x(t)$, at a given time, t, tell us how wealth is distributed in our model. Wealth distribution refers to the probability density function, $\mathcal{P}_x(x)$, and not to the activity of distributing wealth among people.

We interpret the PDF as follows. Imagine a population of N individuals, where N is large (say, the population of a country). $\mathcal{P}_x(x)\Delta x$ is the approximate fraction of the population with wealth between x and $x + \Delta x$. This is shown graphically as the area of the shaded strip in Fig. 8.1 (left panel). The integral of the PDF, $\int_{-\infty}^{x} \mathcal{P}_x(s)ds$, known as the cumulative distribution function (CDF), is the approximate fraction of the population having wealth less than x. This equals the shaded area in Fig. 8.1 (right panel). These fractions can also be interpreted as the probabilities of a randomly-selected member of the population having wealth in the ranges stated. A broad wealth distribution with a heavy

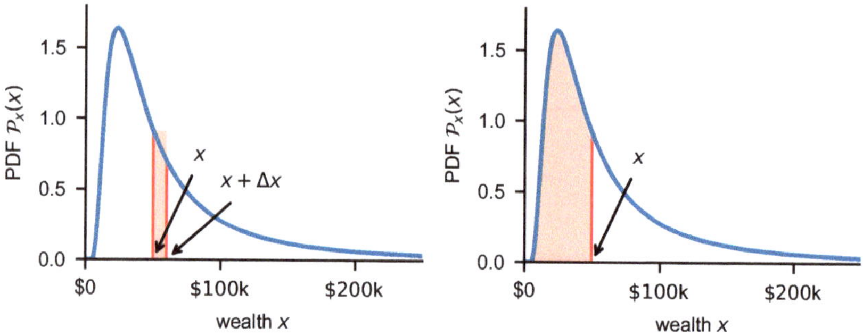

Figure 8.1: Example of a wealth distribution. **Left:** The area of the shaded strip, $\mathcal{P}_x(x)\Delta x$, is the approximate fraction of a large population with wealth between x and $x + \Delta x$. **Right:** The shaded area under the PDF, equal to the CDF, is the approximate fraction of a large population with wealth less than x.

tail indicates greater *wealth inequality*.

8.1.1 Lognormal distribution

Recall from Sec. 4.4 that the SDE for GBM,

$$dx = x(\mu dt + \sigma dW), \tag{8.1}$$

has solution

$$x(t) = x(0) \exp\left[\left(\mu - \frac{\sigma^2}{2}\right) t + \sigma W(t)\right], \tag{8.2}$$

which, at a given time t, can be viewed as a lognormally-distributed random variable with time-dependent parameters,

$$\ln x(t) \sim \mathcal{N}\left(\ln x(0) + \left(\mu - \frac{\sigma^2}{2}\right) t, \sigma^2 t\right). \tag{8.3}$$

In our model population, we will assume that all individuals have the same starting wealth, $x(0)$.[1]

Using the results in Sec. 4.1.2, let's state some of the basic properties of this distribution. The PDF, now time-dependent, is

$$\mathcal{P}_x(x;t) = \frac{1}{x\sqrt{2\pi\sigma^2 t}} \exp\left(-\frac{[\ln x - \ln x(0) - (\mu - \frac{\sigma^2}{2})t]^2}{2\sigma^2 t}\right). \tag{8.4}$$

[1]We could relax this assumption and assume a distribution of starting wealths. This would add complexity to the analysis and would be worth doing only if relevant to the problem at hand.

The expectation value is

$$\langle x(t) \rangle = x(0) \exp(\mu t) \tag{8.5}$$

or, equivalently, $\ln \langle x(t) \rangle = \ln x(0) + \mu t$, and the variance is

$$\text{Var}[x(t)] = x(0)^2 \exp(2\mu t)[\exp(\sigma^2 t) - 1]. \tag{8.6}$$

We remind ourselves that the lognormal distribution, indeed any distribution, is a mathematical object. It is a part of our model economy. Its properties, expressed in statistics such as the expected value $\langle x(t) \rangle$, are those of an imaginary infinite ensemble. Real populations are finite and, therefore, more realistically modelled as finite ensembles. We might consider a model population of N individuals at time t having wealths $\{x_i(t)\}$ drawn independently from (Eq. 8.3), with which we can compare the observed wealths in a real population.

It would be very handy if the statistics of finite ensembles were well approximated by those of the distribution, which we can simply look up. This would allow us, for example, to replace in our calculations the finite-ensemble average, $\langle x(t) \rangle_N$, which is a random variable, with the ensemble average, $\langle x(t) \rangle$, which is a known quantity. This replacement will be acceptable when N is large because $\langle x(t) \rangle$ is simply the $N \to \infty$ limit of $\langle x(t) \rangle_N$. In what follows, we will assume our model populations are large enough to make this replacement. We will specify what we mean by "large enough" in Sec. 8.2.

8.1.2 Two growth rates

We recap the result, derived in Sec. 4.4, that the ensemble average of all possible trajectories of GBM grows at a higher rate than that of a single trajectory over a long time. This difference was the key to developing a coherent theory of individual decision-making. We will see here that it is also crucial to understanding how wealth becomes distributed in the GBM model and how the inequality in such a distribution can be measured.

Let's start with a reminder of the result. Suppose personal wealth follows (Eq. 8.1). Then the growth rate of the ensemble-average wealth,

$$g_{\langle\rangle} = \frac{\Delta \ln \langle x \rangle}{\Delta t} = \mu, \tag{8.7}$$

is larger than the time-average growth rate of wealth,

$$\overline{g} = \left\langle \frac{\Delta \ln x}{\Delta t} \right\rangle = \mu - \frac{\sigma^2}{2}. \tag{8.8}$$

In (Eq. 8.8) we have used the ergodic property of the growth rate to express the time average as an ensemble average.

These two growth rates are deterministic properties of our model in two limiting regimes: infinitely many systems and infinitely long time. For finite populations and finite time, let's imagine a population of constant size, N, and denote individual wealths by $x_i(t)$ for $i = 1 \dots N$. A single wealth trajectory generated by (Eq. 8.1) evolves over a finite time period Δt as

$$x_i(t + \Delta t) = x_i(t) \exp\left[\left(\mu - \frac{\sigma^2}{2}\right)\Delta t + \sigma W_i(\Delta t)\right]. \tag{8.9}$$

The growth rate realised in this trajectory over this period is

$$g_i = \frac{\Delta \ln x_i}{\Delta t} = \mu - \frac{\sigma^2}{2} + \frac{\sigma W_i(\Delta t)}{\Delta t}, \tag{8.10}$$

which is random variable with a normal distribution,

$$g_i \sim \mathcal{N}\left(\mu - \frac{\sigma^2}{2}, \frac{\sigma^2}{\Delta t}\right). \tag{8.11}$$

Each growth rate in the population is drawn independently from this distribution. We compute the following two growth rates.

Plutocratic growth rate

$g_{\langle\rangle} = \mu$ is the growth rate of the ensemble-average wealth. In a finite population, we compute the growth rate of the finite-ensemble-average wealth, which we call the *plutocratic growth rate* following [38]:

$$g_{\text{plu}} \equiv \frac{\Delta \ln \langle x \rangle_N}{\Delta t} = \frac{1}{\Delta t} \ln\left[\frac{\sum_{i=1}^N x_i(t + \Delta t)}{\sum_{i=1}^N x_i(t)}\right]. \tag{8.12}$$

Put simply, g_{plu} is the growth rate of the average wealth. We call it "plutocratic" because it depends only on the growth of the total wealth of the population, and not on how that growth is experienced by individuals.[2]

This type of averaging weights each person's growth rate roughly in proportion to that person's wealth, as we will show now. We use the approximation $\Delta \ln x_i \approx \Delta x_i / x_i$, valid for small relative changes in wealth, and define the plutocratic weight as the ratio of individual to

[2]Plutus is the god of wealth in Greek mythology, and also the title of a comedy by Aristophanes, which may well be the most insightful text on economics ever produced.

total wealth, $w_i^{\text{plu}} = x_i / \sum_i^N x_i$. The plutocratic growth rate becomes

$$
\begin{aligned}
g_{\text{plu}} &= \frac{\Delta \ln \langle x \rangle_N}{\Delta t} && (8.13)\\
&\approx \frac{1}{\Delta t} \frac{\Delta \langle x \rangle_N}{\langle x \rangle_N} && (8.14)\\
&= \frac{1}{\Delta t} \frac{\sum_i^N \Delta x_i}{\sum_i^N x_i} && (8.15)\\
&= \frac{1}{\Delta t} \sum_i^N \left(\frac{x_i}{\sum_i^N x_i} \right) \frac{\Delta x_i}{x_i} && (8.16)\\
&\approx \sum_i^N w_i^{\text{plu}} \frac{\Delta \ln x_i}{\Delta t} && (8.17)\\
&= \sum_i^N w_i^{\text{plu}} g_i. && (8.18)
\end{aligned}
$$

Thus g_{plu} is approximately equal to the wealth-weighted average of the individual growth rates in the population. In this sense, it is indeed a plutocratic measure of growth – not one-person-one-vote, but one-dollar-one-vote.

Democratic growth rate

The time-average growth rate, achieved by any single wealth trajectory in the long-time limit, is $\overline{g} = \mu - \sigma^2/2$. By its ergodic property, it is also the ensemble average of the finite-time growth rate, (Eq. 8.8). In our finite population, we can compute the corresponding finite-ensemble average, which we call the *democratic growth rate*:

$$
g_{\text{dem}} \equiv \left\langle \frac{\Delta \ln x_i}{\Delta t} \right\rangle_N = \frac{1}{N} \sum_{i=1}^N g_i. \qquad (8.19)
$$

In the literature, this has been called the "people's growth rate" [59] or the "population-weighted growth rate" [38]. It is tricky to avoid politically loaded terms, but their technical origin in this case is clear: each growth rate g_i (and, therefore, each person i) has the same weight in this average, namely the democratic weight, $w_i^{\text{dem}} = 1/N$. It is common to call systems democratic if each person has the same say. If we had given additional weight to the growth rates of women, then we might have called the result a "matriarchal growth rate." But in (Eq. 8.19), each person has the same influence on the average growth rate, so we call it "democratic."

In the GBM model, $g_{\text{dem}} \to \mu - \sigma^2/2$ as $N \to \infty$. Therefore, for large enough N, we can make the approximation $g_{\text{dem}} \approx \mu - \sigma^2/2$. In this case, it is relatively easy to quantify what we mean by "large enough" because g_{dem} is simply an average of N normal variates. This is itself a normal random variable,

$$g_{\text{dem}} \sim \mathcal{N}\left(\mu - \sigma^2/2, \frac{\sigma^2}{N\Delta t}\right). \tag{8.20}$$

We may insist that the variance of this distribution be smaller than some small value, Var_{max}, that is important to us for some reason. This translates directly into a condition on N:

$$N > \frac{\sigma^2}{\text{Var}_{\text{max}}\Delta t}. \tag{8.21}$$

We have to be careful because under GBM all entities experience growth rates independently. This is clearly an unrealistic aspect of using GBM to model real wealths or incomes: recessions often simultaneously reduce the growth rates of a significant part of a population. But leaving this issue to one side for the moment, if we model annual growth rates, $\Delta t = 1$ year, for wealths following GBM with stock market-like volatility $\sigma^2 = (0.2)^2$ per year, then the standard deviation of g_{dem} is 0.002 for $N = 10,000$, and correspondingly very small for nation-sized populations.

Moreover, g_{dem} is a typical growth rate. Although we calculate it as an average over the growth rates of many trajectories, the ergodic property makes it an estimate of the growth rate, $\overline{g}$, to which every trajectory's growth converges almost surely over time. We can explore this idea a little further. Imagine an individual whose wealth, $x_{\text{dem}}(t)$, grows at exactly g_{dem}. Writing this as

$$x_{\text{dem}}(t + \Delta t) = x_{\text{dem}}(t) \exp(g_{\text{dem}}\Delta t) \tag{8.22}$$

$$= x_{\text{dem}}(t) \exp\left(\sum_{i=1}^{N} \frac{g_i \Delta t}{N}\right) \tag{8.23}$$

shows that such an individual spends an equal amount of time, $\Delta t/N$, experiencing the growth rate of each person in the population. Thus, in a single period Δt the individual shares everyone's experiences of the national economy in equal measure. We might think of this individual as the "representative agent" of EE.

Let's invent a story contrasting the two growth measures we've just discussed, to solidify their meanings in our minds.

Imagine you're sitting in the library, and as an exercise compute the plutocratic growth rate, g_{plu}, of those in the room. If Jeff Bezos (or whoever happens to be the Croesus of your era) walks in, this will simplify your calculation immensely: you can forget about everyone else, since the total wealth is indistinguishable from his. Because each dollar rather than each growth rate is weighted roughly equally, the plutocratic growth rate is that of Jeff Bezos.

Had you been computing the democratic growth rate, g_{dem}, the story would have been different. Jeff Bezos's arrival wouldn't have made much difference. In g_{dem} his growth rate has the same $1/N$ weight as that of the underpaid librarian. g_{dem} is, by construction, a one-person-one-vote measure of economic growth.

Curiously, despite being atypical in a population, the growth rates reported most widely in economics and the media are similar in structure to g_{plu}. Most importantly, the *growth rate of GDP* is a plutocratic (income-weighted) growth rate. In public discussions GDP is used as a proxy for the "size of the economy". Of course, the size of the economy is an important statistic for a government that must monitor the resources available for public spending. However, if income is well modelled as a multiplicative process, then the GDP growth rate will be akin to g_{plu} and it will be larger than g_{dem}, which represents the typical growth rate of members of the population. Using the plutocratic growth rate as the only measure of economic growth risks creating a disconnect between a government, which sees total income growing at $g_{\text{plu}} = \mu$, and the electorate, most of whom experience income growth closer to $g_{\text{dem}} = \mu - \sigma^2/2$. EE tells us that wise leadership would account for both growth rates.

8.1.3 Measuring inequality

In the case of GBM we have just seen how to compute exactly the full wealth distribution, $\mathcal{P}_x(x)$. This is interesting but often we want only summary measures of the distribution. One summary measure of particular interest to economists is inequality. How much inequality is there in a distribution like (Eq. 8.3)? And how does this quantity increase over time under GBM, as we have suggested it does?

Clearly, to answer these questions, we must quantify "inequality". In this section, and also in [2], we develop a natural way of measuring it.

The two extremes – perfect equality and perfect inequality – are easily identified. Minimum inequality means that everyone has the same wealth, so the wealth distribution is a *Dirac delta function* at the average wealth of the population, *i.e.* the finite-ensemble average. The *minimally unequal distribution* is

$$\mathcal{P}_x(x) = \delta(x - \langle x \rangle_N). \tag{8.24}$$

If we assume, for the moment, that individuals cannot have negative wealth, then maximum inequality means that one individual has all the wealth and everyone else has nothing. The *maximally unequal distribution* is, therefore, composed of two Dirac delta peaks, one at zero wealth

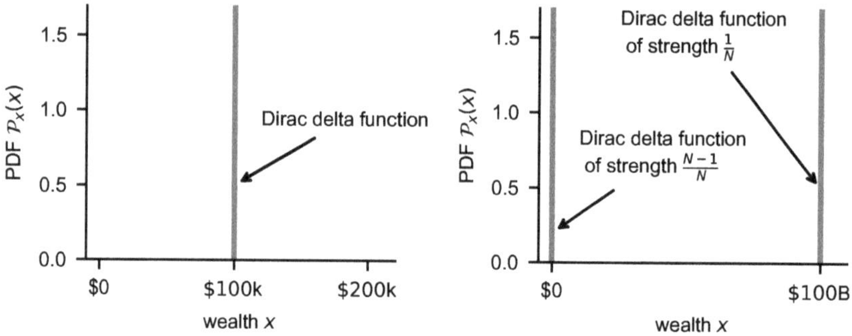

Figure 8.2: Extreme wealth distributions in a population of 1 million people. **Left:** The maximally equal distribution in which everyone has the same wealth (here \$100,000, as an example). **Right:** The maximally unequal distribution (assuming no negative wealth) in which one person owns everything (here \$100 billion).

and one at the total wealth,

$$\mathcal{P}_x(x) = \frac{N-1}{N}\delta(x-0) + \frac{1}{N}\delta(x - N\langle x\rangle_N), \tag{8.25}$$

as shown in Fig. 8.2.

Quantifying inequality in a distribution is reminiscent of the gamble problem. Recall that for gambles we wanted to make statements of the type "this gamble is more desirable than that gamble". We did this by collapsing distributions, in this case of wealth changes, to scalars which can be ranked. Depending on the question that was being asked, the appropriate way of collapsing the distribution and the resulting scalar can be different. For example, the scalar relevant to an insurance company may not be relevant to an individual. In the case of inequality we also have a distribution – the wealth distribution – and we want to make statements of the type "this distribution is more unequal than that distribution". Again, this is done by *collapsing the distribution to a scalar* and, again, many different choices of scalar are possible. The *Gini coefficient* is a well-known example, as is the 80/20 ratio. Indeed, there is a whole menagerie of inequality measures in economics.

An inequality measure of particular interest for us is the so-called *mean logarithmic deviation*,

$$\ln\langle x(t)\rangle_N - \langle \ln x(t)\rangle_N. \tag{8.26}$$

In economics, (Eq. 8.26) is also known as *Theil's second index of inequality* [66], and it has an intriguing connection to ergodicity economics.

We established in Sec. 8.1.2 two fundamental growth rates of wealth in a finite population. The plutocratic growth rate, g_{plu}, is the growth rate of the average wealth, $\langle x \rangle_N$. Assuming constant population size, it is also the growth rate of the total wealth, $N \langle x \rangle_N$. For large populations, g_{plu} is well approximated by the ensemble-average growth rate, $g_{\langle\rangle}$, which equals μ in GBM.

The democratic growth rate, g_{dem}, is the average of the growth rates of wealth. For large populations, it resembles the time-average growth rate, $\overline{g}$, which is the typical growth rate to which any wealth trajectory converges almost surely in the long term. This has the value $\mu - \sigma^2/2$ in GBM.

Total wealth in GBM thus grows at a higher rate than the typical wealth, $g_{\text{plu}} > g_{\text{dem}}$, indicating that inequality increases as time passes. This suggests a way of measuring wealth inequality in GBM as the quantity which grows at the difference between the plutocratic and democratic growth rates,

$$\frac{dJ}{dt} = g_{\text{plu}} - g_{\text{dem}}. \tag{8.27}$$

With (Eq. 8.27) defining the dynamic of inequality in GBM, inequality itself is found by integrating over time:

$$J(t) = J(0) + \int_0^t [g_{\text{plu}}(s) - g_{\text{dem}}(s)]ds, \tag{8.28}$$

where the constant of integration, $J(0)$, is inequality at time $t = 0$.

In the GBM model, we can write the difference in growth rates as

$$\frac{dJ}{dt} = \frac{d \ln \langle x \rangle_N}{dt} - \frac{d \langle \ln x \rangle_N}{dt} \tag{8.29}$$

and integrate from time 0 to t to get

$$J(t) = \ln \langle x(t) \rangle_N - \langle \ln x(t) \rangle_N, \tag{8.30}$$

where $J(0) = 0$ under our assumption that all trajectories have equal starting wealth, $x(0)$. Indeed, in (Eq. 8.30), perfect equality of wealth occurring at any time t would correspond to $J = 0$, while any other arrangement of wealth would yield $J > 0$ by Jensen's inequality,

$$f(\langle x(t) \rangle_N) \geq \langle f(x(t)) \rangle_N \tag{8.31}$$

for a strictly concave function f, with equality if and only if all $x_i(t)$ are equal. Equation (8.30) is identical to Theil's expression in (Eq. 8.26) and we denote it by J to indicate the connection to Jensen's result.

For the general wealth dynamics studied in Chap. 6, the general quantity $J(t) = v(\langle x(t) \rangle_N) - \langle v(x(t)) \rangle_N$ will have properties that depend on the concavity or convexity of the ergodicity transformation $v(x)$. These may or may not lead to an easily-interpreted inequality measure. Nevertheless, knowing both the plutocratic and democratic growth rates of wealth is always informative of the dynamics of inequality.

We find it remarkable that the simple difference between the plutocratic and democratic growth rates, evaluated for the important case of GBM, leads to an established measure of inequality, (Eq. 8.30), identified by economists who did not consider the ergodicity problem. Merely by insisting on measuring inequality well, Theil derived an inequality measure that arises naturally in EE when we assume multiplicative growth.[3]

Substituting the known approximations of the finite-ensemble averages for large populations into (Eq. 8.30), we can evaluate the mean logarithmic deviation as a function of time and of the parameters of the GBM model:

$$J(t) = \frac{\sigma^2 t}{2}. \tag{8.32}$$

Those who go forth and multiply, their inequality shall increase without bound!

8.1.4 Wealth condensation

The lognormal distribution generated by GBM, (Eq. 8.6), broadens indefinitely. Likewise, the inequality present in the distribution grows indefinitely, (Eq. 8.32). A related property of GBM is the evolution towards wealth condensation. Wealth condensation means that a single individual owns a non-zero fraction of the total wealth of the population in the $N \to \infty$ limit [12]. In the present case, an arbitrarily large share of the total wealth will be owned by an arbitrarily small share of the population.

One simple way to see this is to compute the proportion of individual wealths that are smaller than the expected wealth, *i.e.* $x(t) < x(0)\exp(\mu t)$. To do this, we define a new random variable, $z(t)$, constructed by change of location and scale to have a standard normal distribution:

$$z(t) \equiv \frac{\ln x(t) - \ln x(0) - (\mu - \sigma^2/2)t}{\sigma t^{1/2}} \sim \mathcal{N}(0,1). \tag{8.33}$$

We want to know the mass of the distribution with $\ln x(t) < \ln x(0) + \mu t$. This is equivalent to $z < \sigma t^{1/2}/2$, meaning that the proportion below the expected wealth is

$$\Phi\left(\frac{\sigma t^{1/2}}{2}\right), \tag{8.34}$$

where Φ is the CDF of the standard normal distribution. This increases over time and tends to 1 as $t \to \infty$, see Fig. 8.3.

[3] Like Kelly's ideas about gambling [25], Theil's inequality measures emerged from information theory.

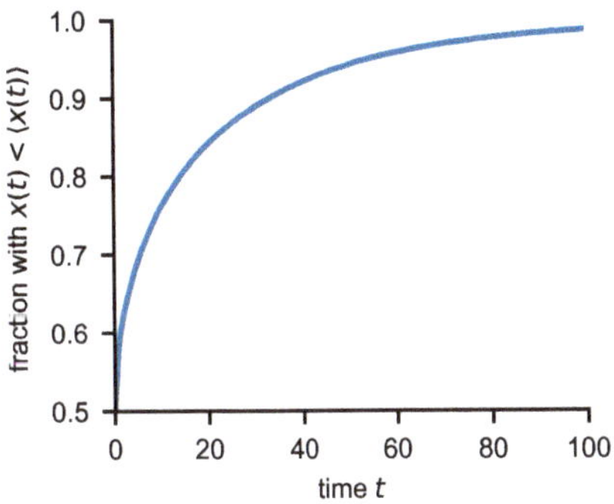

Figure 8.3: Fraction of GBM wealth trajectories below the expectation value, $x(t) < \langle x(t) \rangle$. In the long-time limit, each wealth trajectory falls behind the expectation value almost surely, and the fraction tends to 1. **Parameters:** $\sigma^2 = 0.2$ per unit time.

8.1.5 Rescaled wealth

Economists have arrived at many inequality measures, and have drawn up a list of conditions that particularly useful measures of inequality satisfy. Such measures are called "*relative measures*" [61, Appendix 4] and J is one of them.

One of the conditions is that inequality measures should not change when the observable of interest, *e.g.* wealth, is divided by the same factor for everyone. Since we are primarily interested in inequality in this section, we can forget about absolute wealth levels and study instead an object called *rescaled wealth.*

DEFINITION: **Rescaled wealth**

The rescaled wealth of individual i in a population $i = 1 \dots N$ is the ratio of the individual's wealth to the average wealth of the population (*i.e.* the finite-ensemble average):

$$w_i(t) \equiv \frac{x_i(t)}{\langle x(t) \rangle_N}. \tag{8.35}$$

This quantity is useful because its numerical value does not depend on the currency used: it is a dimensionless number. Thus if your rescaled wealth is $w_i(t) = 1/2$, it means that your wealth is half the average wealth, irrespective of whether you measure it in Kazakhstani Tenge or Swiss Francs. The finite-ensemble average of rescaled wealth is easily calculated:

$$\langle w_i(t) \rangle_N = \left\langle \frac{x(t)}{\langle x(t) \rangle_N} \right\rangle_N = 1. \tag{8.36}$$

For the populations we study, the finite-ensemble average wealth, $\langle x(t) \rangle_N$, is close to the ensemble-average wealth, $\langle x(t) \rangle$, which is simply its $N \to \infty$ limit. Thus, the rescaled wealth is well approximated as

$$w(t) = \frac{x(t)}{\langle x(t) \rangle} = \frac{x(t)}{x(0)\exp(\mu t)}, \tag{8.37}$$

where we have dropped the trajectory index, i.

Now that we have an expression for w in terms of x and t, we can derive the dynamic for rescaled wealth using Itô's formula (just as we did to find the wealth dynamic for a general utility function in Sec. 6.6.2). We start with

$$dw = \frac{\partial w}{\partial t}dt + \frac{\partial w}{\partial x}dx + \frac{1}{2}\frac{\partial^2 w}{\partial x^2}dx^2 \quad (8.38)$$

$$= -\mu w dt + \frac{w}{x}dx, \quad (8.39)$$

and then substitute (Eq. 8.1) for dx to get

$$dw = \sigma w dW. \quad (8.40)$$

So $w(t)$ follows a very simple GBM with zero drift and volatility σ. This means that rescaled wealth has an ever-broadening lognormal distribution,

$$\ln w(t) \sim \mathcal{N}\left(-\frac{\sigma^2}{2}t, \sigma^2 t\right). \quad (8.41)$$

Rescaled wealth trajectories converge to $w = 0$ almost surely over time, even though the expectation value remains $\langle w \rangle = 1$, consistent with our previous observation of wealth condensation in Sec. 8.1.4.

Finally, noting that $\langle \ln w \rangle_N = \langle \ln x \rangle_N - \ln \langle x \rangle_N$ gives us a simple expression for our inequality measure in (Eq. 8.30) in terms of the rescaled wealth:

$$J(t) = -\langle \ln w(t) \rangle_N. \quad (8.42)$$

8.1.6 Power-law resemblance

It is an established empirical observation [42] that the upper tails of real wealth distributions look more like a power law than a lognormal. Our trivial model does not strictly reproduce this feature, but it is instructive to compare the lognormal distribution to a power-law distribution. A power-law PDF has the asymptotic form

$$\mathcal{P}_x(x) \sim x^{-(1+\zeta)}, \quad (8.43)$$

for large arguments x. This implies that the logarithm of the PDF is proportional to the logarithm of its argument, $\ln \mathcal{P}_x(x) = -(1+\zeta)\ln x$. Plotting one against the other will yield a straight line, the slope being the exponent $-(1+\zeta)$.

Determining whether an empirical observation is consistent with such behaviour is difficult because the behaviour to be observed is in the tail (large x) where data are, by definition, sparse. A quick-and-dirty way of checking for possible power-law behaviour is to plot an empirical

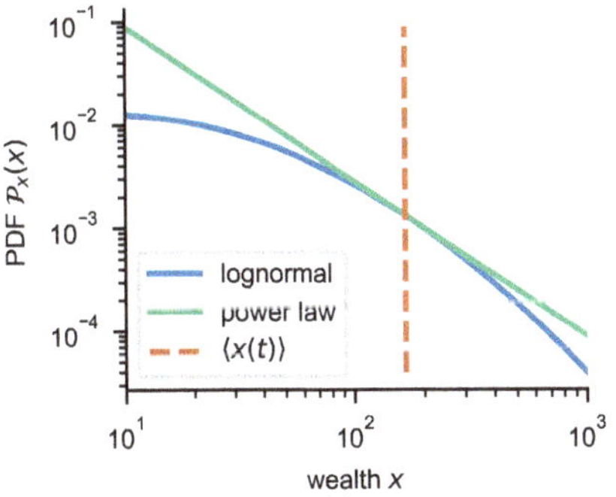

Figure 8.4: The lognormal PDF of GBM (blue line) resembles a power law with exponent $-3/2$ (green line) near the expectation value $\langle x(t) \rangle$ (dashed line). **Parameters:** $x(0) = 100$, $t = 10$, $\mu = 0.05$, $\sigma^2 = 0.2$ (wealth and time units arbitrary).

PDF against its argument on log-log scales, look for a straight line, and measure the slope. However, plotting any distribution on any type of scales results in some line. It may not be a straight line but it will have some slope everywhere. For a known distribution (power-law or not) we can interpret this slope as a local apparent power-law exponent.

What is the local apparent power-law exponent of a lognormal wealth distribution near the expectation value $\langle x \rangle = \exp(\mu t)$, *i.e.* in the upper tail where approximate power-law behaviour has been observed empirically? The logarithm of (Eq. 8.4) is

$$\ln \mathcal{P}(x) = -\ln\left(x\sqrt{2\pi\sigma^2 t}\right) - \frac{[\ln x - \ln x(0) - (\mu - \frac{\sigma^2}{2})t]^2}{2\sigma^2 t} \tag{8.44}$$

The local slope, *i.e.* apparent exponent, is

$$\frac{d \ln \mathcal{P}(x)}{d \ln x} = -\frac{\ln \frac{x}{x(0)}}{\sigma^2 t} + \frac{\mu}{\sigma^2} - \frac{3}{2}. \tag{8.45}$$

Near $\langle x \rangle$, $\ln \frac{x}{x(0)} \sim \mu t$ so that the first two terms cancel approximately. Here the distribution will resemble a power law with exponent $-3/2$ when plotted on doubly logarithmic scales, Fig. 8.4. (The distribution will also look like a power law where the first term is much smaller than the others, *e.g.* where $\ln \frac{x}{x(0)} \ll \sigma^2 t$.)

We don't believe that empirically observed power laws are merely a manifestation of this mathematical feature. Important real-world mechanisms that broaden real wealth distributions, *i.e.* concentrate wealth, are missing from the null model. We will see in Sec. 9.2 that including interactions among individuals produces a proper power-law tail in the distribution whose exponent is closer to observations than $-3/2$. However, it is interesting that the trivial model of GBM reproduces so many qualitative features of empirical observations.

8.2 Finite populations

So far we have considered the properties of the random variable, $x(t)$, generated by GBM at a fixed time, t. We know its distribution at any time, and we know that expectation values under this distribution are averages over N realisations in the limit $N \to \infty$. For example, the expected wealth, $\langle x(t) \rangle$, is the $N \to \infty$ limit of

$$\langle x(t) \rangle_N \equiv \frac{1}{N} \sum_{i=1}^{N} x_i(t), \tag{8.46}$$

which we introduced in Sec. 2.3 as the finite-ensemble average.

If N represents the size of a real population, it will certainly be finite – nothing real is infinite. Therefore, we need to be diligent and ask under what conditions the results we have derived in the large-N limit are valid for finite populations. In particular, we will focus on the finite-ensemble average wealth under GBM. For what values of μ, σ, t, and N is this well approximated by the expectation value? And when it is not, what does it resemble?

8.2.1 How long is a long time?

We know that at a given time t, $x(t)$ is a random variable with a lognormal distribution. Therefore, the object of our interest is a sum of lognormal variates (divided by N to turn the sum into an average). Here we sketch out some simple arguments about how this object depends on N and t, see also [53, 49].

Considering the two growth rates in Sec. 8.1.2, we anticipate a tension between two limiting scenarios:

- for large N, the finite-ensemble average resembles the expectation value, $x(0) \exp(\mu t)$;
- for large t, all trajectories in the finite ensemble, and therefore the finite-ensemble average itself, grow like $x(0) \exp[(\mu - \sigma^2/2)t]$.

The first scenario, when a finite-ensemble average resembles the corresponding expectation value, is known in statistical physics as "*self-averaging*". A simple way of checking whether we are in the self-averaging regime is this: compare the magnitude of typical fluctuations in the finite-ensemble average to the finite-ensemble average itself. To capture this comparison in a number, we divide the variance of the finite-ensemble average by the expected value of the finite-ensemble average squared, and call the result the Ginzburg ratio (after the 2003 Physics Nobel Laureate, Vitaly Ginzburg),

$$\mathcal{G} \equiv \frac{\mathrm{Var}[\langle x(t) \rangle_N]}{\langle \langle x(t) \rangle_N \rangle^2}. \tag{8.47}$$

To be explicit, the $\mathrm{Var}[\cdot]$ and $\langle\cdot\rangle$ operators, without the subscript N, refer to the mean and variance over all possible realisations of the random variables enclosed, which in (Eq. 8.47) are finite-ensemble averages. The finite-ensemble averages themselves, taken over finite samples of wealth realisations, are denoted by the $\langle\cdot\rangle_N$ operator, with subscript N indicating the sample size.

In statistical physics, the condition

$$\mathcal{G} \ll 1 \tag{8.48}$$

is known as the Ginzburg criterion , see *e.g.* [20, p. 415]. If it is satisfied, then fluctuations in the finite-ensemble average are small on the relevant scale, and we expect self-averaging to hold. This exemplifies Ginzburg's very general reasoning: if the fluctuations around the mean of a thing are much smaller than the mean of the thing, then we might get away with neglecting fluctuations and working with means only. In statistical physics this argument is widely used to estimate where models which ignore fluctuations cease to be valid.

Equation (8.47) simplifies to

$$\mathcal{G} = \frac{\frac{1}{N}\mathrm{Var}[x(t)]}{\langle x(t)\rangle^2}, \tag{8.49}$$

into which we insert (Eq. 8.5) and (Eq. 8.6) to get an expression in terms of the GBM model parameters:

$$\mathcal{G} = \frac{\exp(\sigma^2 t) - 1}{N}. \tag{8.50}$$

If (Eq. 8.48) is satisfied, then the finite-ensemble average will likely be close to its own expectation value, which is equal to the expectation value of the GBM. This condition holds approximately when

$$t < \frac{\ln N}{\sigma^2}. \tag{8.51}$$

Therefore, we have

$$\langle x(t)\rangle_N \approx \langle x(t)\rangle = x(0)\exp(\mu t), \tag{8.52}$$

provided (Eq. 8.51) is satisfied.

The Ginzburg criterion tells us roughly when self-averaging holds: yes, for large enough samples, as we anticipated, but equivalently for short enough time or low enough volatility. It is instructive to note that there's no t small enough for it to hold for $N = 1$: where individuals are concerned, expected wealth is never relevant according to this criterion. When $\sigma = 0$, (Eq. 8.51) is undefined: taking expectation values has no effect in the absence of fluctuations.

A more careful estimate of the critical time when self-averaging breaks down is twice as large [49], but its scaling with sample size and volatility is identical. We will not reproduce the derivation of this result here but nonetheless define the critical crossover time as

$$t_c = \frac{2\ln N}{\sigma^2}. \tag{8.53}$$

We can say more about the way in which *self-averaging breaks down* if we think in terms of extremes: self-averaging must stop when even the "luckiest" trajectory (the extreme) is no longer close to the expectation value $x(0)\exp(\mu t)$. This is guaranteed to happen eventually because the probability for a trajectory to reach $x(0)\exp(\mu t)$ decreases towards zero as t grows, as we saw in Sec. 8.1.4. Naturally, this takes longer for larger samples, which have more chances to contain a lucky trajectory.

For $t > t_c$, the growth rate of the finite-ensemble average transitions from μ to its $t \to \infty$ limit of $\mu - \sigma^2/2$. For finite N and t, we can estimate the value of the finite-ensemble average by thinking about what dominates the average. At early times in the process, all trajectories are close together and none dominates the finite-ensemble average. However, as time goes by the distribution broadens exponentially. Since each trajectory contributes with the same $1/N$ weight to the finite-ensemble average, we speculate that after some time the finite-ensemble average will be dominated by the maximum in the sample, *i.e.*

$$\langle x(t)\rangle_N \approx \frac{1}{N}\max_{i=1}^{N}\{x_i(t)\}. \tag{8.54}$$

This speculation is consistent with the numerical simulations in Fig. 8.5.

The maximum (or minimum) of a sample of realisations of a random variable is a central object of study in extreme-value theory. Of course, the maximum is itself a random variable, since it depends on the realisations of the members of the sample. In our case, we can write

$$x_i(t) = x(0)\exp\left[\left(\mu - \frac{\sigma^2}{2}\right)t + \sigma t^{1/2}\xi_i\right] \tag{8.55}$$

where $\xi_i \sim \mathcal{N}(0,1)$ are standard normal variates. Noting that this is monotonic in ξ_i converts the problem of finding the largest $x_i(t)$ to that of finding the largest in a sample of N standard normal variates. In the large-N limit, this follows a *Gumbel distribution* with expectation value,

$$\left\langle \max_{i=1}^{N}\{\xi_i\}\right\rangle \approx \sqrt{2\ln N}, \tag{8.56}$$

to leading order in N. We quote this result without proof. Further details, including a more complete parametrisation of the limiting distribution, can be found in [18, Chapter 3].

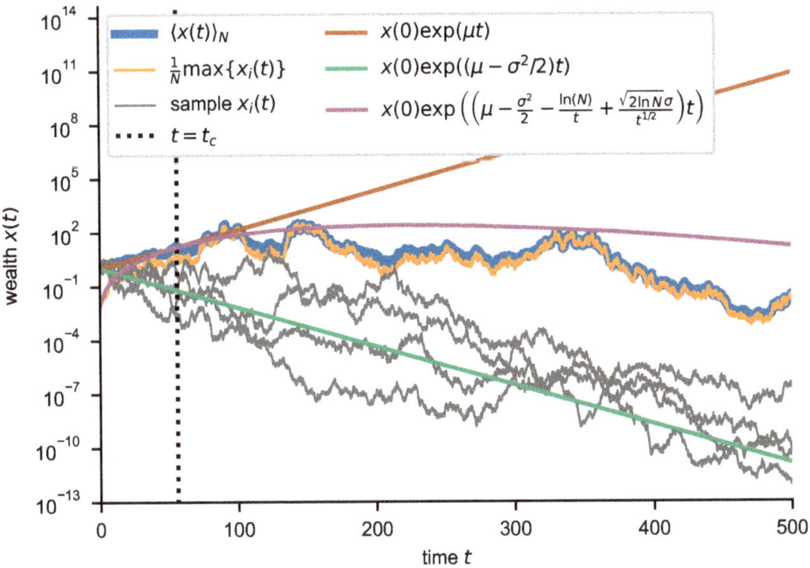

Figure 8.5: A finite ensemble of GBM trajectories. **Blue line:** finite-ensemble average $\langle x(t)\rangle_N$. **Yellow line:** contribution of the maximum value of any trajectory at time t to the finite-ensemble average. **Grey lines:** randomly chosen trajectories – any typical trajectory soon grows at the time-average growth rate. **Dotted line:** Critical time – for $t > t_c = \frac{2\ln N}{\sigma^2}$ the maximum begins to dominate the finite-ensemble average (the yellow line approaches the blue line). **Red line:** expectation value $\langle x(t)\rangle$. **Pink line:** finite-ensemble average, growing at rate $g_N(t)$, second line in (Eq. 8.59). **Green line:** exponential growth at the time-average growth rate. In the $t \to \infty$ limit all trajectories grow at this rate. **Parameters:** $N = 256$, $x(0) = 1$, $\mu = 0.05$, $\sigma^2 = 0.2$ (wealth and time units arbitrary).

Inserting this result for standard normal variates back into our expression for $x_i(t)$ yields the approximation

$$\langle x(t)\rangle_N \approx \frac{x(0)}{N}\exp\left[\left(\mu-\frac{\sigma^2}{2}\right)t+\sqrt{2\ln N}\sigma t^{1/2}\right], \tag{8.57}$$

which we expect to hold outside the self-averaging regime, *i.e.* when $t > t_c$. Note that the first term in the exponent dominates as $t \to \infty$, so the growth rate tends to that of a single trajectory, $\mu - \sigma^2/2$, as we have argued it must.

We now have two approximations, (Eq. 8.52) and (Eq. 8.57), for the finite-ensemble average in and out of the self-averaging regime. We can express these as approximations of the growth rate, $g_N(t)$, of a finite-ensemble average of size N after time t:

$$g_N(t) = \frac{\ln\langle x(t)\rangle_N - \ln\langle x(0)\rangle_N}{t-0} \tag{8.58}$$

$$\approx \begin{cases} \mu, & 0 < t < t_c; \\ \mu - \frac{\sigma^2}{2} - \frac{\ln N}{t} + \frac{\sqrt{2\ln N}\sigma}{t^{1/2}}, & t > t_c. \end{cases} \tag{8.59}$$

The pink line in Fig. 8.5 shows this to be a good approximation of the growth rate of the finite-ensemble average.

Chapter 9

Interactions

9.1 Cooperation

We have seen that fluctuations reduce time average growth rates in multiplicative growth. Consider two stochastic processes following GBM with the same drift parameter, μ, but with different volatilities, $\sigma_1 < \sigma_2$. Although their expectation values grow at the same rate, μ, the time average growth rates of their individual trajectories are different,

$$\mu - \frac{\sigma_1^2}{2} > \mu - \frac{\sigma_2^2}{2}. \tag{9.1}$$

The process with the lower volatility will outgrow the process with the higher volatility almost surely over long time.

For this reason it is desirable to reduce the size of fluctuations. One protocol that achieves this is pooling and sharing of resources. In Sec. 8.1 we explored the world created by a model of independent GBMs,

$$dx_i = x_i \left(\mu dt + \sigma dW_i\right) \tag{9.2}$$

for $i = 1 \dots N$. This is a world in which everybody experiences the same long-run growth rate and nobody interacts. Here we explore the effect of cooperation, by which we mean specifically the sharing of resources. It turns out that cooperation increases long-run growth rates by reducing volatility. This is a crucial insight which, we believe, goes a long way to explaining why we see so much cooperative structure in society and, more generally, in nature.

This ubiquity of cooperation may, at first glance, seem puzzling. The better-off member of a cooperating pair must voluntarily relinquish something of value to the worse-off member to maintain the cooperative pact. So, if pure generosity is an unsatisfactory explanation of cooperation, we must expose the advantage – in the form of faster growth – derived by the better-off member in such an arrangement.

We will start with an illustration of our model in the form of a fable about farmers who pool and share their grain. Marc Elsberg devised this story with us for his economics thriller *Greed* [17]. An interactive version of the fable is available online at `https://www.farmersfable.org`. We will then present our mathematical model, GBM with a pooling and sharing mechanism [51].

9.1.1 Farmers' fable

Imagine two farmers, Ann and Bill. Both have plenty of land to grow crops, but conditions vary from year to year and from farm to farm. We follow their fortunes over two harvests, first assuming that each works independently and then assuming that they pool and share their grain equally after each harvest.

We denote Ann's and Bill's grain holdings respectively by $x_A(t)$ and $x_B(t)$ in the non-cooperative case and by $y_A(t)$ and $y_B(t)$ in the cooperative case. Time t is measured in harvests. In both cases, each farmer starts with 100kg of grain. Conditions in the first growth season are good for Ann, who triples her grain, but meagre for Bill, who breaks even. In the second season, their fortunes are reversed. Let's see how they get on:

> As independent farmers
>
> Both Ann and Bill triple their grain over the two harvests, $x_A(2) = x_B(2) = 300$kg. See Fig. 9.1, left panel.
>
> As a cooperative
>
> Ann and Bill share their grain after each harvest. After the first harvest, Ann's 300kg and Bill's 100kg give them 200kg each, $y_A(1) = y_B(1) = 200$kg. Next season, both farmers sow their grain and realise the same growth factors as they did without cooperation, nature being unaffected by their pact. Ann breaks even and keeps her 200kg of grain, while Bill triples his grain to 600kg. They pool and share again, and each ends up with $y_A(2) = y_B(2) = 400$kg. See Fig. 9.1, right panel.

The agreement to pool and share after each harvest leads to an end wealth of each partner of 400kg of grain, rather than the 300kg they achieve without the pact. The extra 100kg is the per-person *cooperation benefit.*

Cooperative behaviour of this type is common in humans. There are real-life versions of this fable: farming cooperatives. Real farmers have known about the cooperation benefit for a long time. In the mediaeval practice of *land scattering*, peasants held several separate plots of land in preference to one large plot [36]. This synthetic creation of many

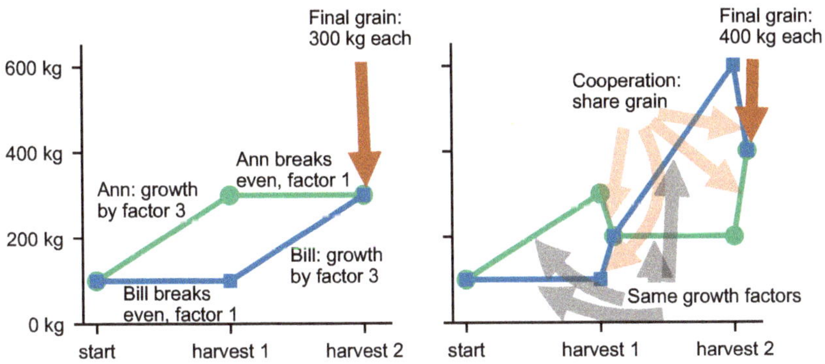

Figure 9.1: The *cooperation benefit*. **Left:** farmers Ann and Bill grow crops independently. There is no difference in skill or quality of land but, by sheer luck, Ann's first season goes well and her second season less well. For Bill the sequence is reversed. Both turn 100kg of grain into 300kg after two harvests. **Right:** Ann and Bill agree to pool and share their grain after each harvest. While grain is conserved in the sharing phase, the growth phase introduces a non-zero-sum element. Under the same environmental conditions, each farmer turns 100kg of grain into 400kg, achieving a cooperation benefit of 100kg each.

'Anns' and 'Bills' within a single farmer's ownership is a direct real-world application of the fable and persists among subsistence farmers to this day.

Nor is cooperation the preserve of humans. Life exists not as minimal self-reproducing chemical units, but as cells, organisms, families, herds, companies, institutions, nations, and so on. Cooperation is ubiquitous in nature, and what we see in nature is what has survived. In our model, entities which grow their resources at the highest time average growth rate will come to dominate their environment over time. Therefore, strategies which increase $\mu - \sigma^2/2$, regardless of their effect on μ, confer an evolutionary advantage.

9.1.2 Model

We return to the familiar setting of people and wealth, though feel free to replace 'people' by 'cells,' 'organisms,' 'herds,' 'nations' and so on; and 'wealth' by 'resources,' 'food,' 'biomass,' and so on. *Cooperation* occurs in many domains and at many scales.

The situation we imagine is as follows. N people decide to meet up periodically, put all their money on a table, divide it into N equal amounts, and then go back to their business of making wealth follow GBM. How does this arrangement alter their wealth dynamics?

Our baseline is N non-cooperating people. Let $x_i(t)$ be the wealth of non-cooperator i at time t and consider a discretised version of (Eq. 9.2),

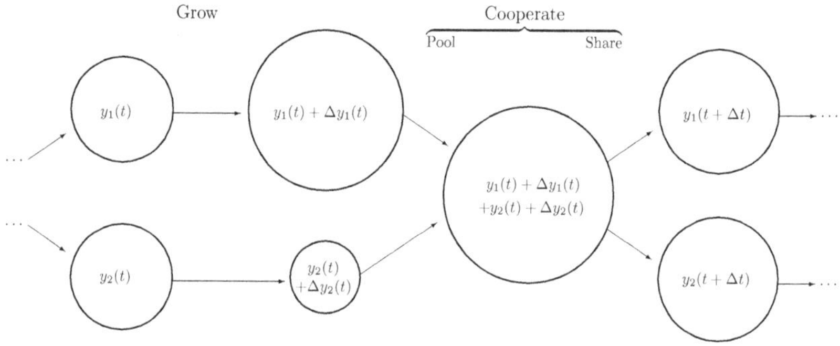

Figure 9.2: Cooperation dynamics. Two cooperators start each time step with the same wealth. Then they grow independently according to (Eq. 9.6). Then they cooperate by pooling their wealth and sharing it equally, according to (Eq. 9.7). Then the next time step begins.

such as would be used in a numerical simulation. Wealths grow according to

$$\Delta x_i = x_i(t)\left(\mu \Delta t + \sigma \Delta W_i\right), \tag{9.3}$$
$$x_i(t + \Delta t) = x_i(t) + \Delta x_i, \tag{9.4}$$

where $\Delta W_i \sim \mathcal{N}(0, \Delta t)$ are discrete Wiener increments, realised independently across individuals and over time.

Now we add the *pooling* and *sharing* mechanism, summarised pictorially for $N = 2$ in Fig. 9.2. The previously independent people start to cooperate. We denote the wealths of the cooperators by $y_i(t)$ to distinguish them from the wealths, $x_i(t)$, of the equivalent non-cooperators. For simplicity we assume equal sharing of wealth,

$$y_i(t) = y^{(N)}(t) \tag{9.5}$$

for all $i = 1 \dots N$, where $y^{(N)}(t)$ denotes the per-person wealth of N equal cooperators.

We treat each discrete time step as having two phases. First there is a growth phase, analogous to (Eq. 9.3), in which each cooperator increases their wealth by an amount

$$\Delta y_i = y^{(N)}(t)\left(\mu \Delta t + \sigma \Delta W_i\right). \tag{9.6}$$

This is followed by a cooperation phase, replacing (Eq. 9.4), in which wealth is pooled and shared equally among the cooperators,

$$y^{(N)}(t + \Delta t) = \frac{1}{N} \sum_{i=1}^{N} \left(y^{(N)}(t) + \Delta y_i\right) = y^{(N)}(t) + \frac{1}{N} \sum_{i=1}^{N} \Delta y_i. \tag{9.7}$$

Equation (9.7) is equivalent to equal sharing of the sum of the individual increments, *i.e.*

$$\Delta y^{(N)} = \frac{1}{N} \sum_{i=1}^{N} \Delta y_i. \tag{9.8}$$

We note that cooperation has no *cost* in our model. In reality, sharing requires coordination, which is seldom free. For example, human societies have administrative systems to redistribute goods and services, and land scatterers would have borne the costs of coordinating their work across several plots. Such costs may be large enough to make cooperation disadvantageous. If desired, costs could be included as a negative term proportional to Δt in (Eq. 9.8).

Nor do we consider the problem of *defection*. We assume our cooperators are unable to leave the cooperative, although we will discuss later when doing so would be beneficial.

Substituting (Eq. 9.6) into (Eq. 9.8) yields the dynamic followed by the wealth of each cooperator,

$$\Delta y^{(N)} = y^{(N)}(t) \left(\mu \Delta t + \frac{\sigma}{N} \sum_{i=1}^{N} \Delta W_i \right). \tag{9.9}$$

The key insight comes from simplifying the final term. The sum of independent normal increments is itself normal. Therefore, we can define a single normal increment,

$$\Delta W^{(N)} \equiv \frac{1}{\sqrt{N}} \sum_{i=1}^{N} \Delta W_i \sim \mathcal{N}(0, \Delta t), \tag{9.10}$$

with the same distribution as the individual increments. Inserting this back into (Eq. 9.9) yields

$$\Delta y^{(N)} = y^{(N)}(t) \left(\mu \Delta t + \frac{\sigma}{\sqrt{N}} \Delta W^{(N)} \right), \tag{9.11}$$

showing that the net effect of N individual fluctuations, pooled and shared, is a single fluctuation whose amplitude is reduced by a factor $1/\sqrt{N}$ compared to that of the individual fluctuations. In other words, *cooperation reduces volatility.*

Letting the time increment $\Delta t \to 0$ produces a stochastic differential equation of the same form as (Eq. 9.2), but with the volatility reduced from σ to $\sigma/\sqrt{N}$:

$$dy^{(N)} = y^{(N)} \left(\mu dt + \frac{\sigma}{\sqrt{N}} dW^{(N)} \right). \tag{9.12}$$

The effect of this volatility reduction on the time average growth rate of wealth provides our answer to the cooperation conundrum, as we shall now show.

Solution of the cooperation puzzle

The expectation values of the wealth of a non-cooperator, $\langle x_1(t)\rangle$, and the corresponding cooperator, $\langle y_1(t)\rangle$, with the same initial wealth, $x_1(0)$, are identical: $x_1(0)\exp(\mu t)$. From this perspective there is no incentive to cooperate. Moreover, immediately after the growth phase, (Eq. 9.6), the better-off member of a cooperating pair, say $y_1(0) > y_2(0)$, could increase its future expectation value from $[(y_1(0) + y_2(0))/2]\exp(\mu t)$ to $y_1(0)\exp(\mu t)$ by breaking the cooperative pact. From this perspective, cooperation looks pointless and fragile, and its frequent observation seems puzzling.

However, a central claim in EE is that people are more concerned about the time-average growth rate of their wealth than the growth rate of their expected wealth. We know that the wealth of a non-cooperator grows at $\overline{g} = \mu - \sigma^2/2$ in the long run. Under cooperative dynamics, (Eq. 9.12), the volatility decreases to $\sigma/\sqrt{N}$ and the time average growth rate increases to

$$\overline{g}^{(N)} = \mu - \frac{\sigma^2}{2N}. \tag{9.13}$$

So, for non-zero volatility, cooperators grow faster than non-cooperators. The premium increases with the number of cooperators as

$$\overline{g}^{(N)} - \overline{g} = \frac{\sigma^2}{2}\left(1 - \frac{1}{N}\right), \tag{9.14}$$

implying that larger cooperatives are favoured over smaller ones. Note that this growth rate premium increases most rapidly when N is small, from individuals, to pairs, to triplets. As the cooperative expands, the benefit gained by adding each new member diminishes.

In the world created by our model, cooperators will eventually dominate the environment and cooperation will become ubiquitous. The effect is illustrated in Fig. 9.3 by direct simulation of (Eq. 9.3)–(Eq. 9.4) and (Eq. 9.6)–(Eq. 9.7). Even without effects of specialisation or the emergence of new function, cooperation pays in the long run.[1]

Note that $\overline{g}^{(N)}$ in (Eq. 9.13) approaches the growth rate of the ensemble average wealth of a non-cooperator as N grows large,

$$\lim_{N\to\infty} \overline{g}^{(N)} = \mu. \tag{9.15}$$

The red dashed line in Fig. 9.3 shows the evolution of this ensemble average wealth. It bears little resemblance to the wealths of non-cooperators (green) and members of small cooperatives (blue). Indeed, (Eq. 9.15) exposes the expectation value, which grows at μ, to be a fiction in which

[1] An interactive app, to explore the effects of cooperation on different time scales and sizes of cooperatives, is available at https://ergodicityeconomics.com/2023/08/29/for-to-withhold-is-to-perish/

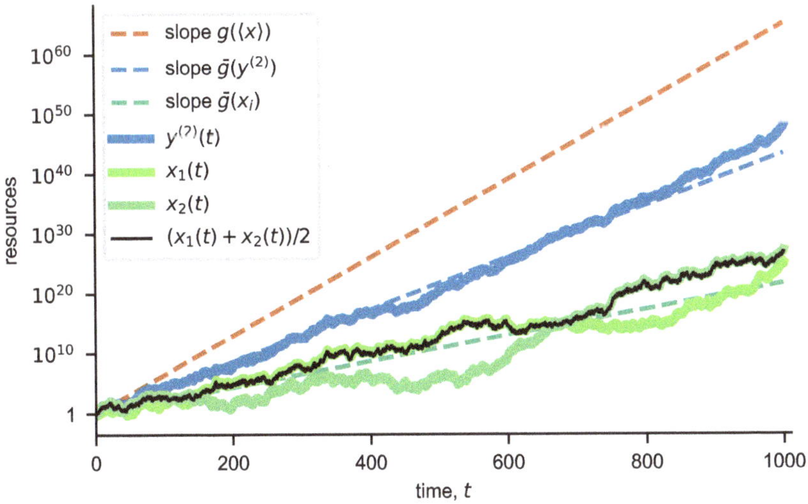

Figure 9.3: Simulated trajectories for two non-cooperators (green) and the corresponding cooperators (blue) on a logarithmic vertical scale. Over time, noise reduction for cooperators leads to faster growth. The thin black line shows the average wealth of the non-cooperators, which is far less than the wealth of each cooperator. In a literal mathematical sense, the whole, $y_1(t) + y_2(t)$, is more than the sum of its parts, $x_1(t) + x_2(t)$. The red dashed line grows at the ensemble average growth rate, which is the growth rate in the limit of infinitely many cooperators. **Parameters:** $\mu = 0.15$ per time unit; $\sigma^2 = 0.2$ per time unit; $\Delta t = 0.1$ time units. Noise realisations in the growth phases – (Eq. 9.3) for non-cooperators and (Eq. 9.6) for cooperators – were kept identical to prevent differences in outcomes arising by chance alone.

all the cooperation that could possibly happen has happened already. It follows that judging cooperation by its effect on ensemble average wealth leads to the conclusion that it is, at best, futile. Of course, this conclusion is misleading when we ask why individuals may be cooperating: *the ensemble average is irrelevant to individuals.*

Idiosyncratic parameters

Real cooperatives have members of *differing abilities* as well as differing fortunes. The latter we model already as different realisations of the noise in (Eq. 9.2). The former we can treat by generalising (Eq. 9.2) so that individuals have idiosyncratic drifts and volatilities, *i.e.*

$$dx_i = x_i\left(\mu_i dt + \sigma_i dW_i\right) \tag{9.16}$$

for $i = 1 \ldots N$. The individual time average growth rates, $\overline{g}_i = \mu_i - \sigma_i^2/2$, are now idiosyncratic. Some people, if left to their own devices, will grow their wealth faster than others. This raises questions. Out of sheer self-interest, should leaders share with laggards? When should a non-cooperator join a cooperating group? When should the group allow it?

We repeat the protocol of growing and then pooling and sharing. This creates a modified dynamic,

$$\begin{aligned} \Delta y^{(N)} &= y^{(N)}(t)\left(\frac{1}{N}\sum_{i=1}^{N}\mu_i\Delta t + \frac{1}{N}\sum_{i=1}^{N}\sigma_i\Delta W_i\right) \\ &= y^{(N)}(t)\left(\mu^{(N)}\Delta t + \sigma^{(N)}\Delta W^{(N)}\right), \end{aligned} \tag{9.17}$$

where $\Delta W^{(N)} \sim \mathcal{N}(0, \Delta t)$ is the effective Wiener increment in (Eq. 9.10) and

$$\mu^{(N)} \equiv \frac{1}{N}\sum_{i=1}^{N}\mu_i, \quad \sigma^{(N)} \equiv \frac{1}{N}\sqrt{\sum_{i=1}^{N}\sigma_i^2} \tag{9.18}$$

are effective drift and volatility parameters. Therefore, the wealths of the cooperators evolve according to

$$dy^{(N)} = y^{(N)}\left(\mu^{(N)}dt + \sigma^{(N)}dW^{(N)}\right), \tag{9.19}$$

with time average growth rate,

$$\overline{g}^{(N)} = \mu^{(N)} - \frac{(\sigma^{(N)})^2}{2} = \frac{1}{N}\sum_{i=1}^{N}\left(\mu_i - \frac{\sigma_i^2}{2N}\right). \tag{9.20}$$

We can now answer our questions. Out of sheer self-interest, person j should remain in the cooperative if

$$\frac{1}{N}\sum_{i=1}^{N}\left(\mu_i - \frac{\sigma_i^2}{2N}\right) > \mu_j - \frac{\sigma_j^2}{2}. \tag{9.21}$$

Similarly, the cooperative should retain person j as a member if

$$\frac{1}{N}\sum_{i=1}^{N}\left(\mu_i - \frac{\sigma_i^2}{2N}\right) > \frac{1}{N-1}\sum_{\substack{i=1\\ i\neq j}}^{N}\left(\mu_i - \frac{\sigma_i^2}{2(N-1)}\right). \tag{9.22}$$

In real life, we interpret these conditions as saying that individuals motivated by nothing but self-interest can gain by being part of society even if they are unusually skillful; and that society can benefit from a broad and inclusive membership, from weak to strong.

Correlated fluctuations

A second generalisation concerns *correlations*. So far, fluctuations experienced by different people have been uncorrelated in our model: we have treated the dW_i in (Eq. 9.2) and the ΔW_i in (Eq. 9.3) onwards as independent random variables. In reality, cooperators are often localised spatially or connected socially, such that they experience similar environmental or economic conditions. By allowing ΔW_i and ΔW_j to be correlated at each time step, our model can be adapted to describe such situations.

Suppose the $\Delta W_i \sim \mathcal{N}(0, \Delta t)$ realised from t to $t + \Delta t$ are jointly normal and cross-correlated such that $\langle \Delta W_i \Delta W_j \rangle = \rho_{ij}\Delta t$. We assume for simplicity that

$$\rho_{ij} = \begin{cases} 1, & i = j, \\ \rho, & i \neq j, \end{cases} \tag{9.23}$$

i.e. fluctuations for all pairs of people have the same covariance, $\rho\Delta t$. The more general case of a covariance matrix with unequal off-diagonal elements is also solvable, but adds complexity without illumination.

The presence of cross-correlations alters the evaluation of the sum of the normal variates in (Eq. 9.9). We have now

$$\sum_{i=1}^{N} \Delta W_i \sim \mathcal{N}(0, N\Delta t + N(N-1)\rho\Delta t). \tag{9.24}$$

Positive variance requires $-1/(N-1) \leq \rho \leq 1$, meaning that perfect anticorrelation can exist for $N = 2$ only and that anticorrelation becomes impossible as $N \to \infty$. Equation (9.24) suggests defining, analogously to (Eq. 9.10), an effective Wiener increment,

$$\Delta W^{(N)} \equiv \frac{1}{\sqrt{N + N(N-1)\rho}} \sum_{i=1}^{N} \Delta W_i \sim \mathcal{N}(0, \Delta t). \tag{9.25}$$

The change in $y^{(N)}(t)$ can be written as

$$\Delta y^{(N)} = y^{(N)}(t)\left(\mu\Delta t + \sigma\sqrt{\frac{1+(N-1)\rho}{N}}\,\Delta W^{(N)}\right), \tag{9.26}$$

analogous to (Eq. 9.11) in the uncorrelated case.

Without correlations, cooperation reduces the amplitude of fluctuations from σ to $\sigma/\sqrt{N}$. With them, the fluctuation amplitude becomes

$$\sigma_{\text{corr}} \equiv \sigma\sqrt{\frac{1+(N-1)\rho}{N}}. \tag{9.27}$$

McCloskey [36] obtains the same expression for the variance of the annual yield of peasant farmers with scattered plots, as does Winterhalder [70] for teams of foragers sharing food.

Let us explore the dependence of σ_{corr} on ρ and N. Firstly, as a consistency check, we note that $\sigma_{\text{corr}} \to \sigma/\sqrt{N}$ as $\rho \to 0$ for fixed N, recovering the uncorrelated result in the appropriate limit.

For all $N > 1$, we have $0 \leq \sigma_{\text{corr}} \leq \sigma$, with $\sigma_{\text{corr}} = \sigma$ if and only if $\rho = 1$. In other words, provided fluctuations are not perfectly correlated, a cooperation benefit always exists. This makes intuitive sense. With perfect correlation, all the ΔW_i are identical and sharing achieves nothing. The cooperative is equivalent to a giant individual following a single trajectory of (Eq. 9.2). As soon as some variation is introduced between the fluctuations of individual wealths, the cooperation mechanism can begin to mitigate the negative effect of this variation on growth.

Furthermore, in the $N \to \infty$ limit we have $\sigma_{\text{corr}} \to \sigma\sqrt{\rho}$ with $\rho \geq 0$. The maximum time average growth rate achievable by adding cooperators is, therefore,

$$\lim_{N\to\infty} \overline{g}^{(N)} = \mu - \frac{\sigma^2\rho}{2}, \tag{9.28}$$

cf. (Eq. 9.15). This cannot exceed μ and decreases as ρ increases. Again, this matches intuition: as fluctuations become more correlated, the variation between them diminishes and the scope for beneficial cooperation narrows. In our setup, cooperation is more useful when there is *diversity* in individual outcomes. A corollary is that forms of cooperation which suppress diversity could be self-defeating.

Of course, cooperation need not be total. Another generalisation of our model is to partial cooperation, where people share only a fraction of their wealth, resembling taxation and redistribution in human societies. We discuss this now.

9.2 Reallocation

In Sec. 8.1 we created a model world of independent trajectories of GBM. We studied how the distribution of the resulting random variables evolved over time. We saw that this is a world of broadening distributions, increasing inequality, and wealth condensation.

We introduced cooperation in Sec. 9.1 and saw how this increases the time average growth rate for those who pool and share all of their resources. In this section we study what happens if a large number of individuals pool and share a fraction of their resources. This reminds us of taxation and redistribution in the real world, and more generally of interactions that couple individual wealths together: an employer paying an employee, a worker buying food at a supermarket co-owned by a pension fund, co-owned by a retiree. We call this general coupling *reallocation*, and we call the corresponding model reallocating geometric Brownian motion (RGBM).

We find that sufficiently fast reallocation from richer to poorer in a large population has two effects. First, everyone's wealth grows in the long run at a rate close to that of the ensemble average. Second, the distribution of rescaled wealth converges over time to a stable form. This means that, although wealth can be distributed very unequally, wealth condensation and the divergence of inequality no longer occur in this model. Of course, for this to be an interesting finding, we must quantify what we mean by "sufficiently fast reallocation".

We also find that no stable rescaled wealth distribution exists when reallocation is too slow or, in particular, when it goes from poorer to richer, which we label as negative reallocation. In the latter case, the population splits into groups with positive and negative wealths, whose magnitudes grow exponentially.

Finally, having understood how our model behaves in each of these regimes, we fit the model parameters to historical wealth data from the real world, specifically the US. This tells us which type of model behaviour best describes the dynamics of the US wealth distribution over the last 100 years. You might find the results surprising – we certainly did!

9.2.1 The ergodic hypothesis in economics

Of course, we are not the first to study resource distributions in economics. The topic has a long history, going back at least to Vilfredo Pareto's work [43] of the late 19th century, when he introduced the power-law distribution we discussed in Sec. 8.1.6. It is worth spending a few moments to consider how the subject is treated classically, before we say how we do it.

Typically, economists model the distribution of wealth (or of income) assuming it converges over time to a unique and stable form, regardless of initial conditions. This allows them to study the stable distribution and ignore the transient phenomena preceding it, which are far harder to analyse. Paul Samuelson called this assumption the "*ergodic hypothesis*"

[60, pp. 11-12]. Not in a strict mathematical sense – Samuelson was an economist – but "in analogy to the use of this term in statistical mechanics," as he put it.

Economics is often concerned with growing quantities, which cannot be ergodic because their distributions never stabilise. Doesn't this imply that the ergodic hypothesis is never valid? Well, not quite. Under GBM, for example, we found that whereas wealth x is not ergodic, the multiplicative growth rate is ergodic. Even in non-ergodic processes, there may be transformations of the process which are ergodic.

The transformation used most in the present context is that from wealth to rescaled wealth, whose definition in (Eq. 8.35) we recall here:

$$w_i(t) \equiv \frac{x_i(t)}{\langle x_i(t) \rangle_N}. \tag{9.29}$$

The hope is that this operation, which scales out the growth of the total wealth, will make rescaled wealth ergodic. We know this does not work in GBM because, as we saw in Sec. 8.1.5, rescaled wealth has an ever-broadening lognormal distribution in that model. And we have already said that it works in RGBM only when reallocation is sufficiently fast. This suggests it is *unwise to assume rescaled wealth is ergodic* in a model without checking that it is true for parameter values consistent with real data. For example, we would be foolish to make the ergodic hypothesis in RGBM unless we knew that reallocation rates fitted to data were always in the "sufficiently fast" category.

Surprisingly, to us at least, the ergodic hypothesis is routinely made without test in studies of resource distributions in the economics literature. We could not find a single example where the assumption was validated empirically. This means that the ergodic hypothesis is effectively "baked in" to mainstream models of inequality, regardless of whether it is realistic.

9.2.2 Reallocating geometric Brownian motion

Our model, RGBM, is a system of N individuals whose wealths, $x_i(t)$, evolve according to the SDE,

$$dx_i = x_i \left[(\mu - \tau)dt + \sigma dW_i\right] + \tau \langle x \rangle_N \, dt. \tag{9.30}$$

In effect, we have added to GBM a simple reallocation mechanism. Over a small time step, δt, each individual pays a fixed proportion of its wealth, $\tau x_i \delta t$, into a central pot ("contributes to society") and gets back an equal share of the pot, $\tau \langle x \rangle_N \delta t$, ("benefits from society"). We can think of this as applying a wealth tax, say of 1% per year, to everyone's wealth and then redistributing the tax revenues equally. Note that the reallocation parameter, τ, is, like μ, a rate with dimensions per unit time. Note also that when $\tau = 0$ we recover our old friend, GBM.

RGBM with positive reallocation is not a new model. Interestingly, at least three other groups of physicists arrived at it independently when attempting to model economic distributions [35, 12, 30]. This is no coincidence: RGBM is the simplest way to incorporate the two mechanisms – growth and reallocation – that seem most important in describing how resources are distributed in a population. It is usually a good sign when scientists asking the same questions arrive at substantially the same answers.

It is instructive to write (Eq. 9.30) as

$$dx_i = \underbrace{x_i(\mu dt + \sigma dW_i)}_{\text{Growth}} \; \underbrace{- \; \tau(x_i - \langle x \rangle_N)dt}_{\text{Reallocation}}. \tag{9.31}$$

This exposes the importance of the sign of τ, highlighting that RGBM with positive τ is nothing but GBM to which a mean-reversion term has been added. With negative τ, the extra term becomes mean-repelling. We discuss the two regimes in turn, and summarise them graphically in Fig. 9.4.

9.2.3 Positive reallocation

With positive τ, the reallocation term acts as a stabiliser on the relative-wealth distribution. To analyse its effects quantitatively, we first ask how much reallocation it takes for the finite-ensemble average, $\langle x_i(t) \rangle_N$, to be in the *self-averaging regime*, meaning

$$\langle x(t) \rangle_N \approx \langle x(t) \rangle = x(0) \exp(\mu t), \tag{9.32}$$

where we assume that everyone starts out at the same wealth, $x(0)$.

A rigorous derivation of the required reallocation rate, τ_c, is possible but difficult [11], and we will use an intuitive argument to get the right answer.

In Sec. 8.2.1 we presented arguments for why GBM is self-averaging for short time, and we found that "short time" means $t < t_c$, where $t_c = 2 \ln N / \sigma^2$. We can think of this as follows: t_c is the timescale over which the inequality-increasing effects of fluctuations drive wealths apart, such that a finite ensemble of wealths becomes dominated by a few trajectories.

Under RGBM, τ is the reallocation rate, so τ^{-1} is the reallocation timescale, *i.e.* the timescale over which the inequality-reducing effects of reallocation pull wealths together. If $\tau^{-1} > t_c$, then mean reversion is too slow to overcome the inequality-increasing effect of GBM. Conversely, if $\tau^{-1} < t_c$, then reallocation pulls wealths together more quickly than they get driven apart, continually 'resetting' the finite ensemble and

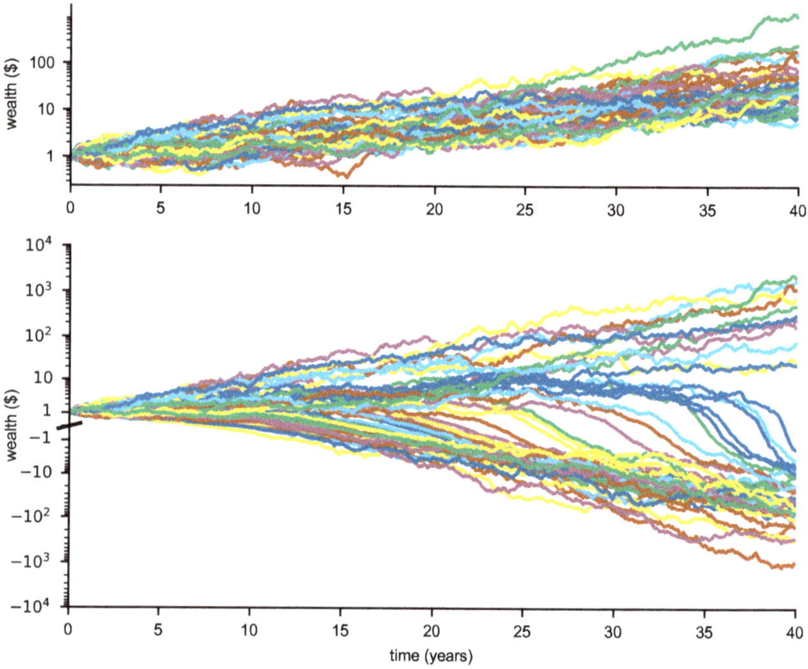

Figure 9.4: Regimes of RGBM. $\tau \approx 0$ separates the two regimes of RGBM. **Top:** for $\tau > 0$ (here 5% per year), a stable rescaled wealth distribution exists. **Bottom:** for $\tau < 0$ (here -5% per year), no stable rescaled wealth distribution exists, and wealths diverge away from the mean, both positively and negatively. The y-axis is scaled with the Yeo-Johnson function, a transformation which allows negative arguments and is otherwise similar to the logarithm. $N = 50$ trajectories are shown, using $\mu = 0.08$ year^{-1}, $\sigma = 0.25$ year$^{-1/2}$, $x_i(0) = \$1$.

maintaining self-averaging indefinitely. Converting this condition into one on the reallocation rate, we get

$$\tau > \tau_c \equiv \frac{\sigma^2}{2 \ln N}, \tag{9.33}$$

which is indeed the correct result.

For realistic parameter values, τ_c is small. Typical parameters for US wealth are $N = 10^8$ people and $\sigma = 0.2$ year$^{-1/2}$, giving $\tau_c = 0.1\%$ year^{-1}. Accounting for the uncertainty in these parameter values makes τ_c statistically indistinguishable from zero.

To good approximation, therefore, (Eq. 9.32) holds for $\tau > 0$. Self-averaging is useful to us because it means we can find rescaled wealth using the ensemble average, *i.e.*

$$w_i(t) = \frac{x_i(t)}{x(0)\exp(\mu t)}, \tag{9.34}$$

thus avoiding pesky finite-N effects.

In Sec. 8.1.5 we used Itô's formula to obtain the SDE for the rescaled wealth in GBM, (Eq. 8.40). Starting from (Eq. 9.34) and following the same procedure, we find the corresponding SDE for RGBM,

$$dw_i = \sigma w_i dW_i - \tau(w_i - 1)dt. \tag{9.35}$$

Note that the ensemble-average growth rate, μ, has been scaled out, just as it was in GBM.

Rather fortuitously, it is possible to find the asymptotic ($t \to \infty$) rescaled-wealth distribution generated by (Eq. 9.35). Equation (9.35) is an Itô equation with drift term $a_w = \tau(w - 1)$ and diffusion term $b_w = \sigma w$. Such SDEs are associated with second-order partial differential equations, called *Fokker-Planck equations*, which describe the evolution of the PDF, $\mathcal{P}(w,t)$. The probability density changes due to the action of the drift term (like advection in a fluid) and the diffusion term (like heat spreading). In this case, the Fokker-Planck equation is

$$\frac{\partial}{\partial t}\mathcal{P}(w,t) = \frac{\partial}{\partial w}[a_w \mathcal{P}(w,t)] + \frac{1}{2}\frac{\partial^2}{\partial w^2}[{b_w}^2 \mathcal{P}(w,t)]. \tag{9.36}$$

The asymptotic distribution is found by requiring the Fokker-Planck equation to be in a steady state, which we achieve by setting the time derivative to zero. This produces the ODE,

$$\frac{\sigma^2}{2}\frac{d^2}{dw^2}(w^2\mathcal{P}) + \tau\frac{d}{dw}[(w-1)\mathcal{P}] = 0. \tag{9.37}$$

Positive wealth following multiplicative dynamics with non-negative reallocation in continuous time can never reach zero, so we apply the boundary condition $\mathcal{P}(0) = 0$. Under this condition, (Eq. 9.37) has solution

$$\mathcal{P}(w) = \frac{(\zeta - 1)^\zeta}{\Gamma(\zeta)} e^{-\frac{\zeta - 1}{w}} w^{-(1+\zeta)}, \tag{9.38}$$

where

$$\zeta = 1 + \frac{2\tau}{\sigma^2} \tag{9.39}$$

and $\Gamma(\zeta) = \int_0^\infty s^{\zeta-1}e^{-s}ds$ is the gamma function.[2]

The distribution (Eq. 9.38) is called the *inverse gamma distribution.* It has a power-law tail as $w \to \infty$, like (Eq. 8.43) in Sec. 8.1.6. This is reminiscent of Pareto's oft-confirmed observation that the frequency of large wealths tends to decay as a power law [43], and indeed ζ is called the Pareto tail index and is sometimes used as a measure of inequality.

Equation (9.39) makes intuitive sense: the larger σ (more randomness in the returns) and the smaller τ (slower reallocation), the smaller the tail index ζ and the fatter the tail of the distribution (higher inequality). Fitted τ values give typical ζ values between 1 and 2, consistent with observed tail indices between 1.2 to 1.6, see [8, 7] for details. So, not only does RGBM with positive τ predict a realistic functional form for the distribution of rescaled wealth, but also it admits fitted parameter values which match observed tails.

9.2.4 Negative reallocation

For negative reallocation, or reallocation from poor to rich, $\tau < 0$, the model exhibits *mean-repulsion* rather than reversion. The ergodic hypothesis is invalid and no stable rescaled wealth distribution exists. The population splits into those above the finite-ensemble average and those below it. Whereas in RGBM with positive reallocation (from rich to poor, $\tau > 0$), it is impossible for positive wealth to turn negative, negative reallocation leads to negative wealth. No longer is total economic wealth a limit to the wealth of the richest individual because the poorest develop large negative wealth. The wealth of the rich in the population increases exponentially away from the finite-ensemble average, and the wealth of the poor becomes negative and exponentially large in magnitude, see Fig. 9.4 (bottom panel).

Such splitting of the population is a common feature of non-ergodic processes. If rescaled wealth were an ergodic process, then individuals would, over long enough time, experience all parts of its distribution. People would spend 99% of their time as "the 99 percent" and 1% of their time as "the 1 percent." The *social mobility* implied by models that assume ergodicity may not exist in reality.

9.2.5 Fitting US wealth data

We have introduced the RGBM model and understood its basic properties. It is a simple model of an interacting population of noisy multiplica-

[2] As an exercise, you can verify this by substituting (Eq. 9.38) for $\mathcal{P}$ in (Eq. 9.37) and carrying out the differentiations.

tive growers. We expect it to be more realistic than GBM, $\tau = 0$, because we know that real people interact. In particular, large populations have, over centuries, developed public institutions and infrastructure, to which everyone contributes and from which everyone benefits. Therefore, we might anticipate that RGBM with positive τ will fit real wealth data better than GBM or, indeed, better than RGBM with negative τ.

If this is true and if associated convergence times are shorter than the timescales of policy changes, then the ergodic hypothesis applied in the context of economic inequality will be justified. If not, then it will be an unwarranted constraint on models, potentially generating misleading analyses and conclusions.

We thus arrive at two related empirical questions. Are real data consistent with a stable rescaled wealth distribution in the model? In other words, would a model-fit to real data find a robustly positive reallocation rate τ? The related question is about time scales: how long would convergence to the asymptotic relative-wealth distribution take after a change of parameters? If, for example, our aim is to estimate the effect of a tax policy over the next election cycle then we will fail if the model indicates that convergence takes longer than all of human history. Therefore, treating a stable model distribution as representative of an empirical distribution implies an assumption not only of convergence but of fast convergence. As the late Tony Atkinson pointed out: "the speed of convergence makes a great deal of difference to the way in which we think about the model" [5].

In the following we will use the *relaxation time scale* $(\tau)^{-1}$ as an estimate for the time scale of convergence. There are many ways of quantifying convergence, namely by choosing a distance measure between a distribution and its asymptotic form. The choice of measure will somewhat affect the convergence time scale based on it, but in the context of the uncertainty in real data the details are not significant, and simply using $(\tau)^{-1}$ seems appropriate.

In [8, 7] we fit the RGBM model to historical wealth data from the US for the last hundred years. We won't include a full description of this empirical analysis here, since our main aim is to communicate how we think about problems and build models. However, since the results were, to us at least, rather shocking, we include a brief summary.

The basic setup is to fix the values of μ, σ, and N in our RGBM model using data about, respectively, aggregate economic growth, stock market volatility, and population size. Then we find, by numerical simulation of (Eq. 9.30), the time series of $\tau(t)$ values which best reproduces historical *wealth shares* in the US. The wealth share is a type of inequality measure. It is defined as the proportion of total wealth owned by the richest fraction of the population. So, for example, saying that "the 10%-wealth share is 50%" means that the richest 10% of the population own 50% of the total wealth. Reproducing the historical wealth shares is one way of reproducing the approximate level of inequality in the wealth distribution. Helpfully, economists Emmanuel Saez and Gabriel Zucman have estimated about a century's worth of wealth shares for the US in [58].

Fitting the model to these addresses our two main questions:

- Are fitted values of $\tau(t)$ robustly positive such that the ergodic hypothesis for rescaled wealth is consistent with US data?
- When $\tau(t) > 0$, is convergence to the stable distribution fast enough for it to be representative of the empirical distribution?

Figure 9.5 shows the results of fitting the RGBM model to the annual 1%-wealth share data in [58]. Because annual fluctuations are large and we are more interested in longer-term changes in reallocation driven by structural economic and political changes, we take a 10-year moving average (blue line). We also show the uncertainty in this moving average (grey envelope).

The take-home message is this: the fitted reallocation rate, $\tilde{\tau}_{1\%}(t)$, is not robustly positive over the last hundred years and, indeed, it is consistently negative – indicating net reallocation from poorer to richer – since the mid-1980s. Furthermore, even when reallocation is positive, associated convergence times are very long compared to times between policy changes – typically at least several decades, see Fig. 9.5 (bottom panel). This makes the answer to both our questions above a resounding "No!"

What shocked us most when we first encountered these results was the existence of long periods with negative reallocation. We began the analysis imagining that GBM was unrealistic because it has no positive-reallocation component. After all, we pay our taxes and use public services. We expected to see $\tau > 0$ and the only question in our minds was how large it would be. Instead we found that reallocation has been consistently negative in recent US history, not at all robustly positive. In our model, this corresponds to wealths being driven apart, populations splitting into groups with positive and negative wealths, and no convergence to a stable distribution of rescaled wealth.

In retrospect, perhaps we shouldn't have been so surprised. Qualitatively, our results echo the findings that the rich experience higher growth rates of their wealth than the poor [54, 71] and that the cumulative wealth of the poorest half of the American population has been negative in recent years [56, 65].

Important economic phenomena, such as *diverging wealth inequality*, social immobility, and the emergence of *negative wealth*, are difficult to reproduce in a model that assumes ergodicity. In our simple model, it is easy to see why: in the regime of ergodic relative wealth, with $\tau > 0$, our model cannot reproduce these phenomena at all. However, when

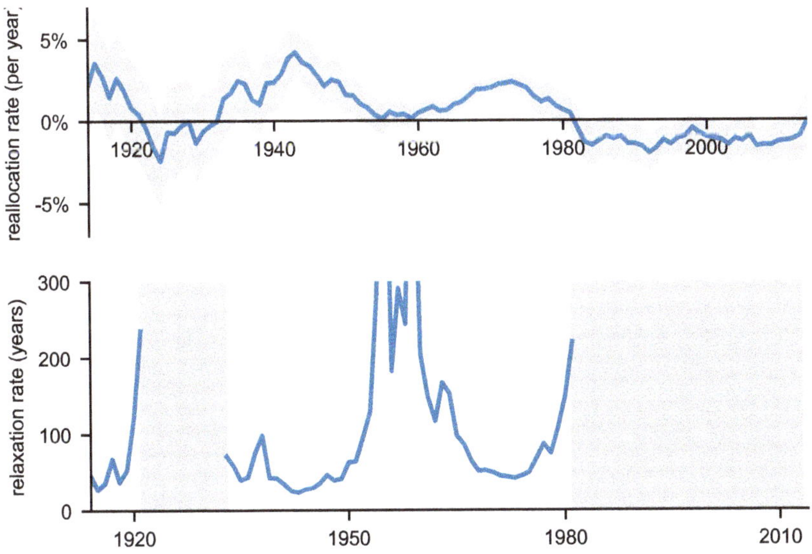

Figure 9.5: **Top:** effective reallocation rates, fitted using one-percent wealth shares. 10-year moving average, $\widetilde{\tau}_{1\%}(t)$ (blue line), with grey envelope indicating one standard error in the moving average. Fitting assumes $\mu = 0.021$ year^{-1} and $\sigma = 0.16$ year$^{-1/2}$. **Bottom:** inverse of top, estimated relaxation time $\widetilde{\tau}_{1\%}(t)^{-1}$. We interpret this as the time scale at which relative-wealth distributions converge to their asymptotic forms. The grey shaded areas indicate time periods when $\widetilde{\tau}_{1\%}(t) < 0$, the non-ergodic regime of RGBM where no stationary distribution for rescaled wealth exists. In these periods, the distribution never stabilises and the convergence time is undefined (or infinitely large).

we admit the possibility of non-ergodicity, $\tau \leq 0$, it becomes clear that these phenomena can emerge in an economy that does not actively guard against them.

Chapter 10

Markets

In this final chapter, we address a basic question about prices of freely traded assets: why do they fluctuate so much (or so little)? In the general spirit of ergodicity economics, we will eschew personality-type arguments and see how far we get with mechanistic reasoning only.

Consider the following gedankenexperiment: there are two banks, bank A offering to lend or borrow at 3% per annum, and bank B offering to lend or borrow at 5% per annum, without any restrictions on how much you can borrow or deposit. This situation seems unlikely because it violates a simple *stability* argument. If these imagined banks really existed, borrowing \$100 from bank A and depositing it in bank B would produce a \$2 annual profit, and of course doing the same with \$1,000,000,000 would give you \$20,000,000 per year. Presumably many people would notice this, and a torrent of cash would flow from bank A to bank B. In reality, this torrent would be so forceful that at least one of the banks would soon change its practices, or collapse.

We learn: two riskless investments providing returns at different rates cannot exist for long. Their combined existence is unstable. We will generalise this argument to risky investments. The riskless investments are a limiting case, namely the limit of volatility approaching zero. We will perturb away from this special limiting case and arrive at a *theory of noise*. The prices of freely traded assets whose expected values grow at different rates must fluctuate, for reasons of stability. We will make this statement quantitative, test it on real-world data, and find that stability alone explains much of the apparent trade-off between risk and return observed in financial markets.

Throughout the chapter, we will illustrate the concepts we develop with real data. As anyone who has worked with real data knows, the choices among data sets are limitless, and often compromises and judgement calls have to be made. We could have stuck to pure theory, but decided against it to illustrate the applicability of the theory to the real world. Where we quote numbers and show data, they are representative of many more analyses that we and others have performed. Nonetheless, we stress that the point of this chapter is to develop theory and analysis, and not a comprehensive description of financial markets. If actual numbers matter to you, we recommend applying our techniques to the data that interest you.

10.1 The portfolio selection problem

We will work with a model market where asset prices follow multiplicative dynamics, modelled by GBM. We do this not only because we have learned a lot about GBM in this book, but also because it is the canonical model of asset price evolution in the financial industry. In other words, the model is entirely standard, even if our perspective on it will be new.

An amount x invested in such an asset evolves according to the SDE,

$$dx = x(\mu dt + \sigma dW), \tag{10.1}$$

where μ is the drift and σ is the volatility. By now we are very familiar with this equation and how to solve it.

10.1.1 Riskless and risky assets

To keep things simple, we imagine a market of two assets. One asset is riskless: the growth in its value is known deterministically and comes with a cast-iron guarantee.[1] This might correspond in reality to a bank deposit. The other asset is risky: there is uncertainty over what its value will be in the future. This might correspond to a share in a company or to a stock index. We will think of it simply as stock.

An amount x_r invested in the *riskless asset* evolves according to

$$dx_r = x_r \mu_{\mathrm{r}} dt. \tag{10.2}$$

μ_{r} is the riskless drift, known in finance as the riskless rate of return. There is no volatility term. In effect, we have set $\sigma = 0$. We know with certainty what x_r will be at any point in the future:

$$x_r(t_0 + \Delta t) = x_r(t_0) \exp(\mu_{\mathrm{r}} \Delta t). \tag{10.3}$$

An amount x_s invested in the *risky asset* evolves according to

$$dx_s = x_s(\mu_{\mathrm{s}} dt + \sigma_{\mathrm{s}} dW), \tag{10.4}$$

[1]Such guarantees are easy to offer in a model. In the real world, one should be very suspicious of anything that comes with a "cast-iron guarantee".

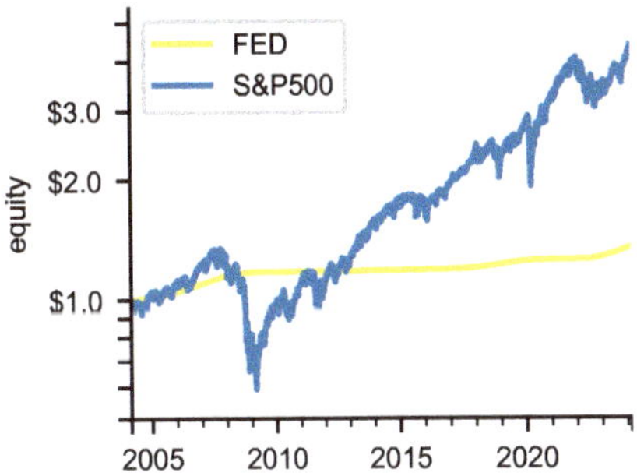

Figure 10.1: **Yellow:** 20-year performance of \$1 deposited at overnight FED interest rates (modelled as a riskless asset). **Blue:** 20-year performance of \$1 invested in the S&P500 (modelled as a risky asset).

where $\mu_\mathrm{s} > \mu_\mathrm{r}$ is the risky drift and $\sigma_\mathrm{s} > 0$ is the volatility (the subscript s stands for stock). μ_s is also known in finance as the expected return.[2] This equation has solution

$$x_s(t_0 + \Delta t) = x_s(t_0) \exp\left[\left(\mu_\mathrm{s} - \frac{{\sigma_\mathrm{s}}^2}{2}\right) \Delta t + \sigma_\mathrm{s} W(\Delta t)\right], \qquad (10.5)$$

which is a random variable.

We will refer to the difference

$$\mu_\mathrm{e} = \mu_\mathrm{s} - \mu_\mathrm{r} \qquad (10.6)$$

as the *excess drift*.

For a concrete example of what this setup is supposed to model, Fig. 10.1 shows the performance of \$1 deposited from 2004 till 2024 at the US effective federal funds rate (overnight) (FED) and that of \$1 invested in the S&P500 index (S&P500). These are two available investments (derivatives written on the value of the S&P500 make it a tradable asset) whose best-fit volatilities differ by orders of magnitude. The blue line in Fig. 10.1 fluctuates up and down violently, whereas the yellow line is much smoother.

10.1.2 Leverage

Let's turn to the concept of *leverage*. Imagine a very simple portfolio of value x_ℓ, out of which ℓx_ℓ is invested in stock and the remainder, $(1-\ell)x_\ell$, is put in the bank. ℓ is known as the leverage. It is the fraction of the total investment assigned to the risky asset. $\ell = 0$ corresponds to a portfolio consisting only of bank deposits. $\ell = 1$ corresponds to a portfolio only of stock.

You would be forgiven for thinking that prudence dictates $0 \leq \ell \leq 1$, *i.e.* that we invest some of our money in stock and keep the rest in the bank. However, the financial markets have found all sorts of exciting

[2] Probably because it's the growth rate of the expected value, see (Eq. 10.16).

ways for us to invest almost any amount in any asset. For example, we can make $\ell > 1$ by borrowing money from the bank to buy more stock than we could have bought with only our own money.[3] We can even make $\ell < 0$ by borrowing stock (a negative investment in the risky asset), selling it, and putting the money raised in the bank. In the financial world this practice is called *short selling.*

Each investment in our portfolio experiences the same relative fluctuations as the asset in which it has been made. The overall change in the portfolio's value is, therefore,

$$dx_\ell = (1-\ell)x_\ell \frac{dx_r}{x_r} + \ell x_\ell \frac{dx_s}{x_s}. \tag{10.7}$$

Substituting in (Eq. 10.2) and (Eq. 10.4) gives the SDE for an investment in a portfolio of leverage ℓ,

$$dx_\ell = x_\ell[(\mu_\mathrm{r} + \ell\mu_\mathrm{e})dt + \ell\sigma_\mathrm{s} dW], \tag{10.8}$$

with solution,

$$x_\ell(t_0+\Delta t) = x_\ell(t_0)\exp\left[\left(\mu_\mathrm{r} + \ell\mu_\mathrm{e} - \frac{\ell^2{\sigma_\mathrm{s}}^2}{2}\right)\Delta t + \ell\sigma_\mathrm{s} W(\Delta t)\right]. \tag{10.9}$$

When $\ell = 0$, x_ℓ follows the same evolution as x_r; and when $\ell = 1$, it evolves as x_s.

In our model, once ℓ is chosen, it is held constant over time. This means that our model portfolio must be *continuously rebalanced* to ensure that the ratio of stock to total investment stays fixed at ℓ. For example, imagine our stock investment fluctuates up a lot over a short time-step, while our bank deposit only accrues a little interest. Immediately we have slightly more than ℓ of the portfolio's value in stock, and slightly less than $1-\ell$ of its value in the bank. To return the leverage to ℓ, we need to sell a small amount of stock and deposit the proceeds in the bank, Fig. 10.2. In (Eq. 10.8) we are imagining that this happens continuously.

In reality, of course, that's not possible. In Fig. 10.3 we show the performance over almost 100 years of daily rebalanced S&P500-FED portfolios at different leverages.

We compute these performances via simple backtests. Specifically, a portfolio of leverage ℓ is backtested using two time series, $r_s(t)$ (risky returns) and $r_r(t)$ (returns on FED deposits) as illustrated in Fig. 10.2.

1. We start with equity of $x_\ell(t_0;\ell) = \$1$, consisting of $\$\ell$ in the risky asset and $\$(1-\ell)$ in bank deposits.

[3] This doesn't immediately affect the portfolio's value. The bank loan constitutes a negative investment in the riskless asset, whose value cancels the value of the stock we bought with it. Of course, the change in the portfolio's composition will affect its future value.

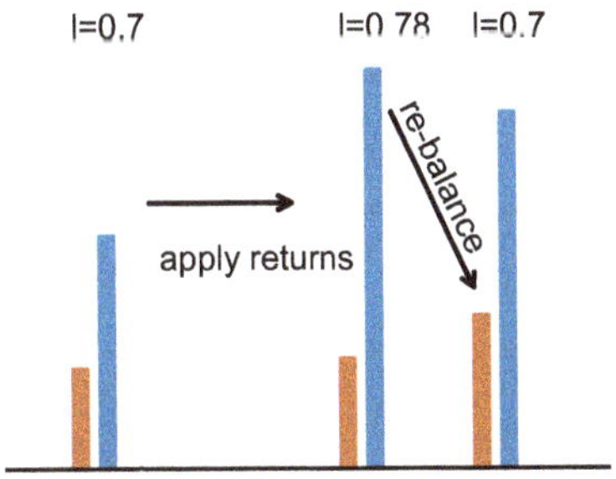

Figure 10.2: **Red:** investment in a riskless asset. **Blue:** investment in a risky asset. Leverage starts at $\ell = 0.7$, meaning 70% is invested in the risky asset, and 30% in the riskless. The investment then experiences the relative returns of the market. In this case the risky asset goes up quite a bit, and the riskless asset goes up less. Consequently, the leverage changes. To maintain a constant leverage, some risky asset has to be sold in return for some riskless, a step known as *rebalancing*.

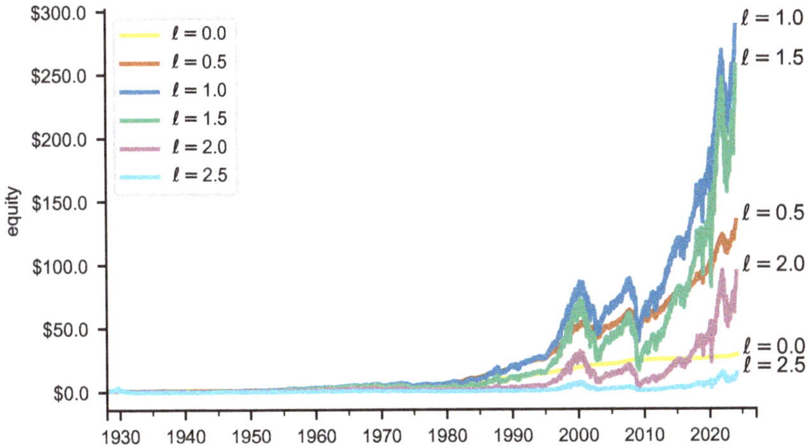

Figure 10.3: Equity in daily rebalanced portfolios consisting of S&P500 and FED at different leverages. Performance is shown from 31 December 1927 until 1 March 2024. Final equity is not monotonic in leverage, but peaks somewhere between leverage 0.5 and 1.5.

2. Each day the values of these holdings are updated according to the historical returns, so that

$$\begin{aligned} \ell x_\ell(t;\ell) &\rightarrow r_s(t)\ell x_\ell(t;\ell) && (10.10) \\ (1-\ell)x_\ell(t;\ell) &\rightarrow r_r(t)(1-\ell)x_\ell(t;\ell). && (10.11) \end{aligned}$$

3. The portfolio is then rebalanced, *i.e.* some risky holdings are bought or sold so that the leverage remains ℓ.

In real life, frequent rebalancing can be costly. Typically, we would pay extra fees when we borrow cash or stock, and *transaction costs*, such as broker's fees and transaction taxes, every time we buy or sell an asset. The simple model (Eq. 10.8) assumes no such costs and, to keep our illustrations close to the theory, we assume the same in the backtests in Fig. 10.3. We could include estimates of realistic costs in our simulations and, indeed, did so in [50], although this additional realism has surprisingly little effect on our key results.

Steps 1–3 result in the following protocol, which is a discretised version of (Eq. 10.8)

$$x_\ell(t) = \underbrace{r_s(t)\ell x_\ell(t-\Delta t)}_{\text{new risky holdings}} + \underbrace{r_r(t)(1-\ell)x_\ell(t-\Delta t)}_{\text{new bank deposits}}. \tag{10.12}$$

We apply this protocol repeatedly until the final day of the backtest, $t_{\max}$, when the final equity $x_\ell(t_{\max})$ is recorded. If at any time the equity falls below zero, the investment is declared bankrupt and the backtest is considered invalid for the corresponding leverage. This happens when the leverage is very high and the risky asset drops in value, or when it's very negative and the risky asset rises in value.

Note that the final equity in these portfolios is not monotonic in leverage. For instance, the risky asset ($\ell = 1$) outperforms the riskless asset ($\ell = 0$) here, but the daily rebalanced portfolio at leverage $\ell = 2.5$ underperforms the riskless asset. We will have more to say about these non-linear effects of leverage in Sec. 10.1.4.

10.1.3 Classical portfolio theory

Our simple model portfolio parametrised by ℓ allows us to ask the following question.

> What is the optimal value of ℓ?

This is similar to choosing between stochastic wealth processes, for which we developed a decision theory in Chap. 6. The main difference is that we are now choosing from a continuum of processes, each characterised by a value of ℓ, whereas previously we were choosing between a discrete set of processes.

Markowitz's efficient frontier

Before we use EE once more, let's review the classical treatment of the problem so that we appreciate the wider context. Intuitively, people understand there is some kind of trade-off between risk and reward. In our model of a generic multiplicative asset (Eq. 10.1) we could use σ as a proxy for risk and μ as a proxy for reward. Ideally we want an investment with large μ and small σ, but we also acknowledge the rule of thumb that assets with larger μ tend to have larger σ.[4] This is why we model our risky asset as having a positive excess return, $\mu_{\mathrm{e}} > 0$, over the riskless asset.

Intuition will only take us so far. A rigorous treatment of the portfolio selection problem was first attempted by Markowitz in 1952 [32]. He suggested defining a portfolio i, with drift and volatility (σ_i, μ_i), as efficient if there exists no rival portfolio, j, with drift and volatility (σ_j, μ_j) with $\mu_j \geq \mu_i$ and $\sigma_j \leq \sigma_i$. Markowitz argued that it is unwise to invest in a portfolio which is not efficient.

In our problem, we are comparing portfolios with parameters $(\ell\sigma_{\mathrm{s}}, \mu_{\mathrm{r}} + \ell\mu_{\mathrm{e}})$. These lie on a straight line in the (σ, μ)-plane,[5]

$$\mu = \mu_{\mathrm{r}} + \left(\frac{\mu_{\mathrm{e}}}{\sigma_{\mathrm{s}}}\right)\sigma, \tag{10.13}$$

shown schematically in Fig. 10.4. Under Markowitz's classification, all of the leveraged portfolios on this line are efficient. Indeed, in finance this line is called the *efficient frontier*. Therefore, any leverage we choose gives a portfolio which the classification would recommend. This does not help answer our question. By itself, Markowitz's approach is agnostic to leverage: it requires additional information to select a specific portfolio as the optimum. Markowitz was aware of this limitation and argued that the optimal portfolio could be identified by considering the investor's risk preferences [34]: "The proper choice among portfolios depends on the willingness and ability of the investor to assume risk."

The ultimate reliance on personal preferences is a theme that runs through all of economic theory, and we have seen examples of it in previous chapters. Of course, economic theory, or finance theory, is not meant to replace human judgement and imagination, nor is it supposed to force certain products and behaviours on people. But it is supposed to guide decisions. A statement like "this is the action that will eventually

[4] A "no such thing as a free lunch" type of rule.

[5] Derived by eliminating ℓ from the equations $\mu = \mu_{\mathrm{r}} + \ell\mu_{\mathrm{e}}$ and $\sigma = \ell\sigma_{\mathrm{s}}$.

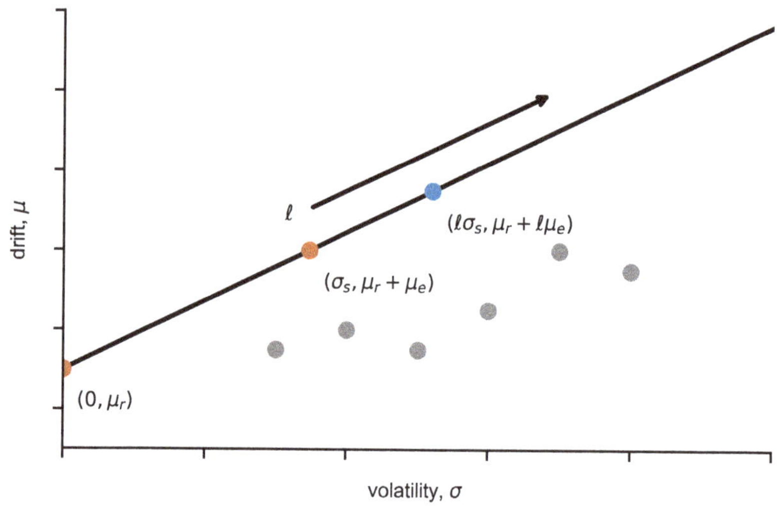

Figure 10.4: The Markowitz portfolio selection picture. The red dots are the locations in the (σ, μ)-plane of portfolios containing only the riskless (left) or risky (right) asset. The blue dot is one possible leveraged portfolio, in this case with $\ell > 1$. All possible leveraged portfolios lie on the black line, (Eq. 10.13). The grey dots are hypothetical alternative portfolios, containing different assets excluded from our simple portfolio problem. Their location below and to the right of the black line makes them inefficient under the Markowitz scheme.

make your wealth grow fastest, assuming we have chosen models and estimated parameters correctly" is helpful and leaves plenty of room for judgement calls. As in decision theory in general, risk preferences are typically included in the portfolio selection problem through a utility function, and thereby the theory of finance inherits a major cornerstone of economics, along with its limitations.

Sharpe ratio

The *Sharpe ratio* [63] for an asset with drift μ and volatility σ is defined as

$$S \equiv \frac{\mu - \mu_\mathrm{r}}{\sigma} \tag{10.14}$$

It is the gradient of the straight line in the (σ, μ)-plane which passes through the riskless asset and the asset in question. S is often used as a convenient shorthand for applying Markowitz's ideas, since choosing the portfolio with the highest S from the set of available portfolios is equivalent to choosing an efficient portfolio. The optimal leverage problem, however, cannot be resolved by this procedure. The reason is this: all of our leveraged portfolios lie on the same line, (Eq. 10.13), and so all of them have the same Sharpe ratio, which is simply the line's gradient:

$$S_\ell = \frac{\mu_\mathrm{e}}{\sigma_\mathrm{s}}. \tag{10.15}$$

This is *insensitive to the leverage* ℓ, resulting in the same non-advice as the Markowitz approach. Sharpe also suggested considering risk preferences to resolve the optimal portfolio: "The investor's task is to select from among the efficient portfolios the one that he considers most desirable, based on his particular feelings regarding risk and expected return" [63]. Once more we encounter the theme of reliance on personal preferences in finance and economics.

Expected return

We noted previously that the growth rate of the expectation value of the risky price is the risky drift, μ_s, also known as the *expected return.* This is because

$$\langle x_s(t_0 + \Delta t)\rangle = \langle x_s(t_0)\rangle \exp(\mu_\mathrm{s} \Delta t), \tag{10.16}$$

which, as a multiplicative process, has growth rate

$$g_\mathrm{m}(\langle x_s\rangle) = \frac{\Delta \ln \langle x_s\rangle}{\Delta t} = \mu_\mathrm{s}. \tag{10.17}$$

It follows immediately from comparison of (Eq. 10.4) and (Eq. 10.8) that the expected value of the leveraged portfolio grows at

$$g_\mathrm{m}(\langle x_\ell\rangle) = \mu_\mathrm{r} + \ell\mu_\mathrm{e}. \tag{10.18}$$

This illustrates why a portfolio theory which is insensitive to leverage, such as that of Markowitz and Sharpe, is potentially dangerous.[6] Because it doesn't alert the investor to the *dangers of over-leveraging* and considers any leverage optimal, the investor must find an additional criterion. There is nothing in the formalism that would prevent the investor from selecting the expected return in (Eq. 10.18) as that additional criterion. Consequently the investor would maximise leverage, $\ell \to \infty$. This, as we will shortly see, would almost surely lead to ruin.

10.1.4 Growth rate maximisation

We now understand the classical approach, as applied to a very simple portfolio problem, and we are aware of its limitations. What does EE have to say?

The time-average growth rate of the leveraged portfolio is

$$\overline{g}_{\mathrm{m}} \equiv \lim_{\Delta t \to \infty} g_{\mathrm{m}}(x_\ell, \Delta t) = \lim_{\Delta t \to \infty} \frac{\Delta \ln x_\ell}{\Delta t}. \tag{10.19}$$

The time-average growth rate will depend on ℓ. Inserting the expression for x_ℓ from (Eq. 10.9) in (Eq. 10.19) gives

$$\overline{g}_{\mathrm{m}} = \lim_{\Delta t \to \infty} \frac{1}{\Delta t} \left[\left(\mu_{\mathrm{r}} + \ell \mu_{\mathrm{e}} - \frac{\ell^2 {\sigma_{\mathrm{s}}}^2}{2} \right) \Delta t + \ell \sigma_{\mathrm{s}} W(\Delta t) \right], \tag{10.20}$$

which, since $W(\Delta t)/\Delta t \sim \Delta t^{-1/2} \to 0$ as $\Delta t \to \infty$, converges to

$$\overline{g}_{\mathrm{m}} = \mu_{\mathrm{r}} + \ell \mu_{\mathrm{e}} - \frac{\ell^2 {\sigma_{\mathrm{s}}}^2}{2}. \tag{10.21}$$

This is a quadratic in ℓ with a maximum[7] at

$$\ell_{\mathrm{opt}} = \frac{\mu_{\mathrm{e}}}{{\sigma_{\mathrm{s}}}^2}. \tag{10.22}$$

This is the key result of the current section. At the start of Sec. 10.1.3 we asked "what is the optimal leverage?" Equation (10.22) is the answer EE gives to this question. ℓ_{opt} is the *optimal leverage* in the sense that it defines the portfolio with the highest time-average growth rate.

ℓ_{opt} is defined objectively, with no reference to idiosyncrasies of the investor. All we need are the parameters μ_{r}, μ_{s}, and σ_{s} of the two assets in our market, and all we learn is how to position ourselves for maximum growth. In Fig. 10.5 we illustrate what this means with real data, once more using S&P500 and FED as our example assets, and now scanning through all possible leverages in daily rebalanced portfolios.

[6] Both recipients of the 1990 Alfred Nobel Memorial Prize in Economic Sciences.

[7] Derived, for example, by setting $\frac{d\overline{g}_{\mathrm{m}}}{d\ell} = 0$.

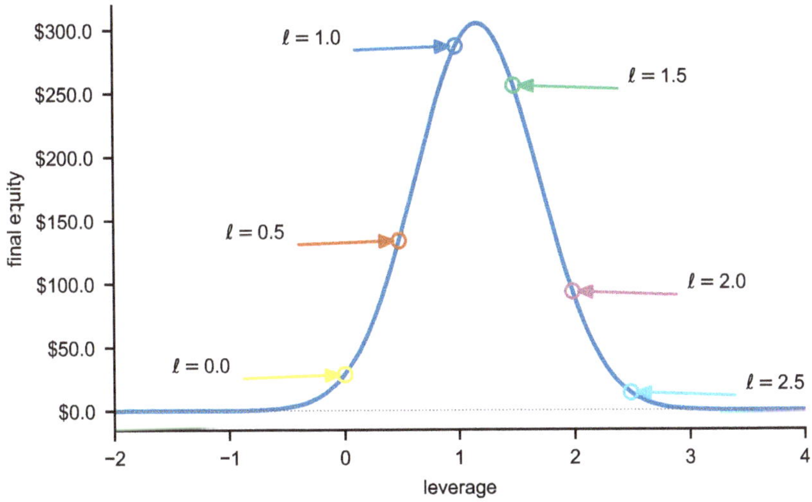

Figure 10.5: Final equity, $x_\ell(t_{\max})$, of the S&P500-FED portfolio at 500 backtested leverages, where $t_{\max}$ is 1 March 2024 and the underlying time series start on 31 December 1927. Each leverage produces a ragged time series of equity, as shown in Fig. 10.3, but the final equity as a function of leverage is a smooth curve. The position of the maximum, *i.e.* the leverage which leads to maximum final wealth, is the optimal leverage for this portfolio between these dates. Here ℓ_{opt} is a little greater than 1.

For $1 invested in 1927, the backtests generate a narrowly peaked curve for the final equity in 2024. The corresponding ℓ_{opt} can be read off in this figure as the position of the maximum. Applying more leverage or less leverage than ℓ_{opt}, irrespective of investor preferences, simply means less final wealth.

Investors who prefer slow growth to fast growth will want to avoid the EE approach to finance. While economists find it important to consider all possible preferences, our approach is useful when it is unknown who the "investor" is. Consider, for instance, a pension fund – it has to position itself in some way, manage its portfolio and the risks it is taking. The portfolio manager often cannot know who the investors are – there may be thousands of them. Optimising the time-average growth rate would be a sensible goal that's easily communicated, whereas trying to optimise the investment according to the investors' risk preferences is simply impossible.

Classical theory is indifferent to where on the line in Fig. 10.4 we choose to be. EE decision theory, however, selects a particular point on that line.[8] (Eq. 10.21) gives the time-average growth rate along the

[8]Subsequently Markowitz became aware of this point, which he called the "Kelly-Latané" point in [33], referring to [25, 28].

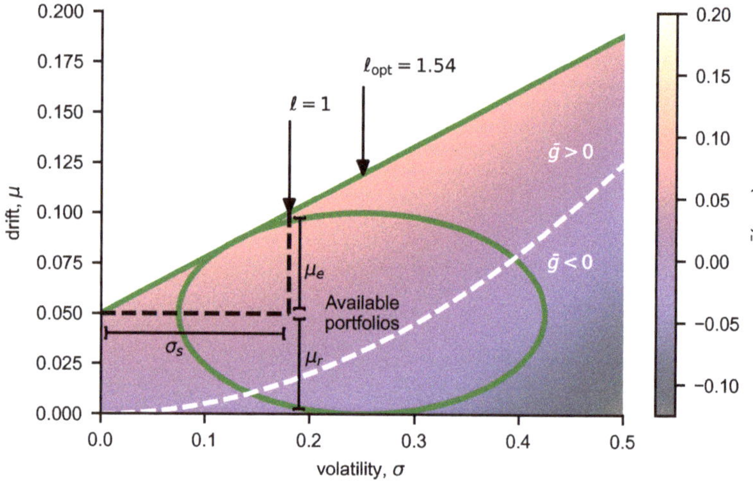

Figure 10.6: The augmented portfolio selection picture. The Markowitz picture is shown in green, with the efficient leveraged portfolios on the straight green line (the efficient frontier) and other (inefficient) available portfolios within the green ellipse (analogous to the grey dots in Fig. 10.4). This is overlaid on a colour plot of the time-average growth rate, $\overline{g}$. The optimal leverage, $\ell_{\text{opt}} \approx 1.54$, is marked at the location of the highest $\overline{g}$ on the efficient frontier. Portfolios on the white curve have $\overline{g} = 0$. Eventually this will intersect the efficient frontier, at which point applying more leverage will produce a portfolio with negative long-run growth. Parameters are $\mu_{\text{r}} = \mu_{\text{e}} = 0.05$ per unit time and $\sigma_{\text{s}} = 0.18$ per square root time. Adapted from [44].

efficient frontier, where all of our leveraged portfolios lie. In fact, it's easy to calculate the growth rate for any point in the (σ, μ)-plane: it is simply $\mu - \sigma^2/2$. Overlaying the Markowitz picture in Fig. 10.4 on the growth rate landscape is illuminating. In effect, it adds the information missing from the classical model, which was needed to distinguish between portfolios. This is shown in Fig. 10.6.

That (Eq. 10.21) defines an inverted parabola means that, even on the efficient frontier, there exist portfolios with $\overline{g}_{\text{m}}(\ell) < 0$. These occur for $\ell < \ell^-$ and $\ell > \ell^+$, where

$$\ell^{\pm} \equiv \ell_{\text{opt}} \pm \sqrt{{\ell_{\text{opt}}}^2 + \frac{2\mu_{\text{r}}}{{\sigma_{\text{s}}}^2}}. \tag{10.23}$$

This confirms our assertion at the end of Sec. 10.1.3: I will lose wealth if I maximise leverage in either direction (provided I can apply enough leverage). Indeed, if my leveraging ability is unlimited, I will find to my horror what is easily seen in (Eq. 10.21), that $\overline{g}_{\text{m}}(\ell)$ diverges negatively as $\ell \to \pm\infty$. I will lose fast.

10.2 Leverage efficiency

Aside from being insensitive to leverage, the Sharpe ratio, $S = \mu_e/\sigma_s$, is a dimensionful quantity. Its unit is (time unit)$^{-1/2}$. This means that its numerical value is arbitrary (since it depends on the choice of time unit) and tells us nothing fundamental about the system under study. For example, a portfolio with $S = 5$ per square root of one year has $S = 5(365)^{-1/2} \approx 0.26$ per square root of one day. Same portfolio, different numbers.

The optimal leverage, $\ell_{\text{opt}} = \mu_e/{\sigma_s}^2$, which differs from the Sharpe ratio by a factor of $1/\sigma_s$, is a dimensionless quantity. Therefore, its numerical value does not depend on choice of units and has the potential to carry fundamental information about the system.[9] We could view ℓ_{opt} as the fundamental measure of a portfolio's quality, similarly to how S is viewed in classical portfolio theory. A portfolio with a high optimal leverage must represent a good investment opportunity to justify such a large commitment of the investor's funds.

However, the significance of ℓ_{opt} runs deeper than this. The portfolio to which ℓ_{opt} refers is that which optimally allocates money between the risky and riskless assets in our model market. Therefore, it tells us much about conditions in that market and, by extension, in the wider economy. A high ℓ_{opt} indicates an economic environment in which investors are incentivised to take risks. Conversely, a low or negative ℓ_{opt} indicates little incentive to take risks. This raises a tantalising question.

> Are there any special numerical values of ℓ_{opt} which describe different market regimes, or to which markets are attracted?

10.2.1 Relaxing the model

Our model market contains assets whose prices follow GBM, which by definition has constant drift and volatility parameters. Once specified, μ_r, μ_s, and σ_s are static and, therefore, so is ℓ_{opt}. This limits the extent to which we can explore the question, since we cannot consider changes in ℓ_{opt}. To make progress we need to relax the model. We must consider which parts of the model are relevant to the question, and which parts can be discarded without grave loss.

The GBM-based model is useful because it motivates the idea of an objectively optimal leverage which maximises the growth of an investment over time. It also provides an expression for ℓ_{opt} in terms of parameters which, in essence, describe the market conditions under which prices fluctuate. These parameters have correspondences with quantities we can measure in real markets. All of this is useful.

[9] See Barenblatt's classic text on scaling [6].

However, we are ultimately interested in real markets, and their asset prices do not strictly follow GBM (because nothing in nature truly does). In particular, real market conditions are not static. They change over time, albeit on a longer time scale than that of the price fluctuations. In this context, the model assumption of constant μ_r, μ_s, and σ_s is restrictive and unhelpful. We will relax it and imagine a less constrained model market where these parameters, and therefore ℓ_opt, are allowed to vary slowly. We will not build a detailed mathematical formulation of this, but instead use the idea to run some simple thought experiments.

10.2.2 Efficiency

One way of approaching the question of special values of ℓ_opt is to invoke the concept of *efficiency*. This has a specific meaning in the context of financial markets, which we will mention imminently. In general terms, an efficient system is one which is already well optimised and whose performance cannot be improved upon by simple actions. For example, a refrigerator is efficient if it maintains a cool internal environment while consuming little electrical power and emitting little noise.[10] Similarly, Markowitz's portfolios were efficient because the investor could do no better than to choose one of them.

The "*efficient market hypothesis*" of classical economics treats markets as efficient processors of information. It claims that the price of an asset in an efficient market reflects all of the publicly available information about it. The corollary is that no market participant, without access to privileged information, can consistently beat the market simply by choosing to buy or sell assets based on their prices. We shall refer to this hypothesis as *price efficiency*.[11]

We will consider a different sort of efficiency, where we think not about the price at which assets are bought and sold in our model market, but instead about the leverage that is applied to them. Let's run a thought experiment.

Thought experiment: efficiency under leverage

Imagine that $\ell_\text{opt} > 1$ in our model market. This would mean that

[10] This is a subtle reference to a fridge whose presence once graced the offices of London Mathematical Laboratory (LML). It was not efficient.

[11] This is not the most precise hypothesis ever hypothesised. What does it mean for a price to "reflect" information? Presumably this involves some comparison between the observed price of the asset and its true value contingent on that information. But only the former is observable, while the latter evades clear definition. Similarly, what does it mean to "beat the market"? Presumably something to do with achieving a higher growth rate than a generic investment in the overall market. But what investment, exactly? We will leave these legitimate questions unanswered here. The interested reader can consult the comprehensive review in [62].

the simple strategy of borrowing money to buy stock will achieve faster long-run growth than buying stock only with our own money. If we associate putting all our money in stock, $\ell = 1$, with an investment in the market, then it would be a trivial matter to beat the market (by doing nothing more sophisticated than investing borrowed money).

Similarly, imagine that $\ell_{\text{opt}} < 1$. In this scenario, the market could again be beaten very easily by leaving some money in the bank (and, if $\ell_{\text{opt}} < 0$, by short selling).

It would strain language to consider our market efficient if consistent outperformance were so straightforward to achieve. This suggests a different, fluctuations-based notion of market efficiency, which we call *leverage efficiency*: it is impossible for a market participant without privileged information to beat a leverage-efficient market simply by choosing the *amount* to invest in stock, *i.e.* by choosing the leverage.[12] We believe real markets to be leverage-efficient. Therefore, we make the following hypothesis.

Leverage efficiency

Real markets self-organise such that

$$\ell_{\text{opt}} = 1 \tag{10.24}$$

is an attracting point for their stochastic properties.

These stochastic properties are represented by μ_{r}, μ_{s}, and σ_{s} in the relaxed model that permits dynamic adjustment of their values.

10.2.3 Stability

Another approach to the question whether there are special values of ℓ_{opt}, whose style owes more to physics than economics, is to consider the *stability* of the system under study (here, the market) and how this depends on the value of the observable in question (here, ℓ_{opt}).

Systems which persist over long time scales tend to be stable. Many of the systems we find in nature therefore include stabilising elements. Unstable systems tend to last for shorter times, so we observe them less frequently.[13] With this in mind, let's think about what different values of ℓ_{opt} imply for *systemic stability*.

[12]The attentive reader will note that this resembles price efficiency with price replaced by leverage.

[13]We use the comparative "shorter" here. This does not mean short. It is quite possible for an unstable system to remain in flux for a long time in human terms, perhaps giving the illusion of stability. Indeed, much of classical economic theory is predicated on the idea that economies are at or close to equilibrium, *i.e.* stable.

Thought experiment: stability under leverage

Imagine that $\ell_{\text{opt}} > 1$ in our relaxed model. Since it is an objectively optimal leverage which does not depend on investor idiosyncrasies, this means that *everyone* in the market should want to borrow money to buy stock. But, if that's true, who's going to lend the money and who's going to sell the stock?

Similarly, imagine that $\ell_{\text{opt}} < 0$. This means that *everyone* should want to borrow stock and sell it for cash. But, if that's true, who's going to lend the stock and who's going to relinquish their cash to buy it?

Unless there are enough market participants disinterested in their time-average growth rate to take the unfavourable sides of these deals, then neither of these situations is globally stable. It's hard to imagine them persisting for long before trading activity causes one or more of the market parameters to change, returning ℓ_{opt} to a stable value.

This thought experiment suggests that markets tend to operate in the regime $0 \leq \ell_{\text{opt}} \leq 1$. To motivate that they operate near the upper end of this range, $\ell_{\text{opt}} \approx 1$, we argue on macro-economic grounds. We've defined optimal leverage as the proportion of one's wealth ideally invested in the risky asset, *i.e.* in stock. The regime $\ell_{\text{opt}} < 1$ therefore probably doesn't correspond to a macro-economically desirable state, in the sense that people would be incentivised to keep money in bank accounts rather than to invest it. An economy in which ℓ_{opt} is close to, or even less than, zero gives people no incentive to invest in productive business. Such an economy would appear paralysed, resembling perhaps those periods in history referred to as economic depressions. Much effort is generally expended to avoid such conditions.

We can also generalise to the case where both assets are risky. What if we're comparing two share indexes or two shares, eliminating cash from our considerations? The same stability arguments would suggest that the optimal leverage in such a portfolio – now defined as the proportion ideally held in one of the assets – should be in the range $0 \leq \ell_{\text{opt}} \leq 1$, which reflects the symmetry between two risky assets. Our original hypothesis then describes the special case where one asset does not fluctuate (is the numeraire) and can be created by a central bank which aims for full investment.

Whether in our original setup real markets spend significant time with $\ell_{\text{opt}} < 1$ is difficult to tell. Realistic optimal leverage depends

Our analysis of real wealth data in Sec. 9.2.5 suggests economies are better viewed as far-from-equilibrium, or even non-equilibrating, systems. If so, they should be modelled as such, even if their dynamics unfold over time scales much longer than our day-to-day affairs.

on factors such as trading costs and access to credit, which may differ between market participants, as well as infrastructure and technology. This suggests that measuring optimal leverage in the simplest way – using market prices only and assuming zero trading costs – will produce an overestimate, compared to the value experienced by real market participants who incur realistic costs.

However, looking back at Fig. 10.5, we no longer think of the position of the maximum as arbitrary happenstance. The proximity, $\ell_{\text{opt}} \approx 1$, is a first hint that leverage efficiency is indeed a concept with real-world relevance.

The dynamical adjustment, or self-organisation, of the market parameters takes place through the trading activity of market participants. In particular, this creates feedback loops, which cause prices and fluctuation amplitudes to change, returning ℓ_{opt} to a stable value whenever it strays. To be truly convincing, we should propose plausible trading mechanisms through which these feedback loops arise. We do this in [50]. Since they involve details about how trading takes place in financial markets (in which we assume the typical reader of this book is disinterested) we shall not rehearse them here. The primary drivers of our hypothesis are the efficiency and stability arguments we've just made.

10.2.4 Prediction accuracy

When we take our theory to the data, we will make systematic errors. For instance, the actual optimal leverage will depend on what actual real asset we choose to represent the risk-free asset – government bonds, probably, but at what maturity? A portfolio of maturities? And should we only consider interest payments or also changes in bond prices? Similarly, we have to choose something with observable prices to approximate the risky asset in our model. An index, maybe, but which one? What about survivorship bias, and what about dividend payments? How are they taxed? What about market impact when positions are bought and sold? In practice, we have to choose something, and it will be systematically off in some way.

Let's ignore these systematic effects for the moment and ask a more basic question. Suppose we estimate an optimal leverage, $\ell_{\text{opt}}^{\text{est}}$, by simulating a leveraged investment over a finite time series of, say, daily asset returns. How close do we expect this to be to the predicted value of $\ell_{\text{opt}} = 1$? Even assuming ideal conditions – that ℓ_{opt} really is attracted to 1 and that any effects that lead to systematic misestimation can be neglected – we expect random deviations from $\ell_{\text{opt}}^{\text{est}} = 1$ to increase as the time series gets shorter. To take an extreme example, with daily data, the observed optimal leverage over a window of one day does not exist. Either $\ell_{\text{opt}}^{\text{est}} \to +\infty$ if the risky return beats the deposit rate on that day; or $\ell_{\text{opt}}^{\text{est}} \to -\infty$ if deposits beat the risky asset. Indeed, the magnitude of the observed optimal leverage will diverge for any window over which the daily risky returns are either all greater than, or all less than, the daily returns on federal funds. This is unlikely for windows of months or years but using daily data it happens commonly over windows of days or weeks. Even without this divergence, shorter windows are more likely to result in larger positive and negative optimal leverages because relative fluctuations are larger over shorter time scales.

To quantify this idea we compute $g_{\mathrm{m}}(x_\ell, \Delta t)$, *i.e.* the time-average growth rate observed in an investment following (Eq. 10.8) after a finite time Δt. That's simply the expression on the right-hand side of (Eq. 10.20) without taking the $\Delta t \to \infty$ limit:

$$g_{\mathrm{m}}(x_\ell, \Delta t) = \mu_{\mathrm{r}} + \ell \mu_{\mathrm{e}} - \frac{(\ell \sigma_{\mathrm{s}})^2}{2} + \frac{\ell \sigma_{\mathrm{s}} W(\Delta t)}{\Delta t} \tag{10.25}$$

Maximising this expression generates a noisy estimate for the optimal leverage over a window of length Δt:

$$\ell_{\mathrm{opt}}^{\mathrm{est}}(\Delta t, N = 1) = \ell_{\mathrm{opt}} + \frac{W(\Delta t)}{\sigma_{\mathrm{s}} \Delta t}. \tag{10.26}$$

Thus, in the model, optimal leverage for finite time series is normally distributed with mean ℓ_{opt} and standard deviation

$$\mathrm{stdev}(\ell_{\mathrm{opt}}^{\mathrm{est}}(\Delta t)) = \frac{1}{\sigma_{\mathrm{s}} \Delta t^{1/2}}. \tag{10.27}$$

In Fig. 10.7 we use this quantity as the standard error for the prediction $\ell_{\mathrm{opt}}^{\mathrm{est}} \approx 1$ and test leverage efficiency, now including uncertainty estimates, once more for S&P500 and for two further risky assets. Like any scientific model, leverage efficiency applies within some range of conditions. In an attempt to explore the limits of this range, we ask how well leverage efficiency applies to Bitcoin, an extremely volatile asset. As a further test, we also run the data analysis on the returns of Berkshire Hathaway (BRK), an exceptionally successful fund. How much greater than for the general market is optimal leverage for this very successful stock-picking fund, selected in hindsight?

The overall impression that emerges is that leverage efficiency is reasonably satisfied. The shaded areas in Fig. 10.7 show the predicted ranges, 2 statistical standard errors to the left and right from $\ell_{\mathrm{opt}} = 1$, and only BRK lies outside its range. We also see that all estimates are a little greater than 1, as might be expected given the assumption of zero trading costs.

So far, we have used the *variance of optimal leverage* that we expect to observe in a finite time series, to arrive at a statistical error estimate, a scale on which to judge whether leverage efficiency holds or not. But

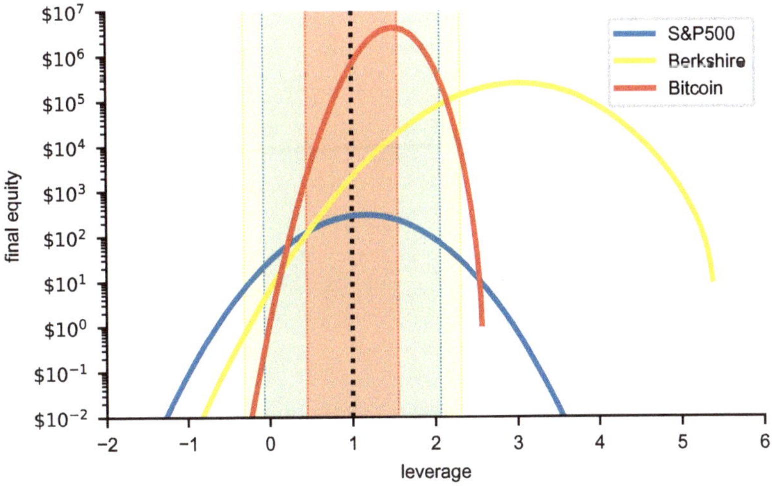

Figure 10.7: Final equity $x_\ell(t_0;\ell)$ for investments of initially \$1. **Blue:** in the S&P500. **Yellow** in BRK. **Red** in Bitcoin (red). Shaded areas around leverage 1 indicate two standard errors from the prediction, in the corresponding colour. The maximum for the much more volatile Bitcoin is also near the predicted optimum of $\ell_{\text{opt}} = 1$ – within 2 standard errors of the prediction, without any correction for the biases introduced by neglecting trading costs. For BRK the picture is a little different: for this extremely successfully managed fund it would have been optimal to leverage up over the course of its existence.

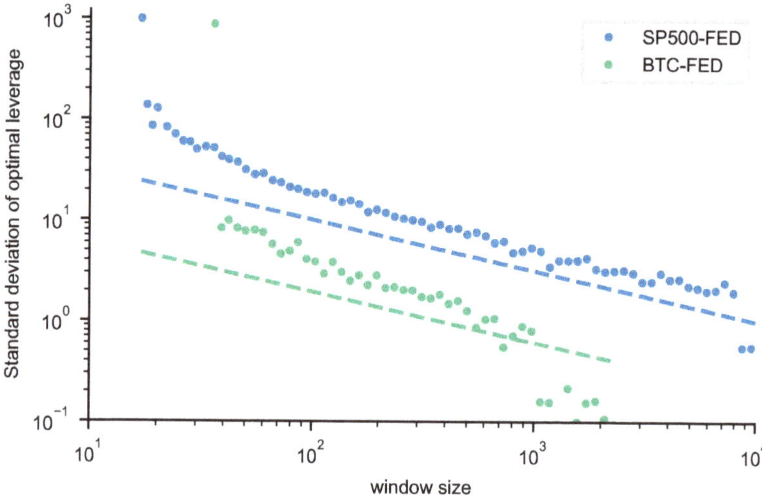

Figure 10.8: Dots show the standard deviation of samples of $\ell_{\text{opt}}^{\text{est}}(\Delta t)$ as a function of window length measured in days. Dashed line shows the prediction of (Eq. 10.27) using the estimate of σ_{s} obtained by fitting a parabola to curves like in Fig. 10.7 (blue for S&P500, green for Bitcoin).

we can also use (Eq. 10.27) as a prediction in itself: is the sample variance of ℓ_{opt}, measured in many windows of size Δt, well described by (Eq. 10.27)? We can't make the time series longer than they are, but we can make them shorter. In Fig. 10.8 we collect statistics of $\ell_{\text{opt}}^{\text{est}}$ estimated in non-overlapping time windows and find good agreement with the model-specific prediction.

The structure we have identified – leverage efficiency – operates on all time scales from weeks to decades. This broad range of applicability supports our theory of noise which we will turn to in Sec. 10.3.1: it is a requirement of stability that asset prices fluctuate, and the shorter the time scales the less significant any economic information becomes. Thinking of price changes as a reflection of new economic information may be relevant on time scales of years or decades, where the real economic fortunes of companies become apparent. On time scales of days or minutes, let alone milliseconds, price movements usually have nothing to do with economic information.

10.3 Applications of leverage efficiency

Our solution of the portfolio selection problem, and the concept of leverage efficiency that follows from it are important developments in the theory of financial markets. While in a sense the puzzle pieces necessary for these developments have been around for a while, it seems that they haven't so far been put together in quite the way we've presented them. This is evident from many puzzles and questions in finance and economics, which have straightforward solutions using the concepts developed in this book. We now turn to some of these famous puzzles.

10.3.1 A theory of noise

According to leverage efficiency, prices of risky assets must fluctuate if an excess drift exists, $\mu_e > 0$, simply because the market would otherwise become unstable. But, if price fluctuations are necessary for stability, then the intellectual basis for price efficiency – that changes in price are driven by the arrival of new economic information – cannot be the whole truth. Or – depending on what is meant by "information" – it may be an empty circular statement. At least some component of observed fluctuations must be driven by the leverage feedbacks described in section Sec. 10.2, which enforce leverage efficiency and which have little to do with the arrival of meaningful economic information.

Fisher Black differentiated between information-based and other types of price fluctuation, referring to the latter as "noise" and regarding them as symptoms of inaccurate information and market *inefficiency* [10]. However, substituting $\ell_{\text{opt}} = 1$ in (Eq. 10.22) yields

$$(\sigma_s)^2 = \mu_e. \tag{10.28}$$

Purely based on leverage efficiency, prices must fluctuate, and we can even quantify by how much. An asset whose expectation value grows faster than the value of the riskless asset must fluctuate; otherwise systemic stability will be undermined. This is a radical departure from conventional thinking, and it has practical consequences. For instance, prices "discovered" at ever higher trading frequencies must necessarily reveal more ups and downs, but this noise is self-generated, imposed by the requirement of leverage stability. That stability creates volatility is a theory of noise requiring no appeal to the arrival of unspecified information, accurate or not.

10.3.2 Solution of the equity premium puzzle

The term "*equity premium*" has been used to describe the premium an investor receives for holding equity – which we interpret as the extra growth rate which stocks (or some other risky asset) experience, compared to riskless rates. We denote this additional growth rate by the symbol ε.

Puzzles usually arise because we look at things from the wrong angle, with a mental model that doesn't reflect reality. The equity premium puzzle is no exception. The researchers who first studied the equity premium had a model in mind whereby equity prices are set based on the consumption preferences of the population [37]. We won't go into these models in detail, but the story is this: consumption-based asset pricing models come to the conclusion that no one should ever hold cash. In these models only people who are pathologically terrified of losing money would hold cash, and such people just don't exist. But with the assumption that they don't exist, the models predict a very different equity premium from what's observed. So something is not working.

In 2016 LeRoy summarised the state of the debate as follows [29]: "Most analysts believe that no single convincing explanation has been provided for the volatility of equity prices. The conclusion that appears to follow from the equity premium and price volatility puzzles is that, for whatever reason, prices of financial assets do not behave as the theory of consumption-based asset pricing predicts."

Of course the difference between the time-average growth rates of the risky asset ($\ell = 1$) and the riskless asset ($\ell = 0$) can be measured. It is

$$\varepsilon \equiv \overline{g}_{\mathrm{m}}(x_s) - \overline{g}_{\mathrm{m}}(x_r) \tag{10.29}$$

$$= \mu_{\mathrm{e}} - \frac{(\sigma_{\mathrm{s}})^2}{2}. \tag{10.30}$$

What value would we expect the equity premium to take in a real market? Substituting (Eq. 10.28) into (Eq. 10.30), it follows that the equity premium is attracted to

$$\varepsilon = \frac{(\sigma_{\mathrm{s}})^2}{2}. \tag{10.31}$$

It is important to remember that any theoretical prediction comes with a band of uncertainty around it. The next step is, therefore, to estimate the uncertainty in the equity premium. We do this by considering finite measurement times and substitute (Eq. 10.25) into (Eq. 10.29)

$$\mathrm{stdev}(\varepsilon(\Delta t)) = \frac{\sigma_{\mathrm{s}}}{\Delta t^{1/2}}. \tag{10.32}$$

We will use this as our definition of one statistical standard error.

The equity premium puzzle is an interesting case study of economic science in operation. The literature on the puzzle is large and often takes a psychological and individual-specific perspective. For instance, a more risk-averse individual will demand a higher equity premium. Models of human behaviour enter both into the definition of the equity premium and into its analysis. In a review of 150 textbooks discussing the equity premium, Fernández [19] finds estimates for ε in a range from 3%*p.a.* to 10%*p.a.*, broadly consistent with our predictions. For instance, in [50] we measured values between 0.4%*p.a.* and 6.4%*p.a.* using (Eq. 10.29), for S&P500 versus FED, depending on how dividends were treated and which maturities were chosen. The values were statistically plausible. The higher value breaches 2 standard errors of the prediction based on $\ell_{\text{opt}} = 1$ and the relevant measured volatility, but in that case the choice of assets introduces a systematic bias for a high estimate, which the statistical error does not capture.

We hasten to add that Fernández finds the 150 textbooks to be inconsistent in their definitions of the equity premium, so these numbers can only be a rough guide. The problem is often treated in wordy essays and in complicated formal models. But this additional complexity generates less, rather than more, comprehension compared to our treatment: it fails to explain the equity premium. It seems to be a result of science incrementally going in one direction and failing to retrace its steps and try a different angle.

The framework we have developed here takes a psychologically naïve perspective, and assumes that market participants simply want to maximise the growth rate of their investments. It ignores consumption. It is analytically simple. It makes use of only one key insight: performance over time is not performance of the ensemble. We regard the correct prediction of the equity premium by leverage efficiency as the long-sought resolution of the equity premium and price volatility puzzles. From the perspective of classical economics, the equity premium puzzle is the fact that observed equity premia cannot be explained with consumption-based asset pricing models. In our view, this simply suggests that the consumption-based asset pricing models used should be questioned.

10.3.3 Central-bank interest rates

Our observations are also relevant to the issue of setting a central bank's lending rate. The rate setter would interpret the total drift μ_{s} of an appropriate asset or index as given, and the risk-free drift μ_{r} as the rate under their control. Setting a central-bank *interest rate* is a multi-objective process, but if we focus on the objective to achieve full investment in productive activity without fuelling an asset bubble, then setting this rate so that $\ell_{\text{opt}} = 1$ is a good starting point. Since $\ell_{\text{opt}} = \mu_{\text{e}}/(\sigma_{\text{s}})^2$ and $\mu_{\text{e}} = \mu_{\text{s}} - \mu_{\text{r}}$, this is achieved by setting

$$\mu_{\text{r}} = \mu_{\text{s}} - (\sigma_{\text{s}})^2. \tag{10.33}$$

Using values for μ_{s} and σ_{s} estimated from the shapes of parabolas like those in Fig. 10.7, we can determine the corresponding optimal interest rate. Of course, this depends on the assets we choose to represent the riskless and risky. For example, using interest rates for ten-year maturity Treasury bills as the return for the riskless asset, and the S&P500 total return index for the risky, between 1988 and 2020 the optimal interest rate comes out as 8.2% *p.a.*, suggesting that actual interest rates over the analysed period have been in a region where they can inflate leverage bubbles (the geometric average on 10-year maturity Treasury bills was lower than this at around 4.6% *p.a.*). The effect is mitigated by trading costs, and our estimate of its magnitude depends on what we think are good assets to use in the analysis. So these numbers should be thought of as a proof of principle – choose your own assets, and build more realistic models to come to a comprehensive understanding of where we are. It is hard to deny, of course, that asset bubbles were observed over this period.

One task of the central banker can be seen as the task of estimating μ_s and σ_s in the relevant way. This will involve choices about data and timescales which are far from trivial. For instance, in our data analyses at any given time there is an estimate for μ_s and one for σ_s for each possible length of lookback window.

However, operational matters aside, stability with respect to leverage is an important consideration for any central bank. Leverage efficiency provides one simple quantitative input for a rate setting protocol and may contribute to qualitative discussions about interest rates in a useful way.

10.3.4 Fraud detection

We have seen that leverage efficiency is real. Prices of real traded assets obey the constraints dictated by systemic stability as well as one might statistically expect.

But what if it doesn't? What if there is an asset that consistently and at low volatility outperforms bank deposits? First of all, we now know that such behaviour is a challenge to systemic stability. Because of this, we don't expect it to survive for long. Where it does survive for long, one possible explanation is fraud. A common type of fraud is the so-called *Ponzi scheme*: the fraudster fabricates an attractive past performance of a portfolio or asset value, which entices new investors to give him their money. Instead of investing the money in the fictitious asset, it is passed on to pay off earlier investors and the fraudster siphons off a handy profit. Since the performance of the asset price is invented, there is no strong reason for it to obey leverage efficiency. We will now test this for Bernard L. Madoff Investment Securities (MAD), a giant Ponzi scheme exposed in 2008, and ask: was it too good to be true from the perspective of leverage efficiency?

This takes the idea of finding the limits of the range of applicability of leverage efficiency one step further. MAD has officially been declared a Ponzi scheme. Monthly returns were included in a now famous complaint filed with the Securities and Exchange Commission (SEC) by

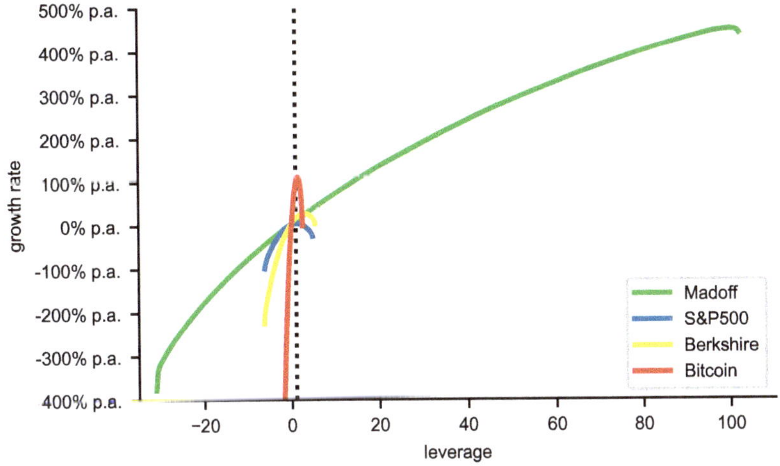

Figure 10.9: Annual growth rate for investments in S&P500 (blue), BRK (yellow), Bitcoin (red), and MAD (green). The maxima for the real assets cluster near the predicted value $\ell_{\text{opt}} = 1$. Madoff's concocted performance had such low volatility that a leverage of 100 would have been optimal, even if rebalancing could have only occurred once per month. At higher rebalancing frequencies (had the asset actually existed) the green curve would be seen to be the left end of a parabola whose maximum may well be at 200 or 300.

Harry Markopolos in 2005 [31]. The SEC did not act on the complaint, and Madoff happily continued his scheme until the turbulent financial events of 2008 brought to light what he'd been up to. We digitised the returns in Markopolos's complaint and ran the same backtests for MAD as for the other assets, Fig. 10.9.

Of course, in principle Madoff could have chosen the invented returns of his fund in a way that's consistent with leverage efficiency. But it is significant that he didn't. He wouldn't have known how to do it because he didn't know about leverage efficiency, an EE concept which hadn't been discovered when he set up the fraud. Nor did this hinder the fraud: among his victims were some of the most sophisticated investors, large institutions with departments full of quantitative analysts. But they, too, didn't know about leverage efficiency and had no formal reason to suspect malfeasance.

That leverage efficiency doesn't apply to MAD is a good sign – showing that a theory fails to predict things it shouldn't be able to predict is important. A theory about asset price fluctuations that applies even to fictitious prices like Madoff's would be suspicious – it would probably not say much about prices at all but just be a statement that's generally true for a much broader class of phenomena. Having said this, introducing realistic transaction costs, leveraging something by a factor of 100 or 200 is extremely expensive, and the MAD optimal leverage comes down significantly in a more realistic setup. Nonetheless, in Fig. 10.9 the MAD returns have a statistical signature that is unequivocally different from prices arising through trading that we have investigated.

10.4 Discussion

The primary aim of this final chapter was to demonstrate that the mathematical formalism we have developed to conceptualise randomness in economics, which started with a simple model of wealth evolution by repetition of a gamble, is very powerful. It does more than simply create a rigorous and plausible foundation for economic theory. In particular, because the framework is epistemologically sound, we can make testable predictions, which we can corroborate empirically using real economic data. We could not have guessed from our simple coin-tossing game that we would end up making a prediction about the fluctuations of stock markets or those of Bitcoin. The simple-but-deep conceptual insight that the ergodicity question has been overlooked ultimately shone light on the equity premium puzzle, informed the debate of how to set central-bank interest rates, and provided a new way of thinking about noise and the stabilising role of price fluctuations. What other surprising predictions can we make in this formalism? That, dear reader, is a question for you.

Acronyms

BM Brownian motion. 41, 42, 45, 46, 48–50, 52, 54–56, 73, 91–93, 95–97, 192

BRK Berkshire Hathaway. 178, 179, 185

CDF cumulative distribution function. 123, 124, 132, 192

EE ergodicity economics. 1, 17, 26, 28, 32, 38–41, 51, 58, 79–83, 86–88, 90, 95, 98–100, 102–105, 108–111, 113, 117, 118, 128, 129, 132, 146, 167, 170, 171, 185

EUT expected utility theory. 80, 83, 86, 89–93, 98–102, 104, 108, 109, 111

EVT expected-value theory. 87–90, 99–103, 105, 106, 113–116, 118, 119

FED effective federal funds rate (overnight). 163–165, 170, 171, 183

GBM geometric Brownian motion. 50, 52–56, 74, 91, 93, 123–125, 128, 129, 131–137, 139, 141–143, 150, 152, 153, 155, 157, 158, 162, 173, 174

GDP gross domestic product. 6, 129

iid independent identically distributed. 28, 47, 48

LML London Mathematical Laboratory. 174

MAD Bernard L. Madoff Investment Securities. 184–186

ODE ordinary differential equation. 47, 48, 55, 155

PDF probability density function. 11, 13, 15, 19, 20, 30, 32, 39, 41, 123, 124, 134, 135, 155

RGBM reallocating geometric Brownian motion. 151–159, 194

S&P500 S&P500 index. 163–165, 170, 171, 178–180, 183, 185

SDE stochastic differential equation. 46–48, 51–55, 73, 92, 94–96, 124, 152, 155, 162, 164, 189

SEC Securities and Exchange Commission. 184, 185

US United States. 151, 155–158

List of Symbols

Δt A general time interval. 21, 22, 25–27, 30, 31, 34, 60, 61, 63–66, 68, 77, 87, 100, 105, 117, 125–128, 144, 145, 147–150, 162–164, 166, 169, 170, 178, 180, 182, 191

δ Most frequently used to express a difference, for instance δx is a difference between two wealths x. It can be the Kronecker delta function, a function of two arguments with properties $\delta(i, j) = 1$ if $i = j$ and $\delta(i, j) = 0$ otherwise. It can also be the Dirac delta function of one argument, $\int f(x)\delta(x - x_0)dx = f(x_0)$. 12, 42–45, 47, 84, 85, 87–89, 117, 118

δt A time interval corresponding to the duration of one round of a gamble or, mathematically, the period over which a single realisation of the constituent random variable of a discrete-time stochastic process is generated. 2, 17, 21, 25–28, 35, 36, 42, 44, 45, 48, 54, 80–82, 84–86, 88, 92, 114, 117, 152, 193

E A subset of a sample space for defining an event. 10–12

$\mathbf{E}$ Expectation value. 13, 15, 20, 30, 31, 36, 39–41

ε Equity premium in our model. 181, 182

η Risk aversion parameter in an isoelastic function (q-logarithm), used as a utility function or ergodicity transformation. 110, 111, 190

$\eta_{\mathbf{Alice}}$ Alice's estimate for η, or her risk aversion parameter. 111, 112

η_c Critical risk aversion parameter of a pair of gambles. 110–112

F Fee to be paid. 81, 100–105, 107, 114–119

F^{max} Maximum fee a player is willing to pay. 101–104

f Generic function. 51–53, 64, 75, 131

G Gain from one round trip of the ship. 114, 115, 117

$\mathcal{G}$ Ginzburg ratio. 136, 137

g Growth rate. 27, 54, 55, 61, 64, 66, 74, 75, 77, 78, 110, 126–128, 139, 140

$g_{\langle\rangle}$ Growth rate of the expectation value. 26, 29, 95, 125, 126, 131

$\overline{g}$ Time-average ergodic growth rate. 77, 79, 88, 93, 94, 103, 104, 117, 118, 125, 127, 128, 131, 146, 148, 150, 170, 172, 182, 191

$\ell_{\mathbf{opt}}$ Optimal leverage. 170–181, 183, 185

$\ell_{\mathbf{opt}}^{\mathbf{est}}$ Estimate of optimal leverage from data. 177, 178, 180

m Index specifying a particular wealth process or gamble. 87, 89

μ Drift term in BM. 39–41, 45–50, 53–56, 91, 124–129, 131–141, 143–150, 152–155, 157, 159, 162, 167–169, 172

$\mu_{\mathbf{e}}$ Excess drift. 163, 164, 167, 169, 170, 172, 173, 178, 181–183

$\mu_{\mathbf{r}}$ Drift of riskless asset. 162–164, 167, 169, 170, 172–175, 178, 183

$\mu_{\mathbf{s}}$ Drift of risky asset. 162, 163, 169, 170, 173–175, 183, 184

N Ensemble size, number of realisations. 4, 5, 12, 14–17, 19, 26, 29–31, 35, 40, 41, 49, 100, 123, 125–134, 136–141, 143–146, 148–150, 152–155, 157, 194, 195

$\mathcal{N}$ Normal distribution, $x \sim \mathcal{N}(\langle p \rangle, \mathrm{Var}(p))$ means that the variable p is normally distributed with mean $\langle p \rangle$ and variance $\mathrm{Var}(p)$. 36, 39–43, 45, 47–50, 54, 124, 126, 128, 132, 134, 138, 144, 145, 148, 149, 192, 194, 195

$\mathbb{N}^+$ Set of all positive integers. 100

n n_j is the number of times outcome j is observed in an ensemble. 12, 15, 16, 27, 84, 86

Ω Sample space. 9–11

P Probability distribution. 9–12, 44

$\mathcal{P}$ Probability density function. 11–13, 20, 30, 31, 34, 37, 39, 41, 123, 124, 129, 130, 134, 135, 155, 156

p Probability, p_j is the probability of observing event j in a realisation of a random variable. 10, 11, 13, 15, 16, 18, 20, 80, 81, 86, 100, 102, 114, 115, 117, 192

π The ratio of a circle's circumference to its diameter. 39, 41, 124, 135

Φ CDF of the standard normal distribution. 132

ϕ Parameter of AR(1) process. 35, 36

Q Random variable defining a gamble through additive wealth changes. 80–82, 84, 85, 87, 89, 100–103, 106, 114, 115, 119, 193

q Possible values of Q. We denote by q_i the value Q takes in the ith realisation, and by q_j the jth-smallest possible value. 16, 80–82, 84, 100, 102, 193

R Random multiplier of wealth in one round of a gamble. 17, 85, 86, 103

$\mathbb{R}$ Set of real numbers. 9

r Realisation of random multiplier of wealth in one round of a gamble. 2, 17, 25–29, 85, 86

r_r Factor whereby wealth deposited in a bank changes. 164, 166

r_s Factor whereby wealth invested in stock changes. 164, 166

r_T Effective per round wealth multiplier after T rounds of the coin game. 27

$r_{\mathbf{time}}$ Effective per round wealth multiplier as the number of rounds of the coin game diverges. 27–29

ρ Covariance. 149, 150

S Sharpe ratio. 169, 173

s Dummy variable in an integration. 21, 22, 30, 34, 46–49, 56, 72, 73, 75, 96, 98, 123, 131, 156, 191

σ Magnitude of noise in a Brownian motion. 39–41, 45–50, 53–56, 72–75, 77, 91–98, 124–129, 131–141, 143–150, 152–157, 159, 162, 167–169, 172

$\sigma_{\mathbf{corr}}$ Fluctuation amplitude of wealth of cooperators with correlated noise. 150

$\sigma_{\mathbf{s}}$ Volatility of risky asset. 162–164, 167, 169, 170, 172–175, 178, 180–184

T Number of sequential iterations of a gamble, so that $T\delta t$ is the total duration of a repeated gamble. 17, 21, 25–28, 35, 37, 38, 42–45, 84–86, 193

t Time. 2–4, 12, 17–23, 25–27, 30, 31, 34–37, 42, 45–56, 60–64, 72–75, 77, 81–85, 87, 91–97, 103, 109, 110, 123–126, 128, 130–140, 142–150, 152, 153, 155, 157–159, 162, 164, 166, 191, 194

t_0 Specific value of time t, usually the starting time of a gamble. 84–86, 103, 104, 162–164, 169, 179

t_c Critical time scale in the random energy model. 138–140, 153

$t_{\mathbf{max}}$ Final time in a sequence of repeated gambles. 166, 171

τ Reallocation rate in RGBM. 152–160, 194

τ Dummy variable indicating a specific round in a gamble. 17, 21, 26–28, 35, 42, 43, 84, 85, 157

$\widetilde{\tau}_{1\%}$ Estimate of reallocation rate τ, 10-year moving average based on 1% wealth-share data. 158, 159

τ_c Critical reallocation rate in RGBM. 153, 155

u Utility function. 80, 89, 90, 92, 94, 102

Var Variance. 39–43, 125, 136, 137, 192

$\mathbf{Var}_{\mathbf{max}}$ Maximum variance we consider acceptable for the distribution of g_{dem}. 128

v Ergodicity transformation, so that $v(x)$ has ergodic increments. 61, 64, 66, 69, 72–79, 84, 85, 87, 88, 90–98, 109–111, 117, 131, 189, 194

W Wiener process, $W(t) = \int_0^t dW$ is continuous and $W(t) \sim \mathcal{N}(0, t)$. 46–49, 51–55, 72–75, 77, 91–94, 96, 97, 124, 126, 134, 141, 144, 145, 148–150, 152, 153, 155, 162–164, 170, 178, 189, 194

w Rescaled wealth, $w_i = \frac{x_i}{\langle x \rangle_N}$. 133, 134, 152, 155, 156, 189, 194

$w_i^{\mathbf{dem}}$ Democratic weight, $w_i^{\text{dem}} = \frac{1}{N}$. 127, 194

$w_i^{\mathbf{plu}}$ Plutocratic weight, $w_i^{\text{plu}} = \frac{x_i}{\sum_i^N x_i}$. 127, 194

X Stochastic process. 17–21, 23, 30, 31, 34–37

x Wealth. 2–4, 12, 17–22, 25–27, 30, 31, 34–38, 42–46, 48–56, 72–76, 78–98, 101–105, 107, 109–111, 114, 117, 119, 123–144, 146–148, 152–155, 162–164, 166, 169–171, 178, 179, 182, 189, 191, 192, 194, 195

x Deterministic wealth. 60–64, 66–69, 72–75

$x_{\textbf{dem}}$ Wealth which grows at the democratic growth rate g_{dem}. 128

x_ℓ Value of an investment in a leveraged portfolio. 163, 164, 166, 169–171, 178, 179

x_r Value of an investment in the riskless asset. 162, 164, 182

x_s Value of an investment in the risky asset. 162–164, 169, 182

ξ A standard normal variable, $\xi \sim \mathcal{N}(0, 1)$. 48, 54, 138, 195

Y Generic random variable. 39–41

y Wealth of a cooperator. 142, 144–148, 150, 195

$y^{(N)}$ Trajectory (realisation) of a stochastic process. 144, 145, 148, 150

Z Generic random variable. 9–15, 18, 35–37, 39–41

$\mathbb{Z}$ Set of integers. 9

z Generic value of a random variable. 10–15, 18, 35–37, 39, 41, 132

ζ Pareto tail index. 13, 134, 155, 156

Index

Bibliography

[1] A. Adamou, Y. Berman, D. Mavroyiannis, and O. Peters. Microfoundations of discounting. *Decision Analysis*, 18(4):257–272, 2021.

[2] A. Adamou and O. Peters. Dynamics of inequality. *Significance*, 13(3):32–35, 2016.

[3] J. Aitchison and J. A. C. Brown. *The Lognormal Distribution*. Cambridge University Press, 1957.

[4] W. B. Arthur. Competing technologies, increasing returns, and lock-in by historical events. *Econ. J.*, 99(394):116–131, Mar. 1989.

[5] A. B. Atkinson. The timescale of economic models: How long is the long run? *Review of Economic Studies*, 36(2):137–152, 1969.

[6] G. I. Barenblatt. *Scaling*. Cambridge University Press, 2003.

[7] Y. Berman, O. Peters, and A. Adamou. Far from equilibrium: Wealth reallocation in the United States. *http://arxiv.org/abs/1605.05631*, May 2016.

[8] Y. Berman, O. Peters, and A. Adamou. Wealth inequality and the ergodic hypothesis: Evidence from the united states. *Journal of Income Distribution*, 30(1), Mar. 2021.

[9] D. Bernoulli. Specimen Theoriae Novae de Mensura Sortis. Translation "Exposition of a new theory on the measurement of risk" by L. Sommer (1954). *Econometrica*, 22(1):23–36, 1738.

[10] F. Black. Noise. *The Journal of Finance*, 41(3):528–543, 1986.

[11] J.-P. Bouchaud. Note on mean-field wealth models and the random energy model. Mimeo, 2015.

[12] J.-P. Bouchaud and M. Mézard. Wealth condensation in a simple model of economy. *Physica A*, 282(4):536–545, 2000.

[13] T. W. Burkhardt. The random acceleration process in bounded geometries. *Journal of Statistical Mechanics: Theory and Experiment*, 2007(7):P07004, 2007.

[14] T. M. Cover and J. A. Thomas. *Elements of Information Theory*. John Wiley & Sons, 1991.

[15] K. Devlin. *The unfinished game*. Basic Books, 2008.

[16] A. Einstein. Über die von der molekularkinetischen Theorie der Wärme geforderte Bewegung von in ruhenden Flüssigkeiten suspendierten Teilchen. *Ann. Phys.*, IV(17):549–560, 1905.

[17] M. Elsberg. *Greed*. Penguin, 2020.

[18] P. Embrechts, C. Klüppelberg, and T. Mikosch. *Modelling Extremal Events*. 3Island Press, 1997.

[19] P. Fernández. The equity premium in 150 textbooks. Working paper, IESE Business School, University of Navarra, 2009.

[20] V. L. Ginzburg. Superconductivity and superfluidity (what was done and what was not). *Physics-Uspekhi*, 40(4):407–432, apr 1997.

[21] J. M. Harrison. *Brownian motion of performance and control*. Cambridge University Press, 2013.

[22] J. C. Hull. *Options, Futures, and Other Derivatives*. Prentice Hall, 6 edition, 2006.

[23] K. Itô. Stochastic integral. *Proc. Imperial Acad. Tokyo*, 20:519–524, 1944.

[24] R. Kaas, M. Goovaerts, J. Dhaene, and M. Denuit. *Modern Actuarial Risk Theory*. Springer, 2 edition, 2008.

[25] J. L. Kelly, Jr. A new interpretation of information rate. *Bell Sys. Tech. J.*, 35(4):917–926, July 1956.

[26] P. E. Kloeden and E. Platen. *Numerical solution of stochastic differential equations*, volume 23. Springer Science & Business Media, 1992.

[27] P. S. Laplace. *Théorie analytique des probabilités*. Paris, Ve. Courcier, 2 edition, 1814.

[28] H. A. Latané. Rational decision-making in portfolio management. *J. Fin.*, 14(3):429–430, 1959.

[29] S. F. LeRoy. excess volatility tests. In S. N. Durlauf and L. E. Blume, editors, *The New Palgrave Dictionary of Economics*, pages 78–80. Springer, 2016.

[30] Z. Liu and R. A. Serota. Correlation and relaxation times for a stochastic process with a fat-tailed steady-state distribution. *Physica A*, 474:301–311, 2017.

[31] H. M. Markopolos. The world's largest hedge fund is a fraud. Filed with the Securities and Exchange Commission, Nov. 2005.

[32] H. Markowitz. Portfolio selection. *J. Fin.*, 1:77–91, Mar. 1952.

[33] H. M. Markowitz. Investment for the long run: New evidence for an old rule. *J. Fin.*, 31(5):1273–1286, Dec. 1976.

[34] H. M. Markowitz. *Portfolio Selection.* Blackwell Publishers Inc., second edition, 1991.

[35] M. Marsili, S. Maslov, and Y.-C. Zhang. Dynamical optimization theory of a diversified portfolio. *Physica A*, 253:403–418, 1998.

[36] D. M. McCloskey. English open fields as behavior towards risk. *Research in Economic History*, 1:124–170, 1976.

[37] R. Mehra and E. C. Prescott. The equity premium puzzle. *J. Monetary Econ.*, 15:145–161, 1985.

[38] B. Milanovic. *Worlds Apart: Measuring International and Global Inequality.* Princeton University Press, 2005.

[39] P. R. Montmort. *Essay d'analyse sur les jeux de hazard.* Jacque Quillau, Paris. Reprinted by the American Mathematical Society, 2006, 2 edition, 1713.

[40] T. Morland. Pólya's urn. *Mathematics in School*, 28(2):35–37, 1999.

[41] H. Morowitz. *Beginnings of cellular life.* Yale University Press, 1992.

[42] M. E. J. Newman. Power laws, Pareto distributions and Zipf's law. *Contemp. Phys.*, 46(5):323–351, 2005.

[43] V. Pareto. *Cours d'Économie Politique.* F. Rouge, Lausanne, Switzerland, 1897.

[44] O. Peters. Optimal leverage from non-ergodicity. *Quantitative Finance*, 11(11):1593–1602, Nov. 2011.

[45] O. Peters. The time resolution of the St Petersburg paradox. *Phil. Trans. R. Soc. A*, 369(1956):4913–4931, Dec. 2011.

[46] O. Peters. Comment on D. Bernoulli (1738). *https://www.researchers.one/article/2019-05-1*, 2019.

[47] O. Peters. Insurance as an ergodicity problem. *Annals of Actuarial Science*, 17(2):215–218, 2023.

[48] O. Peters and A. Adamou. Insurance makes wealth grow faster. *arXiv:1507.04655*, 2015.

[49] O. Peters and A. Adamou. The sum of log-normal variates in geometric brownian motion. *arXiv:1802.02939*, 2018.

[50] O. Peters and A. Adamou. Leverage efficiency. *arXiv:1101.4548*, 2020.

[51] O. Peters and A. Adamou. The ergodicity solution of the cooperation puzzle. *Phil. Trans. R. Soc. A*, 380:20200425, 2022.

[52] O. Peters and M. Gell-Mann. Evaluating gambles using dynamics. *Chaos*, 26:23103, 2016.

[53] O. Peters and W. Klein. Ergodicity breaking in geometric Brownian motion. *Physical Review Letters*, 110(10):100603, Mar. 2013.

[54] T. Piketty. *Capital in the Twenty-First Century.* Harvard University Press, Cambridge, MA, 2014.

[55] S. Redner. Random multiplicative processes: An elementary tutorial. *Am. J. Phys.*, 58(3):267–273, Mar. 1990.

[56] J.-V. Rios-Rull and M. Kuhn. 2013 Update on the U.S. Earnings, Income, and Wealth Distributional Facts: A View from Macroeconomics. *Quarterly Review*, pages 1–75, 2016.

[57] G.-C. Rota. *Indiscrete Thoughts.* Birkhäuser, 1997.

[58] E. Saez and G. Zucman. Wealth inequality in the united states since 1913: Evidence from capitalized income tax data. *Quarterly Journal of Economics*, 131(2):519–578, 2016.

[59] E. Saez and G. Zucman. Progressive wealth taxation. *Brookings Papers on Economic Activity*, 2019.

[60] P. A. Samuelson. What classical and neoclassical monetary theory really was. *The Canadian Journal of Economics*, 1(1):1–15, 1968.

[61] A. Sen. *On Economic Inequality.* Oxford: Clarendon Press, 1997.

[62] M. Sewell. History of the efficient market hypothesis. Technical report, University College London, Department of Computer Science, Jan. 2011.

[63] W. F. Sharpe. Mutual fund performance. *J. Business*, 39(1):119–138, 1966.

[64] B. Skjold, S. R. Steinkamp, O. J. Hulme, O. Peters, and C. Connaughton. Are risk preferences optimal?, September 2023.

[65] The World Inequality Database. USA top 10% and 1%; and bottom 50% wealth shares, 1913–2014. `http://wid.world/data/`, 2016. Accessed: 12/26/2016.

[66] H. Theil. *Economics and Information Theory*. North-Holland Publishing Company, 1967.

[67] E. O. Thorp. *Beat the dealer*. Knopf Doubleday Publishing Group, 1966.

[68] N. G. van Kampen. *Stochastic Processes in Physics and Chemistry*. Elsevier (Amsterdam), 1st edition, 1992.

[69] W. A. Whitworth. *Choice and chance*. Deighton Bell, 2 edition, 1870.

[70] B. Winterhalder. Diet choice, risk, and food sharing in a stochastic environment. *Journal of Anthropological Archaeology*, 5(4):369–392, 1986.

[71] E. N. Wolff. Household wealth trends in the United States, 1983–2010. *Oxford Review of Economic Policy*, 30(1):21–43, 2014.

www.ingramcontent.com/pod-product-compliance
Lightning Source LLC
LaVergne TN
LVHW050006260926
848950LV00033B/1041/J
* 9 7 8 1 0 6 8 6 4 9 1 3 4 *